# New ENTERPRISE

B1+

Student's Book

Jenny Dooley

JN126079

# Express Publishing

# CONTENTS

**Vocabulary:** geographical features; map symbols; road signs
**Grammar:** present simple; present continuous; stative verbs; adverbs of frequency; present perfect; present perfect continuous; *have gone (to)/ have been (to)*
**Everyday English:** asking for/giving directions
**Writing:** a flyer

# On the map

▶ VIDEO

## Vocabulary
### Map symbols

**1** Complete the map key below. Use: *campsite, canal, bridge, footpath, hills, hostel, peak, pond, station, stream, woods, main.*

**1)** mountain
............................

**2)** ............................

**3)** lake or
............................

**4)** river or
............................

**5)** ............................

**6)** ............................

**7)** forest or
............................

**8)** ............................
or hiking trail

**9)** railway line with
............................

**10)** ............................
road

**11)** youth or other
............................

**12)** ............................

# THROUGH - HIKING THE APPALACHIAN TRAIL

The Appalachian National Scenic Trail, more usually known as the Appalachian Trail or the AT, is one of the oldest hiking trails in the world, and still the longest that is for hikers only. Stretching 2,200 miles (3,500 km) in a **roughly** north-east to south-west line, it passes through 14 states between Springer Mountain in Georgia and Mount Katahdin in Maine. Despite its length, it is not an extremely difficult walk, as the Appalachians are an old mountain range, low and covered in thick forests. This makes it a popular **route**, attracting 3-4 million people of all ages and abilities every year. Most people just walk parts of the trail, but some try to complete the **entire** length in a single hike, and the ones that succeed are called 'through-hikers'.

People have been doing the through-hike ever since Earl Shaffer completed the first one in 1948, but lately it has really been **catching on**, so that over 5,000 people are doing or planning a through-hike at this moment. Through-hikers generally begin at the south end of the trail in late spring, when the land has dried out a little. They spend the summer walking through **mainly** hot, humid states to reach Maine in autumn, before winter snow and ice make the final stage impossible. The **record** for completing the through-hike is a little over 41 days, but most through-hikers go far more slowly, taking 165 days on average. The majority don't reach the end at all, dropping out due to injury, **exhaustion** or illness. In fact, just 25% eventually **complete** the through-hike.

Hikers that manage to get to the end, however, have racked up some quite incredible statistics. The average though-hiker takes about five million steps, and passes 165,000 of the rectangular white blazes of paint that mark out the Appalachian Trail on trees along the route. They climb the **equivalent** of 16 Mount Everests. They wear out between four and five pairs of hiking boots and lose 30 pounds (13.6 kg) in weight, despite consuming 5,500 calories per day. They spend around $5,000 on food, stays in hostels and on campsites, and on replacing **worn-out** equipment.

The only large animals on the trail are deer, moose and black bears, and these mostly avoid people. More dangerous by far are poisonous snakes such as rattlesnakes and copperheads, and more **troublesome** are biting insects like black flies and mosquitoes. There is also a lot of poison ivy.

## Reading

**2** Read the text quickly and underline the features from **Ex. 1**. How many are mentioned in the text?

But for most hikers, encounters with nature range from pleasant to **spectacular**: walking through sunbeams in the ancient oak woods of Georgia; watching eagles **soar** above the pines from McAfee Knob on Catawba Mountain, Virginia; standing at the peak of Clingmans Dome, the highest on the trail, with 100 miles of Tennessee in every direction.

Reaching the end of the Appalachian trail gives the through-hiker a feeling of personal satisfaction and **achievement** that is hard to match. Though some through-hikers call that last mile the saddest mile on the Appalachian Trail, since they know their **epic** journey is coming to an end, and photographs never truly **capture** its magic.

> ### ✔ Check these words
> mountain range, humid, majority, drop out, eventually, rack up, on average, blaze, moose, encounter, sunbeam

**3** Read the article again and for questions 1-5, choose the best answer, A, B, C or D. Then explain the words/phrases in bold.

1 The Appalachian Trail is popular because of its
   A length.          C geography.
   B difficulty.       D age.

2 What is true about through-hikers on the Appalachian Trail?
   A There are few alive today.
   B None are as fast as Earl Shaffer was.
   C Most take the north-south route.
   D There are more of them than ever.

3 The Appalachian Trail has
   A no extreme danger from large animals.
   B many poisonous animals to avoid.
   C mountains nearly as high as Everest.
   D little organised accommodation.

4 What would make another good title for the article?
   A The Fastest Through-Hiker
   B The Oldest Trail of Them All
   C The Challenge of a Lifetime
   D The Appalachian Mountains

**4 COLLOCATIONS** Find and complete the words in the text that describe the following. Then use the phrases to make sentences based on the text.

1 ..................... range          5 ................... equipment
2 ..................... forests        6 ................... snakes
3 ..................... stage          7 ................... satisfaction
4 ..................... boots          8 ................... journey

**5 PREPOSITIONS** Choose the correct preposition. Check in your dictionary.

1 You have to walk 8 km a day **at/on** average.
2 The mountains to the north were covered **from/in** snow.
3 I hate it when a journey comes **to/at** an end.
4 There was nothing to see in the desert but sand **in/at** every direction.
5 People **of/at** all ages hike the trail.

**6 WORDS EASILY CONFUSED** Fill in: *grab*, *catch*, *hold*, *capture*. Check in your dictionary.

1 Can you please ..................... my camera for a minute?
2 You should ......................... the opportunity to hike the Appalachian Trail if you get it.
3 We didn't ......................... any fish in the lake.
4 It's almost impossible to ......................... the magic of the forest with a camera.

**7 PHRASAL VERBS** Fill in the correct particle.

> **dry out:** to lose all water and harden
> **dry (sb/sth) off:** to remove water from sb/sth
> **dry up:** (of lakes, rivers) to become dry by being exposed to a heat source

1 You can dry ........... your hair with this towel.
2 Extremely hot weather can cause rivers to dry ......... .
3 Too much exposure to the sun makes your skin dry ........... .

## Speaking & Writing

**8** 👥 (THINK) 🎧 Listen to and read the text. What makes through-hiking the Appalachian Trail an epic journey?

**9** 💬 ICT Collect information about a hiking trail in your country. Prepare and record a three-minute podcast about it. Include: *name*, *route*, *geography*, *wildlife* and *places of interest along the route*. Play your podcast to the class.

# Grammar in Use

## Annie's Blog

### Taking the Appalachian Trail day by day ...

Day 151

Hello readers,

**I'm lying** on my bed, while the other hikers are falling asleep one by one. The hostel **is growing** quiet. I'm trying to sleep too, but I'm still awake. So I'm writing this post to you.

Tomorrow is the last day of my epic through-hike north. I've been walking for 151 days and tomorrow **I'm climbing** Mount Katahdin, the mountain that stands at the northern end of the trail. Then it's down to Millinocket, where my coach **leaves** at 7 am to take me back to the town where I **live**.

I think that's one of the saddest sentences I've ever written. It has just hit me that it's all nearly over. All the pain, the tiredness, the satisfaction, the joy. The little things that **drive** me mad every day. Like the way my left bootlace – and only the left one – **is** always **coming** undone somewhere along the trail. Then there are the countless insect bites. But, the beautiful landscapes made it all worthwhile.

There have been important experiences which have changed the way I see the world. My first day on the trail, full of hope, wearing new boots. The owner of a hostel telling me to keep going when I was about to give up. Hearing another hiker saying, 'I've never felt so alive!' and thinking, 'I know.'

The crazy thing is I'm already thinking about which hike to go on next! I'm looking at brochures about the other two big US trails now: the Continental Divide Trail and the Pacific Coast Trail. They both look great! Any thoughts?

**Post a Comment**

## Present simple – Present continuous – Stative verbs ▸pp. GR1-2

**1** **a)** **Identify the tenses in bold in the text. Match them to the uses.**

- a repeated action • a timetable (future meaning)
- a changing situation • a permanent state
- a fixed future arrangement
- an action happening now • an annoyance

**b)** **Find examples of stative verbs. How does the meaning change in the continuous form?**

**2** **Choose the correct tense. Which are stative verbs?**

**1** Jerry **works/is working** in the forest today.

**2** My brothers **have/are having** some boots we can borrow.

**3** This flower **doesn't smell/isn't smelling** very nice.

**4** Why **do you look/are you looking** at the map? Are you lost?

**5** We don't have to rush. The train **doesn't leave/isn't leaving** until 7 pm.

**6** Where **do you go/are you going** hiking every weekend?

**3** **Put the verbs in brackets into the present simple or the present continuous. Give reasons.**

**1** The campsite shop ..................................................... **(not/open)** on Monday evenings.

**2** More and more people ..................................................... **(enjoy)** outdoor holidays these days.

**3** ..................................................... **(the train/depart)** at 11 am?

**4** It ............................................. **(rain)** a lot in Ireland.

**5** Sea levels ..................................................... **(rise)** due to climate change.

**6** Bob ..................................................... **(sunbathe)** by the river at the moment.

**7** ............................................................. **(it/often/snow)** in Scotland at this time of year?

**8** The swallows ..................................................... **(fly)** south now that the weather is cooler.

**9** ............................................................. **(you/go)** hiking this afternoon?

**10** My brother ..................................................... **(always/take)** my camera without asking. It's so annoying!

**4** **Put the verbs in brackets into the present simple or the present continuous. Give reasons. Explain what each verb means.**

**1** **a** The peak of the mountain ......................................... **(look)** very far away!

**b** Sue ................................................. **(look)** at the map right now.

**2** **a** They ......................................... **(think)** the hostel is very expensive.

**b** He ............................................. **(think)** about going for a hike this weekend.

**3** **a** I ..................................... **(see)** what you mean.

**b** I ..................................... **(see)** my sister tomorrow, so I can tell her about it.

**4** **a** This ice cream ............................... **(taste)** amazing!

**b** The chef ..................................... **(taste)** the soup to check if it needs more salt.

**5** SPEAKING 👥 **Talk about what you do/ don't do in the mornings, what you are doing now and what you are/aren't doing this weekend.**

## Adverbs of frequency ▶ p. GR1

**6** SPEAKING **What do you do when you visit a new place? Use the phrases and the adverbs of frequency to tell the class, as in the example.**

- always (100%)
- usually (90%)
- often (70%)
- sometimes (50%)
- occasionally (30%)
- rarely/seldom (10%)
- never (0%)

• use a map (app) • research the place on the Internet
• upload photos on social media • buy souvenirs
• talk to locals • keep a travel diary • sample local food
• check in online • take a selfie • send postcards

*I always use a map app to explore the area.*

## Present perfect – Present perfect continuous ▶ pp. GR2-3

**7** **Identify the underlined tenses in the text on p. 6. Match them to the uses.**

• a recently completed action • an experience or change • an action that started in the past and continues up to present with emphasis on duration

**8** **Put the verbs in brackets into the present perfect or the present perfect continuous, then choose the correct adverb.**

1 It .......................................... (rain) **for/since** early in the morning and the valley is flooded!
2 Peter ...................................**just/yet (call)** the travel agent to book his trip. He's so excited!
3 .......................................... **(you/visit)** the White Cliffs of Dover **once/yet**? They're spectacular!
4 Dolphins .......................................... **(swim)** by the boat **all morning/just** and I've taken lots of pics!
5 The autumn leaves .......................................... **(not/start)** to fall **yet/before**.
6 We .......................................... **(hike)** up this mountain **all day/once**! I'm exhausted.
7 They .......................................... **(plan)** to see the Black Forest **for/since** years.
8 ............... Mark **ever/already** .......................................... **(book)** the coach tickets?
9 Rebecca ................. **ever/never** .......................................... **(travel)** on a plane.
10 .......................................... **(you/see)** the documentary about Springer Mountain **yet/still**?

**9** **Fill in:** *have/has been to/in, have/has gone to.*

1 Carol .......................................... Italy on a walking tour for a week.
2 I .......................................... the New Forest twice this year.
3 "How long ...................... your parents .......................... Portofino?" "For a week now."
4 My sister and her husband .......................................... their cottage for the summer.
5 "How many times ...................... you .......................... Chile?" "Three times so far."

**10** SPEAKING 👥 **Four friends are on a hike. Say what they have been doing this morning, as in the example.**

• they/walk (since 8 am) • Dan/complain (for an hour)
• Sue/eat three energy bars (since morning) • Peta's feet/hurt (for days) • Mandy/take 30 photos (so far)

*They have been walking since 8 am.*

**11** **Complete the message using the verbs in the list in the correct present tense.**

• you/do • you/enjoy • go • have • hike
• not rain • read • not see • stretch • not visit

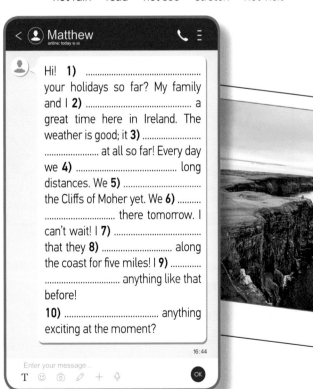

< 👤 **Matthew**  📞 ☰
*online: today 16:55*

👤 Hi! **1)** ..............................................
your holidays so far? My family
and I **2)** ........................................ a
great time here in Ireland. The
weather is good; it **3)** ......................
.......................... at all so far! Every day
we **4)** .......................................... long
distances. We **5)** ................................
the Cliffs of Moher yet. We **6)** ..........
.............................. there tomorrow. I
can't wait! I **7)** ....................................
that they **8)** .............................. along
the coast for five miles! I **9)** ............
.............................. anything like that
before!
**10)** .......................................... anything
exciting at the moment?

16:44

Enter your message...
T  ☺  📷  ✏  +  🎤   OK

**12** WRITING **Imagine you have received the text message in Ex. 11. Write a message with your news. Write where you are, what you are doing and what your plans are.**

7

# Skills in Action

## Vocabulary
### Road signs

**1** **a)** **Complete the gaps. Use:** *crossroads, end, lights, junction, lane, pedestrian, roundabout, speed, way.*

**1** 30-mph ............... limit   **2** stop and give ...............   **3** ...............

**4** ............... ...............   **5** ............... crossing   **6** traffic ...............

**7** cycle ...............   **8** ...............   **9** dead ...............

**b)** 👥 (THINK) **Look at the map. Tell your partner where you might see the road signs from Ex. 1a, as in the example.**

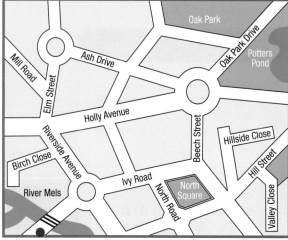

*You might see a cycle lane sign by Oak Park. There's probably a cycle lane there.*

## Listening

**2** 🎧 **Listen to the dialogue and decide if the statements 1-6 are *T* (True) or *F* (False).**

1 The man lives in London.
2 The woman asks for directions to Regent's Park.
3 The bus takes longer than the underground.
4 The nearest underground station to London Zoo is Notting Hill Gate.
5 At Oxford Circus, change onto the blue line to get to London Zoo.
6 The woman decides to take the bus to the zoo.

## Everyday English
### Asking for & Giving directions

**3** **a)** **Read the dialogue. Where is the driver on the map in Ex. 1b and where is she going?**

**b)** **Read the dialogue and fill in the missing words.** 🎧 **Listen and check.**

> **A:** Excuse me ... Is Potters Pond far **1)** ............... here? I was following the map on my phone, but my phone died.
>
> **B:** It's not very far! Let's see ... Once you cross the bridge here in front of you, you come to a roundabout. Go straight **2)** ............... onto Ivy Road.
>
> **A:** OK, got it. Then what?
>
> **B:** Keep going straight **3)** ............... until you reach a junction. That's Beech Street.
>
> **A:** And do I turn left or right there?
>
> **B:** Take a left **4)** ............ Beech Street and you soon come to another roundabout. Take the third exit – that's Oak Park Drive. The park's **5)** ............ your left.
>
> **A:** So ... that's straight on at the first roundabout, left at the junction and third exit **6)** ............... the second roundabout. How long does that take?
>
> **B:** It's a five-minute drive. Maybe a little more.
>
> **A:** Thank you so much for your help!
>
> **B:** Sure, no problem!

**4** 👥 **Act out dialogues similar to the one in Ex. 3, using the language in the box, the red dot as a starting point and these destinations:** *Valley Close, Mill Road.*

| Asking for directions | Giving directions |
|---|---|
| • Excuse me. How do I get to ...?/What's the best way to (get to) ...?/ Could you tell me where the ... is? <br> • Is it far from here?/How long does it take? | • Go up/down/along ... <br> • Turn left/right onto .../Take the first/second right/left. <br> • Keep going straight on until ... <br> • Go straight across the ... <br> • It's five minutes by car/a five-minute drive. |

## Intonation: discourse markers

**5** **a)** 🎧 **Listen and repeat. Which expresses** *determination, arrangement, confirmation, uncertainty*?

1 **Right!** Let's walk home.   3 **Well,** hope that helps!
2 **So,** see you later then.   4 **OK,** I'll be there.

**b)** **Use the words in bold in sentences of your own.**

## Reading & Writing

**6** Read the flyer and fill in the gaps with words derived from the words in brackets.

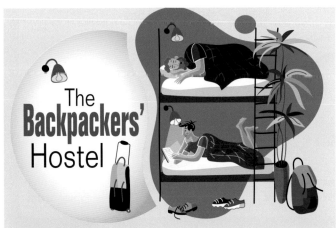

# The Backpackers' Hostel

**Location**

We're right in the heart of the city, around the corner from all the 1) ........................... **(see)** and just a short stroll from one of the most 2) ........................... **(beauty)** rivers in Europe.

**Free facilities**

There's a shared kitchen with a 3) ........................... **(cook)** and fridge that guests are welcome to use, a cosy lounge with free refreshments, and a TV room. We've recently put in three new washing machines in the basement and there's also a 4) ........................... **(space)** back garden with a barbecue.

**Rooms**

Shared rooms are either six-bed or eight-bed, and all beds are bunk beds. Men and women sleep 5) ........................... **(separate)** and there is one bathroom per shared room. Three family rooms are available, which have their own bathroom but no cooking facilities.

**How to find us**

We're only a leisurely five-minute walk from the train station. Take a left coming out of the main entrance and walk along Station Road for about 500 metres. At the first traffic lights, turn left along Mill Street, then take the second right onto Gateshead Road. The hostel is number 122, the 6) ........................... **(impress)** red building on the left. We're looking forward to welcoming you!

**50% off your first night with this flyer!**

**7** Read the writing tip below. Find examples of the underlined features in the flyer in Ex. 6.

 **Writing Tip**

**Writing flyers**

A flyer is a short piece of advertising material which someone hands out to passers-by in the street. It is generally handed out near the place advertised and often contains <u>directions</u> to explain how to get to it. It contains a brief <u>description</u> of what the place offers, and it might have a <u>special offer</u> on it.

**8** As a kind of advertisement, a flyer should use inviting language to sell the place it wants you to visit. Read the text again and find descriptive words or phrases that were used instead of the words below.

| | | | |
|---|---|---|---|
| **1** | tall ............................... | **4** | nicest ........................... |
| **2** | slow ........................... | **5** | warm ........................... |
| **3** | big ............................... | **6** | close to ....................... |

**9** Complete the table with the prompts.

- single rooms with a view • gym • in the town centre
- restaurant • double rooms with large balconies
- near the river • at the junction
- rooftop swimming pool • twin rooms

| location | facilities | rooms |
|---|---|---|
| | | |

## Writing (a flyer)

**10** Use your notes from Ex. 9 and the map below to create a flyer (120-180 words) for the Park Hotel. Think of a special offer and follow the plan.

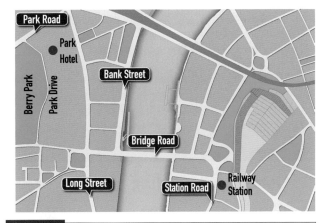

**Plan**

**The Park Hotel**
Location
Facilities
Rooms
Directions
Special offer

**VALUES**

**Direction**
*Direction is so much more important than speed.*

**Anonymous**

# Culture

▶ VIDEO

🏠 Home  @ Connect  # Discover  👤 Me  🔍 Search  ✉ ⚙ ✎

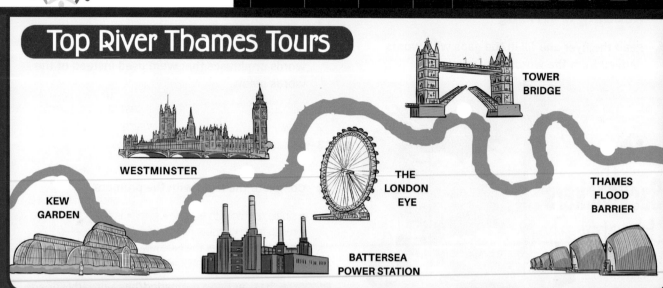

## Top River Thames Tours

WESTMINSTER · KEW GARDEN · TOWER BRIDGE · THE LONDON EYE · THAMES FLOOD BARRIER · BATTERSEA POWER STATION

*Tourists, travellers and visitors to London are getting **choosy** about what they see and how they see it, so here's a list of our top ways to see fabulous London via the mighty Thames for people who think they've seen it all.*

### Ⓐ At top speed

Why see it all at a crawl when you can board a speedboat and take in the lot in 90 minutes? The number of companies who are offering this **thrilling** experience has been steadily growing, and they take passengers past Tower Bridge and the Tower of London in one direction, then down to Greenwich and the Thames Barrier in the other.

### Ⓑ At your leisure

Why not go to the other extreme and book a ticket on one of the long lazy afternoon cruises that head west along the Thames? Starting at Westminster Bridge, these gentle **outings** take you past Battersea Park and the power station there, past Kew Gardens and into the English countryside. Some even reach as far as Hampton Court Palace, and there's usually afternoon tea offered on board. You're sure to see ducks and swans and, if you're lucky, a kingfisher or two.

### Ⓒ By night

Every city looks magical at night and London is no exception. There are a large number of nighttime tours that sail up and down the river, some offering a five-course meal, others a buffet and a guide giving a running **commentary**. All of them offer the unbeatable **cityscape** of London, lit up for your pleasure. Particularly splendid are the London Eye, Tower Bridge and the Palace of Westminster, as well as the lovely street lights along the South Bank.

### Ⓓ By land and water

There are a number of **amphibious** tours, where vehicles designed for travel by road and water take their passengers on an unforgettable ride. After they have done the usual bus tour route past all the famous landmarks, they **splash** into the Thames for a look at the sights from the water. These trips tend to be a little expensive, but seeing as it's two tours for the price of one, it's worth it!

For more ▼

## Listening & Reading

**1** 🎧 **Listen to and read the text. In which tours can you have food and beverages?**

**2** Read the text again. For each question, choose the correct tour (A-D). Explain the words in bold.

**Which tour**

1  costs a lot of money? ..........
2  allows you to spot wildlife? ..........
3  is getting more popular? ..........
4  gives passengers information about the city? ..........
5  goes furthest east? ..........
6  goes furthest west? ..........
7  goes partly along roads? ..........
8  sometimes involves a large dinner? ..........

✓ **Check these words**

crawl, steadily, gentle, on board, kingfisher, splendid, route

## Speaking & Writing

**3** 👥 💬THINK Which of the tours would you like to go on? Why? Tell your partner.

**4** 💬 ICT Find out about ways visitors can see the capital city of your country or another country. Each person in the group should write a section for a webpage entitled 'Top ... tours'. Create an introduction together, then find pictures and present your sections to the class. The class can vote on which tour they would take.

## Vocabulary

**1** **Fill in:** *campsite, trail, routes, final, mountain, railway, hiking, peak, lights, limit.*

1 There's a bear on the hiking .............................!
2 The traffic ............................ are turning red.
3 The highest mountain ............................ in the world is Mount Everest.
4 He stayed at a ......................... for the night.
5 They have raised the speed ......................... to 70 mph.
6 The Andes ...................... range runs along the west coast of South America.
7 This ......................... line goes all the way to the coast.
8 The ......................... stage of the hike was the hardest.
9 These ............................... boots are expensive but comfortable.
10 The Pennine Way is one of the most popular ......................... for UK hikers.

*(10 x 2 = 20)*

**2** **Choose the correct word.**

1 We are now entering **high/thick/entire** forest.
2 You must always use the pedestrian **crossing/ pavement/roundabout**.
3 You don't get opportunities like this often, so **catch/ hold/grab** it!
4 There's a round **pond/canal/river** with ducks in the middle of the village.
5 You have to give **road/lane/way** at this junction.

*(5 X 3 = 15)*

**3** **Fill in:** *up, on, off, to, in.*

1 The lakes in Uyuni dried ............... many years ago.
2 When a journey comes ............... an end, I feel sad.
3 The mountain was covered ............... snow.
4 Dry ............... your wet shoes by the fire.
5 The guide earns $10,000 a year ............... average.

*(5 X 2 = 10)*

## Grammar

**4** **Put the verbs in brackets into the present simple or the present continuous.**

1 Why ......................... **(you/taste)** the soup?
2 Miley ......................... **(not/like)** Texas during the summer.
3 Jim ......................... **(always/make)** fun of me!
4 I can't call Mike, because my phone ............................... **(not/work)** at the moment.
5 Liam usually ......................... **(research)** the country he wants to visit.

*(5 X 4 = 20)*

**5** **Choose the correct tense.**

1 Kevin **has already uploaded/has already been uploading** his photos on his profile.
2 Stella is tired because she **has walked/has been walking** all morning.
3 Dora is out. She **has gone/has been** to the lake to feed the ducks.
4 **Have you been seeing/Have you seen** the new traffic lights on Maple Street?
5 Chris **has done/has been doing** extreme sports for three years.

*(5 X 3 = 15)*

## Everyday English

**6** **Match the sentences.**

1 ☐ Turn left at the junction.
2 ☐ How far is it from here?
3 ☐ Do I take a left or right there?
4 ☐ Thank you so much.
5 ☐ What's the best way to get to Central Park?

a It's a ten-minute walk.
b OK, got it. Then what?
c Sure. No problem.
d Go to the end of the road and turn right.
e Go straight on.

*(5 X 4 = 20)*

*Total 100*

## Competences

GOOD ✓

VERY GOOD ✓ ✓

EXCELLENT ✓ ✓ ✓

| Lexical Competence | Reading Competence | Speaking Competence |
|---|---|---|
| understand words/ phrases related to:<br>• geographical features<br>• map symbols<br>• road signs | • understand texts related to geographical features (read for key information – multiple choice; multiple matching)<br>**Listening Competence**<br>• listen to and understand dialogues asking for/giving directions (listen for specific information – T/F statements) | • ask for & give directions<br>**Writing Competence**<br>• prepare a podcast<br>• write a flyer<br>• write a webpage section |

**Vocabulary:** festivities, celebrations & customs
**Grammar:** past simple – past continuous; past simple vs present perfect; *used to/would; be/get used to*
**Everyday English:** describing an event
**Writing:** an email describing a celebration you attended

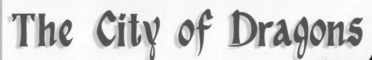

About Us | Support | Contacts   ▶ VIDEO   Search  OK

Try Polish **1)** ........................ like pierogi from street food **2)** ........................ .

See street **3)** ........................ such as dancers and **4)** ........................ .

Attend an open-air show featuring **5)** ........................ and a huge flying dragon **6)** ........................

Watch a **7)** ........................ of people dressed in colourful **8)** ........................ .

# The City of Dragons

*Every June, the people of Krakow, Poland, hold the Dragon Parade. Find out what Lisa Harris thought of it all as she meets a fire-breathing dragon and sees a legend* **brought to life.**

At first, I thought it was just a dragon **sculpture** on the banks of the Vistula River. But while I was taking photos of it, it suddenly roared into life and blew flames into the sky! It nearly scared me to death! **1 ☐** Were they making a film? Kasia, my guide, just laughed, calmed me down and told me about the Wawel Dragon ...

Legend has it that in the days when Krakow used to be the main city of Poland, Wawel Castle was home to King Krakus and his daughter, the princess. These were dangerous times – a terrible dragon was living in a cave nearby and attacking Krakow's residents as well as their cattle and sheep. King Krakus offered his daughter in marriage to anyone who killed the dragon. The brave men of Krakow **set off** hoping to win the princess. **2 ☐** Near the castle, Skuba the shoemaker was working hard when he heard about the King's offer. He wasn't a fighter, but he was very clever, and he **came up with** a plan. He took the skin of a sheep, filled it with sulphur and left it outside the dragon's cave. The dragon ate it hungrily,

but the sulphur made the dragon extremely thirsty. **3 ☐** In fact, it drank so much that it burst – and with the dragon dead, the shoemaker married the princess!

Now that I knew the legend, I was ready to enjoy this amazing event. Everywhere I turned, there were different activities **celebrating** the culture of Krakow. **4 ☐** It was the start of the spectacular open-air show! Huge dragon-shaped balloons soared into the sky surrounded by smoke and colourful lasers. There were dragon boats on the river, too. I've never seen anything like it – it totally blew me away!

The day after, the Old Town parade took place. There was dancing and juggling, and local bands were playing folk music. **5 ☐** Many of them were marching through the town with handmade dragon puppets, each hoping to win the best dragon **contest**! There were also lots of street stalls selling pierogi. **6 ☐** They were absolutely delicious – one of the many highlights of my trip to this amazing city!

✔ **Check these words**

legend, sth roars into life, flame, cave, resident, cattle, sulphur, burst, soar, juggling, march, highlight

## Vocabulary
### Festivities

**1** Look at the pictures and complete the gaps (1-8) with the words below.

- dishes • balloon • parade • fireworks • jugglers
- performers • stalls • costumes

## Reading

**2** What cultural event are the pictures in Ex. 1 about? What is the legend behind it? Read the text quickly to find out.

## Study Skills

**Missing Sentences**

Read the text and the missing sentences. Look closely at the words before and after each gap. Look for hints, e.g. reference words (we, they, etc) or linking words. This will help you do the task.

**3** **Read the text again and fill in the gaps (1-6) with a correct sentence (A-G). One sentence is extra. Then explain the words/phrases in bold.**

**A** But the dragon had each of them for dinner.

**B** Then, all of a sudden, the sky exploded as the fireworks display began.

**C** It's a traditional dish from Poland, similar to a filled dumpling.

**D** Also, the streets were packed with people dressed up in imaginative costumes like characters from the legend!

**E** No one knows where the legend came from.

**F** It was so thirsty that it drank all the water in the river.

**G** I couldn't believe my eyes!

**4** **COLLOCATIONS** **Find the verbs in the text that describe the following. Complete the phrases (1-6) and then make sentences with them.**

1 ................. a parade
2 ................. photos
3 ................. into life
4 couldn't .................... my eyes
5 ................. sb in marriage
6 ................. the contest

**5** **PHRASAL VERBS** **Fill in the correct particle. Check in your dictionary.**

**blow sb away:** to impress sb very much
**blow into (a place):** to arrive somewhere unexpectedly
**blow sb off:** to not meet sb at an arranged meeting
**blow up: 1)** to enlarge a photograph; **2)** to fill (a balloon, etc) with air
**blow sth out:** to extinguish (a candle, etc) using your breath

1 A: Check out this photo of Pawel blowing ................. the candles on his birthday cake.
   B: And there's Anna in the background blowing ................. some balloons.

2 A: Guess what? Kelly's just blown ................. town.
   B: Really! I haven't seen her in ages!

3 A: I thought the art fair was amazing. It really blew me ................. .
   B: It's just a shame Tom wasn't there. I don't know why he blew us ................. .

**6** **PREPOSITIONS** **Fill in:** of, into, in (x2), by, with, to.

# Gudvangen Viking Market

Last week, I went on a trip to the small village of Njardarheimr near Oslo in Norway. It's home **1)** ................. the Gudvangen Viking Market – a festival of all things Viking! The village itself is amazing – it's next to a river and surrounded **2)** ................. snowy mountains. When I got there, the streets were packed **3)** ................. people dressed **4)** ................. Viking costumes. It was like stepping back **5)** ................. time. There was an archery demonstration and people could have a go. I tried my best, but my arrow just went straight up **6)** ................. the sky! Anyway, I had the time **7)** ................. my life there and can't wait to go again next year.

**7** **WORDS EASILY CONFUSED** **Fill in** culture, custom **or** tradition. **Check in your dictionary.**

1 Attending a festival abroad is a great way to experience the local ............................. .
2 It is the ............................. to take off your shoes when entering a house in Japan.
3 It's a ............................. to wear something green on St Patrick's Day.

## Speaking & Writing

**8** **SPEAKING** ICT **Listen to and read the text. Do more research about the legend of the Wawel Dragon and the Dragon Parade. Imagine you were at the event. Prepare a podcast about it.**

## Writing

**9** ICT **Research a legend that is celebrated in your country today. Make notes under the headings:** legend – name of event – when/where – activities. **Use your notes to write an article for an international culture magazine.**

13

# Grammar in Use

SEARCH

Last summer, I **1) saw** a play at Shakespeare's Globe in London. As a child, I **2) went** to the theatre all the time, but this was my first time in the Globe. It's the theatre where actors performed Shakespeare's plays in the late 16th and early 17th century. The original theatre **3) burnt** down, but this one opened in 1997.

A cold wind **4) was blowing** on the evening of the play. I arrived at 7:45, but the doors were still closed. People **5) were standing** outside patiently and they **were chatting**. Then the doors **6) opened** and everyone **rushed** inside. As I **7) was walking** to my seat, I **noticed** that there was no roof! The stage was covered, but most of the audience had no shelter – just like in the original theatre!

The play was a comedy, *Much Ado about Nothing*, and we **8) were** all **enjoying** it. Then, after about an hour, I felt a drop of rain. Soon, it was pouring, but nobody in the audience left. We got soaking wet – but it was a great experience! I haven't returned to the Globe since then, but <u>I've bought</u> tickets for next Wednesday evening. And one thing's for sure – I'll definitely bring a raincoat!

17 ♥   54 💬   74 👍

## Past simple – Past continuous
▶ **pp. GR3-4**

**1** **a)** **Read the blog entry. Identify the tenses in bold. Which past tense do we use for:**

1 background information in a story?
2 an action which happened at a specific time (stated, implied or already known) in the past?
3 past actions which happened one immediately after the other?
4 two or more actions which were happening at the same time in the past?
5 a past action which was in progress when another action interrupted it?
6 past habits?
7 an action which was in progress in the past?
8 a past action which won't take place again?

**b)** **Find examples of time expressions used with past simple or the past continuous in the blog entry.**

**2** **Put the verbs in brackets into the past simple or the past continuous.**

1 A large crowd ................................................. **(watch)** the parade when it ................................. **(start)** raining.
2 Jon and Jane ...................................... **(not/go)** to the puppet show last night; they ........................................ ........................... **(not/feel)** well.
3 The judges ..................................... **(crown)** the king and queen at the end of the parade.
4 ................................................................ **(people/sing)** along while the band ......................................... **(play)**?
5 Jane ..................................... **(not/chat)** online at 5 pm yesterday; she .................................................. **(rehearse)** for her role in the college play.
6 The wind ......................................... **(blow)** strongly and the rain ...................................... **(pour)** down when we got up that morning.
7 "When ................................................................ **(the event/first/take)** place?" "In the 17th century."

**3** **a)** **Complete the sentences with your own ideas.**

1 The sun was shining and ...............................................
2 She entered the shop and ..............................................
3 He was walking down the road when ...........................
4 It started raining, but ...................................................
5 She was sitting on a bench when ................................

**b)** **SPEAKING** **Choose one of the sentences in Ex. 3a and continue the story.**

## Past simple vs Present perfect
▶ **p. GR4**

**4** **Look at the underlined verb in the blog entry in Ex. 1. How is the present perfect different from the past simple? When do we use it?**

**5** **Choose the correct tense. Give reasons.**

1 We **didn't attend/haven't attended** the theatre performance yesterday evening.
2 Hurry up! The show **has started/started**!
3 **Did you take/Have you taken** many interesting pictures of today's parade so far?
4 What time **have they let off/did they let off** the fireworks last night?
5 **I have never flown/I never flew** in a hot-air balloon.
6 The old theatre **has been/was** the most modern building of its time.

**6** Put the verbs in brackets into the past simple, the past continuous or the present perfect.

Hi everyone!

1) ................................................. **(any of you/ever/be)** to Scotland? Well, I'm here now for the Loch Ness Marathon. I **2)** ................................. **(arrive)** in the Highlands capital, Inverness last night. While my taxi **3)** ................................. **(take)** me to my hotel, I noticed signs and pictures around the city that **4)** ................................. **(show)** a strange creature like a sea serpent. The driver **5)** ................................. **(tell)** me why.

Scottish folklore says there is a creature in Loch Ness called the Loch Ness Monster. There is no real proof that it exists, but the local people **6)** ................................. **(take)** it to their hearts and call it 'Nessie'. The first sighting was in the 1870s by D. Mackenzie, but the monster first **7)** ................................. **(attract)** national attention in the 1930s when lots of people reported seeing it. However, scientists believe the sightings were fake and there **8)** ................................. **(not/be)** any reports lately.

Nevertheless, the Loch Ness Marathon attracts 8,000 runners every year and the event **9)** ................................. **(raise)** a lot of money for good causes since it **10)** ................................. **(begin)**. Also, Nessie makes a great mascot. Click <u>here</u> for photos.

### *used to/would – be/get used to*

▶ **pp. GR4-5**

**7** Study the theory. Then cross out the incorrect item in the sentences.

- We use ***used to/would/past simple*** for past habits. *James **used to travel/would travel/travelled** to Melbourne every year when he was younger.*
- We use ***used to/past simple*** for past states. *They **used to be/were** big fans of folk music when they were kids.* (NOT: ~~They would be ...~~) **BUT** *He left last week.* (past action – we can't use ***used to***)
- We use ***be used to*** + noun/pronoun/*-ing* form to show that we are accustomed to (doing) sth. *Sam **isn't used to flying**.*
- We use ***get used to*** + noun/pronoun/*-ing* form/to show that we are getting accustomed to sth gradually. *Mark **got used to living** in York.*

**1** Dave **was going/would go/used to go** to a lot of music performances when he was a teenager.

**2** Richard **didn't use to/wouldn't/didn't** like fireworks until he went to New York for July 4th.

**3** Ben **isn't used to/didn't use to/hasn't got used to** eating Polish food yet, so he still prefers fast food.

**4** **Did you use to go/Would you go/Did you go** to Winterlude when you lived in Canada?

**8** **SPEAKING** Think of various celebrations/ cultural events. Say which of the activities in the list you/your family members used to/didn't use to do when you were 8 years old. Use the prompts below and/or your own ideas.

- put up decorations  • send greeting cards
- prepare/special meal  • take part in/town procession
- watch special TV programmes  • light bonfires
- exchange gifts  • watch/fireworks display

*On my birthday, my family used to **put up decorations** all over our house.*
*I used to **send greetings cards** to all of my relatives for New Year.*

**9** Complete the second sentence so that it means the same as the first. Use between two and five words.

**1** Ben started wrapping gifts at 9:00 and he finished at 10:30. **WAS**
Ben ................................................. at 9:45.

**2** Sarah called during dinner. **EATING**
While we ................................. Sarah called.

**3** The last time I watched a parade was in 2017. **NOT**
I ................................................. since 2017.

**4** When I was younger, I didn't like poetry. **USE**
When I was younger, I .................................................
................................. poetry.

**5** Jon doesn't mind eating spicy food anymore. **GOT**
Jon .................................................
spicy food.

### Listening & Writing

**10** 🎧 Listen to Paul narrating a legend and put the events in the order they happened (1-8).

**A** The two men went to a secret cave.    ........
**B** The bag of gold turned into sand.    ........
**C** The blacksmith replaced a horse's shoe.    ........
**D** The stranger gave the blacksmith a bag of gold.    ........
**E** The stranger asked him to make a horseshoe.    ........
**F** The blacksmith told everyone the secret.    ........
**G** The blacksmith promised not to tell anyone what he saw.    ........
**H** A strange man walked into a blacksmith's shop.    ........

**11** **WRITING** Use the ideas in Ex. 10 to write a summary of the legend.

15

# Skills in Action

## Vocabulary

Types of holidays –
UK Celebrations & Customs

**1** **a)** **Match the UK celebrations (1-6) to the customs (a-f). Make sentences, as in the example. Do you celebrate these events in your country?**

1 ☐ Burns' Night (25th January)
2 ☐ Mother's Day or Mothering Sunday (one Sunday in March)
3 ☐ May Day (1st May)
4 ☐ Bonfire Night (5th November)
5 ☐ Remembrance Day (11th November)
6 ☐ New Year's Eve (31st December)

**a** let off fireworks at midnight and sing Auld Lang Syne
**b** light a huge bonfire, let off fireworks and eat toffee apples
**c** gather flowers and follow a procession led by the May Queen
**d** buy flowers or prepare breakfast for mothers
**e** read Burns' poems aloud, listen to traditional music on the bagpipes and eat haggis
**f** wear poppies and hold a two-minute silence

*On New Year's Eve, people in the UK let off fireworks at midnight and sing Auld Lang Syne.*

**b)** **Think of two important celebrations in your country. How do you celebrate them?**

## Listening

**2** **You are going to hear five people talking about their experiences at different events. Read the sentences below. Match the sentences (A-E) to the speakers (1-4). There is one extra sentence.**

**A** Another person's actions made me feel embarrassed.
**B** The disappointment I felt taught me an important lesson.
**C** A small change made an annual event more memorable.
**D** I was surprised when a custom was introduced to me.
**E** A mistake changed my day in a big way.

| | |
|---|---|
| Speaker 1 | |
| Speaker 2 | |
| Speaker 3 | |
| Speaker 4 | |

## Everyday English

Describing an event

**3** **Read the first two exchanges. What event did Steve attend?**

**Listen and read to find out.**

**P:** Hey, Steve. I haven't seen you in a while.
**S:** Hi, Paul. I've just come back from Scotland. I was there for ten days.
**P:** Wow! What was it like?
**S:** I had the time of my life. The highlight was on my last day when I celebrated Burns' Night with a Scottish friend in Edinburgh.
**P:** I haven't heard of that. What's it about?
**S:** It's a fantastic event where people read Burns' poems aloud and play traditional music on the bagpipes. I also tried the national dish, haggis!
**P:** Really? What did you think of it?
**S:** I liked it! Haggis is very tasty.
**P:** It sounds like you had a wonderful time. I haven't experienced anything like that.
**S:** Well, why don't you come with me next year? I enjoyed it so much that I'm definitely going back.
**P:** Hmm, maybe I will. In fact, count me in!

**4** **Imagine you attended a celebration. Use the phrases in the language box to act out a dialogue similar to the one in Ex. 3.**

| Describing an event | Asking about an event |
|---|---|
| • The highlight was ... | • What was it like? |
| • It's a wonderful event/ evening, etc where ... | • What's it about? |
| • I had a great time. | • What did you think of it? |
| | • It sounds like you ... |

## Intonation: stress-shift

Some words have the same noun and verb forms. These nouns have strong first syllables while the verbs have strong second syllables.

**5** **Identify the forms in bold in the sentences.**

**Listen and repeat. Use the words in bold in sentences of your own.**

1 **a** I'd like a **refund**, please.
  **b** They refused to **refund** our tickets.
2 **a** **Update** me on how preparations are going.
  **b** There is no **update** on the venue.
3 **a** Let me **present** Mr Harris.
  **b** I hope you like my **present**.

## Reading & Writing

**6** Read the email and complete the gaps with the word that derives from the word in bold. What is each paragraph about?

 **INBOX**

Hi Ed,

**A** How's things? Last weekend, I went to the Robin Hood Festival near Nottingham, England. It's a **1)** ......................... **(celebrate)** of the legend of Robin Hood! It takes place every year in Sherwood Forest.

**B** According to the legend, Robin Hood was a **2)** ......................... **(hero)** outlaw in 12th-century England. He hated the way the King treated the people, so he decided to do something about it. He stole money from **3)** ......................... **(wealth)** people and gave it to poor people. The King tried to arrest him, but Robin escaped to Sherwood Forest where he lived **4)** ......................... **(happy)** with other outlaws.

**C** The festival was wonderful! When I entered, **5)** ......................... **(magic)** were doing tricks and experts were giving demonstrations of archery. There were also **6)** ......................... **(perform)** of medieval music and free samples of **7)** ......................... **(taste)** medieval food. The whole event was like stepping back in time!

**D** The Robin Hood Festival is a must for anyone who's **8)** ................ **(fascinate)** by history. It's a pity you missed it. Why not come with me next year?

Kevin

###  Writing Tip

**Using appropriate tenses**
We use **present tenses** to give general information about a celebration and **past tenses** to describe the preparations and the activities on the actual day of the celebration we attended.

**7** Read the Writing Tip. Find examples in the email in Ex. 6.

### Recommending

**8 a)** Fill in: *miss*, *must*, *waste of time*, *well worth*, *disaster*.

1 The International Kite Festival is a ......................... for anyone who likes kites.
2 If you get the chance to visit Japan, don't .................... it!
3 It was a complete .........................; I can't believe I spent so many hours there.
4 It was a huge .........................; I was so disappointed.
5 It's ......................... visiting this festival. You won't regret it.

**b)** How has Kevin recommended the celebration in the email in Ex. 6?

## Writing (an email about a celebration you attended)

**9** Read the task. Underline the key words. What are you going to write? Who is it for? What should it be about? What style should you use?

You have received an email from your penfriend.

Our English teacher has asked us to write about cultural celebrations in various countries that are based on a legend or a historical event. Have you attended one recently? What legend is it based on? How did people celebrate it? Would you recommend it?
Write back and tell me all about it.
Ben

Write your **email** (120-180 words).

**10** **LISTENING FOR IDEAS** 🎧 Listen to Pat's podcast and complete the gaps.

**LEWES BONFIRE NIGHT**

Place: Lewes, **1)** .........................
Date: 5th November
Numbers taking part: 5,000 locals and **2)** ............ visitors
Before bonfires: **3)** ......................... of locals in costumes and marching bands
Number of bonfires and fireworks displays: **4)** .............
Food: toffee apples, burgers and **5)** .................. potatoes

**11** Imagine you attended the Lewes Bonfire Night last week. Use your notes from Ex. 10 to write your email. Follow the plan.

**Plan**

Hi + *(your friend's first name)*
**Para 1:** opening remarks; details of the festival
**Para 2:** legend/historical event behind the festival
**Para 3:** activities during the celebration
**Para 4:** feelings; recommendation; closing remarks
*(your first name)*

**VALUES**
**Traditionalism**
*A people without the knowledge of their past history, origin and culture is like a tree without roots.* **Marcus Garvey**

# 2 Culture

## Listening & Reading

**1** **Which of the following do you think people say bring bad luck in the UK?**

• a building having a 13th floor • finding money • a black cat crossing your path • black birds living in a castle • saying the title of a play • breaking a mirror

🎧 **Listen and read to find out.**

**2** **Read the text and answer the questions.**

**1** How many people in the UK believe in superstitions?
**2** What should actors do if they say the name 'Macbeth' by mistake?
**3** How do high buildings avoid the number 13?
**4** What can tourists see in the Tower of London?
**5** What do people say will happen if the ravens leave the Tower of London?

**3** **Match the words in bold to their synonyms below.**

• one of a kind • ordinary • infrequent • kept • careful • fascinating

**4** **Match the underlined words/ phrases to their opposites below.**

• depressed • add • denying • on purpose • enter • normal

## Speaking & Writing

**5** 👥 THINK **Read the following sayings about luck. What do they mean? Do you agree with any of them? Discuss.**

*It is better to be born lucky than rich.*
*You make your own luck.*
*Bad luck comes in threes.*

**6** ICT 💬 **Find out information about superstitions and/or sayings about good/bad luck in your country or in other countries. Present them to the class.**

▶ **VIDEO**

# Superstitions in the UK

*'Find a penny, pick it up and all day long, you'll have good luck'* is just one of the many sayings about luck that UK citizens have. With over half of them <u>admitting</u> they get at least a little worried if they break a mirror, it is no surprise that they have some **interesting** and, in some cases, **unique** superstitions.

William Shakespeare was one of the world's greatest playwrights. One of his most popular plays is *Macbeth*, first staged in 1606, and people have been performing it all over the world since then. Its name, though, is not popular at all with actors, who believe that saying it will bring bad luck: they call it 'the Scottish play' instead. If an actor <u>accidentally</u> says 'Macbeth', they will try to get rid of the bad luck by reciting a line from one of Shakespeare's other plays. If they are in the theatre at the time, they will <u>exit</u> the theatre, spin around and say 'Macbeth' three times before returning. It seems <u>strange</u>, but, after all, 'the show must go on!'

One of the most **common** superstitions in the UK is the fear of the number 13. There's even a word for it: triskaidekaphobia. Friday 13th is a day to be **cautious** and some people even stay at home to avoid disaster. 13 is not just about Fridays. Lots of blocks of flats and hotels <u>miss out</u> the thirteenth floor; the lift going from the 12th floor directly to the 14th. The London Eye may have 32 capsules for tourists to take in the sights of London, but they have the numbers 1 to 33, without, of course, the number 13.

Visitors to the UK should not miss the Tower of London, where the Crown Jewels are safely **stored**. Another attraction at the Tower is the seven (six plus one spare) coal-black ravens who live there. People call them the Guardians of the Tower. People say that if the ravens ever fly off and leave, then that marks the end of the UK! This may just be a superstition, but it seems British people aren't taking any chances! The ravens' carers keep them <u>content</u> with a diet of raw meat as well as the **occasional** treat – a special biscuit.

 **Check these words**

penny, saying, path, admit, playwright, recite, spin around

## Vocabulary

**1** **Fill in:** *stalls, dishes, costumes, performers, parades.*

1 We tried some delicious Maori ............................. at the festival.

2 Have you seen the ............................. Susan made for her children to wear?

3 There are two ............................. through the city; one at 10 am and one at 6 pm.

4 We can buy something to eat from one of the food ............................. in the square.

5 The street ............................. we saw at the Edinburgh Festival were very talented.

*(5 x 3 = 15)*

**2** **Choose the correct word.**

1 The **flame/highlight/burst** of the event was the dragon contest.

2 A **local/traditional/cultural** man told us about the festival.

3 We **set/recite/hold** a two-minute silence.

4 That was an amazing fireworks **display/show/event**!

5 All the **jugglers/puppets/residents** you can see in the parade are handmade.

6 Lots of people followed the **celebrations/procession/march** through the town.

7 The king **gathered/offered/prepared** his daughter in marriage to the prince.

8 It's the **culture/custom/saying** in my country to kiss people three times when you meet them.

9 The event really **brings/takes/soars** history to life.

10 I couldn't **believe/show/admit** my eyes when the fireworks display started.

*(10 x 2 = 20)*

**3** **Choose the correct item.**

1 They were all dressed **in/on/up** dragon costumes.

2 Jake came **across/over/up** with a fantastic plan.

3 Can you help me blow **into/out/up** these balloons?

4 The Old Town is always packed **for/in/with** people during the festival.

5 Please, blow **away/out/off** all the candles before you go to bed.

*(5 x 3 = 15)*

## Grammar

**4** **Put the verbs in brackets into the past simple, the past continuous or the present perfect.**

1 We were watching the band live on stage when the lights ............................. **(go out)**.

2 ............................. **(they/arrive)** at the festival yet?

3 I ............................. **(learn)** to ice-skate when I was six.

4 Penny ............................. **(not/eat)** Polish food since she left Krakow three months ago.

5 ............................. **(you/drive)** back to your hotel when the storm started?

6 Mary was taking pictures while we ............................. **(walk)** through the festival grounds.

7 The event ............................. **(start)** an hour ago.

8 Steve paid for a ticket and then ............................. **(enter)** the theatre.

9 At 7:30 yesterday evening, they ............................. **(watch)** the mayor letting off fireworks.

10 I ............................. **(not/attend)** the event since I was a young boy.

*(10 x 2 = 20)*

**5** **Choose the correct item.**

1 When I was a child, I **would/used to** have a pet rabbit.

2 Getting up early is hard for me, but my dad **is/gets** used to it because he's been a postman for 12 years.

3 Did you **use/used** to go skating when you were young?

4 Alice couldn't **get/be** used to the hot weather in Dubai.

5 Tom **wouldn't/didn't use to** like traditional music, but now he enjoys it.

*(5 x 2 = 10)*

## Everyday English

**6** **Match the sentences.**

1 ☐ What's it about?
2 ☐ I took part in an archery competition.
3 ☐ What was it like?
4 ☐ Why don't you come?
5 ☐ It sounds like you had fun.

a Really?
b I did.
c Count me in!
d It's a day when people celebrate Burns' poetry.
e I had the time of my life!

*(5 x 4 = 20)*

*Total 100*

## Competences

GOOD ✓

VERY GOOD ✓ ✓

EXCELLENT ✓ ✓ ✓

**Lexical Competence**
understand words/ phrases related to:
• festivities
• celebrations & customs

**Reading Competence**
• understand texts related to festivities (read for key information – gapped text; comprehension questions)
**Listening Competence**
• listen to and understand monologues related to celebrations (multiple matching)

**Speaking Competence**
• describe an event
**Writing Competence**
• write an article
• write a summary of a legend
• write an email about a celebration you attended

# 3 Adventures

| Vocabulary: | adventure activities, types of holidays & travel disasters | Everyday English: | describing an experience – expressing interest & shock |
|---|---|---|---|
| Grammar: | past perfect – past perfect continuous; past simple vs past perfect; past tenses (revision); *a/an – the* | Writing: | a short story |

Daniel's **Blog**  |  about me  |  my photo  |  contact  |  ▶ VIDEO

## UNUSUAL ADVENTURES
### Around the World

*As a young child, I always wanted to try anything new and exciting, and I haven't changed much over the years! I still love trying new things and I especially love travelling. Here are a few of my most interesting stories.*

### A Lionfish Hunting

One of the first places I travelled to by myself was Belize in Central America. As a **fully-trained** diver who loves the ocean, I jumped at the chance to go lionfish hunting there. The locals hunt these fish because there are too many of them and they cause problems for Belize's coral reefs. They also make a delicious meal! I admit I was a little anxious beforehand; I'd never seen a lionfish – the name made them sound quite ferocious! However, they were actually rather small. I felt relieved; I'd been imagining a fish as big as a lion! In the end, I had an amazing time swimming in the warm, crystal-clear waters – I even managed to catch a few lionfish!

### B Diving in Lake Kaindy

One of the most interesting places I've ever been to is Lake Kaindy in Kazakhstan. It's over 2,000 m above sea level and the water is a beautiful blue-green colour. In the centre, there are dozens of **leafless** trees. It's a strange place, but you can't **appreciate** how strange it is from the shore. I got the surprise of a lifetime when I dived into the lake and saw that, underwater, the trees had actually kept their leaves! Apparently, an earthquake had happened over 100 years before, flooding the land. The low temperature of the water means that the trees have stayed in almost perfect condition below the **surface.** Incredible!

### C Canyoning

The first time I visited Asia was on a trip to Japan, and what a trip it was! Forest Canyon, in Nametoko Valley is one of the country's **leading** canyoning spots. People come from all over to try it. I'd never heard of it before I went there. It's a sport which involves jumping into a fast-flowing mountain stream and floating downstream on your back at high speed. Nametoko Valley is home to Yukiwa Waterfall, a 40 m natural water slide with deep pools perfect for jumping into. Instructors carefully explain how to enjoy canyoning, so even a beginner like me could give it a go without any worries. I also tried waterfall abseiling, too. It was a **thrilling** adventure!

### D Virunga Hiking

A couple of years ago, I went on an **extraordinary** hike through the Congo in Africa. It wasn't easy! Our first challenge was climbing Mount Nyiragongo, an active volcano. Some of us experienced headaches and dizziness from climbing so high, and all of us felt absolutely **exhausted**. But it was worth it for the **incredible** sight at the top: an enormous lava lake! We spent the night in cabins next to the lake before descending the volcano the next day. Our guides also took us gorilla tracking through Virunga National Park. We had been walking for hours before we saw a group of them, relaxing in the jungle. We couldn't get too close, but it was **breathtaking** to watch them.

## Listening & Reading

**1** **Look at the pictures. Which places has Daniel visited?**
 **Listen and read to find out.**

✓ **Check these words**

beforehand, ferocious, lifetime, apparently, downstream, slide, pool, abseiling, dizziness, descend

**2** **Read the article again. For questions 1-8, choose from the activities (A-D). The activities may be chosen more than once. Then explain the words in bold.**

**Which activity**

1 involves spending a lot of time with animals? ........
2 includes an overnight stay by a lake? ........
3 helps solve a problem in a local ecosystem? ........
4 happens at a location where a natural disaster occurred? ........
5 offers the opportunity to participate in an unusual sport? ........
6 takes place in cold water? ........
7 includes the possibility of seeing a species of mammal? ........
8 provides food for the local community? ........

**3** THINK **What makes Daniel an adventurous person? Which of these places do you find the most interesting? Why? Tell the class.**

**4** COLLOCATIONS **Find and complete the words in the text that describe the following. Then use the phrases to make sentences.**

1 .................. reef
2 .................. level
3 .................. temperature
4 .................. speed
5 .................. volcano
6 .................. exhausted

**5** PREPOSITIONS **Choose the correct preposition. Check in your dictionary.**

1 We started climbing the mountain at 9 am. **At/In** the end, we reached the top at noon.
2 There are trees **at/in** the centre of the lake.
3 People come from all **under/over** to go canyoning in Forest Canyon.
4 The waterfall is perfect **for/at** abseiling.
5 We waited in the cave **from/for** hours until the rain finally stopped.

**6** WORDS EASILY CONFUSED **Choose the correct word. Check in your dictionary.**

1 Knossos is a famous archaeological **site/sight** in Greece, with ruins thousands of years old.
2 I love travelling, but I feel **ill/anxious** when I travel alone.
3 Some of the group **experienced/felt** seasickness while we were sailing through rough waters.
4 Now that I've graduated from flight school, I'm a fully-**trained/taught** pilot.

## Vocabulary
### Adventure activities

**7** **Fill in**: *explore, come, interact, hire, track, snap*.

① **KILAUEA, HAWAII**
.............................. a helicopter for a flight over this active volcano.

② **DAINTREE RAINFOREST**
............................ face to face with rainforest animals in their natural habitat.

③ **SAHARA DESERT**
Spend a week with the Bedouin and ............................ with another culture.

④ **MAMMOTH NATIONAL PARK**
............................... part of the biggest cave system in the world with an expert guide.

⑤ **MASAI MARA SAFARI**
............................ pictures of Kenya's Big Five – the lion, the leopard, the rhino, the buffalo and the elephant.

⑥ **TANZANIAN HIKE**
Take our ten-day course and learn how to ................... rhinos across the plains of Africa!

**8** PHRASAL VERBS **Fill in the correct particle(s).**

**look around:** to explore an area
**look back:** to think about sth from the past
**look out for:** to try to avoid sth dangerous
**look over:** to examine sth
**look through sth:** to have a quick look at sth

1 I was looking ............................ a holiday brochure.
2 Look ............................ pickpockets at the market.
3 I'll look ............................ all the details and book the flights tonight.
4 Jo spent the morning looking ................... the Old Town.
5 When we're older, we'll look ............................ on this adventure and smile.

## Speaking & Writing

**9** ICT **Research adventure activities in your country or another country. Think about:** *name – place – what to do there – special skills/experience required – who appropriate for*. **Choose one. Imagine you experienced it. Write a text for a travel magazine similar to one of the texts in Ex. 1. Present it to the class.**

# Grammar in Use

**Tom:** Hi, Carrie! I've been thinking about travelling when I finish university. You've visited so many amazing places. Which one was your favourite?

**Carrie:** That's a tough question, Tom, but I'd probably say my trip to Africa last year. I had always thought of Africa as a hot dry place, but my visit to Botswana changed my mind!

**Tom:** How come?

**Carrie:** Well, I went on an amazing safari in the Okavango Delta. It had been raining for weeks before I arrived, and the water had flooded the delta. You could hardly see the river banks! I thought we'd have to cancel the trip, but the guide had been working there for years and knew the way. The scenery was stunning.

**Tom:** It sounds wonderful.

**Carrie:** It was. As we were going down the river, we suddenly heard a loud splash. Ahead of us, some elephants were taking a dip in the water! I was so excited that I had finally seen elephants in the wild.

**Tom:** Wow! What an amazing experience! Well, you've convinced me. Africa's going to be at the top of my list!

## Past perfect – Past perfect continuous ▸ p. GR5

**1** Find examples of the past perfect and past perfect continuous in the dialogue. Which one(s) do we use:

1 for an action which finished before another past action or before a stated time in the past?

2 for an action which finished in the past and whose result was visible at a later point in the past?

3 to put emphasis on the duration of an action which started and finished in the past, before another action or stated time in the past, usually with *for* or *since*?

4 for an action which lasted for some time in the past and whose result was visible in the past?

**2** Put the verbs in brackets into the past perfect or the past perfect continuous.

1 Ben ................................. **(travel)** to three different countries by 2018.

2 ................................................ **(you/wait)** to board the plane for a long time before the flight was cancelled?

3 They missed the bus because they ............................... ................................. **(not/wake up)** early enough.

4 How long ............................................................... **(you/save)** before you could afford to go on a safari?

5 After Simone ................................. **(book)** her flights, she went shopping for some summer clothes.

6 Robert ............................................................... **(hike)** all day so his shoes were covered in mud.

7 I had to go shopping as I ................................. **(not/pack)** enough warm clothes for the trip.

8 ................................. **(the storm/pass)** by the time the plane took off?

**3** Complete the sentences using the ideas in the list.

- not take a map • look for/hotel for hours
- see lots of wild animals on the safari
- not feel well/all morning • rain/for days

1 The tourists were disappointed with the weather.
*It had been raining for days.*

2 We were very satisfied. We ...........................................
......................................................................................... .

3 I decided not to go on the tour. I ....................................
......................................................................................... .

4 John and Kathy were exhausted. They ...........................
......................................................................................... .

5 Paul got lost while exploring. He ....................................
......................................................................................... .

**4** **SPEAKING** One student pretends they took the picture below. The other asks them questions about it, using the past perfect and past perfect continuous, as in the example.

A: *Who had suggested going on the trip?*
B: *My dad. He had been planning it for ages.*

## Past simple vs Past perfect ▶ p. GR5

**5** Put the verbs in brackets into the past simple or the past perfect. Then say which action happened first.

**1** A: Sarah ........................................... **(book)** a diving holiday in Belize last week!

B: Yes, she ............................... **(decide)** to go because her cousin ............................................... **(recommend)** it to her.

**2** A: ........................................... **(you/set off)** on the hike early yesterday morning?

B: No, we ................................... **(leave)** after we ............................................. **(finish)** our breakfast at 10 o'clock.

**3** A: Where did Amy get to last week?

B: She ........................ **(get)** in her car, ......................... **(drive)** all the way to Wales and ............................... **(go)** mountain climbing, even though she ....................................... **(not/do)** it before!

**4** A: ........................................... **(you/see)** any gorillas yesterday?

B: Yes, but then Jon ........................................ **(realise)** that he ................................................... **(not/bring)** our camera.

## Past tenses (Revision)

**6** Put the verbs in brackets into the correct past tense.

Hola Serena!
Thank you for recommending Peru. It's great! **1)** ........................ **(you/go)** to Huacachina when you were here?
Yesterday, I **2)** ........................ **(catch)** a bus from Lima to go there. It was a long trip. We **3)** ........................ **(travel)** for five hours before we **4)** ........................ **(reach)** our destination! While we **5)** ........................ **(drive)** along, I **6)** ........................ **(wonder)** to myself, "Are we going the right way?" All I could see was sand in every direction! But that's what's so special about Huacachina – it's a village built around a lake in the middle of a desert! To be honest, I **7)** ........................ **(not/hear)** of Huacachina before I **8)** ........................ **(speak)** to some other backpackers at the hostel in Lima. They **9)** ........................ **(visit)** the village a week before I met them, and they also recommended hiring a plane for a flight over the Nazca Desert. That sounded great, so I **10)** ........................ **(go)** this morning! We **11)** ........................ **(not/fly)** over the desert for long when we saw the famous Nazca Lines on the ground below. I was thrilled – I **12)** ........................ **(wait)** to see those mysterious markings since I was a child.
I'll send you photos soon.
Zoe

**7** Complete the sentences so they are true for you.

**1** While I was driving to work, ..........................................

**2** Last winter, ...............................................................

**3** After I had finished studying, ...................................

**4** I was eating dinner when ..........................................

**5** I had been learning English for years before ...............

**6** I hadn't been to Poland before so ...............................

## A/an – The ▶ pp. GR5-6

**8** Fill in: *a/an*, *the* or –. Then answer the questions.

**Quiz**

How good is your Geography?
Check your answers online.

**1** Which of these is NOT **1)** .......... continent?
A **2)** .......... South Africa
B **3)** .......... South America

**2** Which landmark is in **4)** .......... USA?
A **5)** .......... Mount Everest
B **6)** .......... Grand Canyon

**3** What is Teotihuacán?
A **7)** .......... ancient city in **8)** .......... Mexico
B **9)** .......... bridge in **10)** .......... Netherlands

**4** Where does **11)** .......... Amazon River start?
A **12)** .......... Rocky Mountains
B **13)** .......... Andes

**5** Which of these is **14)** .......... island in **15)** .......... Japan?
A **16)** .......... Honshu      B **17)** .......... Baffin Island

**6** What is Krakatoa?
A **18)** .......... volcano      B **19)** .......... ocean

**7** **20)** .......... Azores are a group of islands in ...
A **21)** .......... Hudson Bay
B **22)** .......... Atlantic Ocean

**8** Which is **23)** .......... largest island in **24)** .......... Mediterranean Sea?
A Crete                    B Sicily

**9** **25)** .......... Roald Amundsen and his team were **26)** .......... first people to ...
A reach **27)** .......... South Pole
B cross **28)** .......... Australia on foot

**10** Which is **29)** .......... famous place in **30)** .......... London?
A **31)** .......... Oxford Street
B **32)** .......... Central Park

**9** **SPEAKING** 💬 Continue the story. Take turns. Use past tenses and the items in the list.

• London • Big Ben • River Thames • Tower Bridge
• Oxford Street • accident • ambulance • hospital

*Max had arrived in London a day before Tony arrived.*

23

# Skills in Action

## Vocabulary

### Types of holidays & Travel disasters

**1** a) **Match the travel disasters to the type of holiday they would happen on.**

1 ☐ I got seasick and spent the holiday throwing up in my cabin!

2 ☐ I nearly drowned while swimming by a reef!

3 ☐ A poisonous snake bit me during a forest clean-up!

4 ☐ I'm allergic to bees, and one stung me in a park in London!

5 ☐ I burnt my hand badly while lighting a campfire!

6 ☐ I got an infection in my big toe while walking in the mountains!

7 ☐ I fell off a ladder and broke my arm while picking apples!

8 ☐ I twisted my ankle jumping out of the jeep to snap a picture.

| | | | |
|---|---|---|---|
| **a** | agritourism holiday | **e** | safari holiday |
| **b** | diving holiday | **f** | cruise |
| **c** | hiking trip | **g** | city break |
| **d** | camping trip | **h** | ecotourism holiday |

b) **Has anything like the disasters in Ex. 1a ever happened to you while on holiday? What happened? Tell your partner.**

## Listening

**2** **You will hear people talking in four different situations. For questions 1-4, choose the best answer (A, B or C).**

1 You hear two friends talking about an excursion. Why doesn't the man want to go?
   A He doesn't want to travel by boat.
   B The trip costs too much money.
   C He feels ill when he travels by plane.

2 You hear two people talking about a travel problem. What is the man doing?
   A giving advice about travelling abroad
   B explaining how to get a good night's sleep
   C describing how to deal with a travel problem

3 You hear a conversation between two friends. The woman says her burn
   A went away after the injection.
   B is better than it was in the USA.
   C is still causing her pain.

4 You hear an item on the news. What happened to the group?
   A They saved a drowning man.
   B One of them nearly died.
   C Jellyfish stung them all.

## Everyday English

### Describing an experience – Expressing interest & shock

**3** **Joan was on a safari holiday in Kenya. What disaster do you think she experienced?**
   **Listen and read to find out if you were right.**

**Kim:** How was your safari holiday in Kenya, Joan?
**Joan:** It was horrible!
**Kim:** Really? What went wrong? Tell me more!
**Joan:** You'll never believe what happened. My tour group was tracking a rhino, and I was about to take a photo when suddenly a tiny snake bit my ankle!
**Kim:** Really? So what did you do?
**Joan:** I screamed in pain and the rhino obviously ran away!
**Kim:** And what about your leg?
**Joan:** It's fine now, but it was really sore. I had to stay in hospital for the last two days of my trip!
**Kim:** I'm so sorry to hear that, Joan. At least you're OK now.
**Joan:** Tell me about it! I'm never doing that again.

**4** **Think of a nasty experience you had. Act out a dialogue similar to the one in Ex. 3. Use language from the box.**

| Describing an experience | Expressing interest |
|---|---|
| • It was horrible!/It was a disaster. You'll never guess what happened. <br> • It's a long story. You won't believe what happened out there! | • Really? Tell me all about it. <br> • What went wrong? <br> • And what happened next? <br> • And what about ...? <br> • So what did you do? |
| **Expressing shock** ||
| • Oh dear!/Really? <br> • That's awful/terrible!/You're kidding! <br> • I'd never have guessed. ||

## Intonation: sentence stress

**5** **Listen to the sentences. Underline the stressed word(s). What effect does the change of emphasis have on each sentence? What question would each answer?**

1 I asked you to give the keys to the reception.
2 I asked you to give the keys to the reception.
3 I asked you to give the keys to the reception.
4 I asked you to give the keys to the reception.

## Reading & Writing

**6** Read the story and fill in the gaps with words derived from the words in brackets. Is it a *first-* or *third*-person narrative?

### A Close Call at the Lake

It was a **1)** ............................. (sun) summer's day. Jack and his friends Anna, Joe and Dean were at the local lake, where they had all gone paddle boarding. They were all laughing and enjoying **2)** ............................. (them).

They had been paddling for ages and everybody was feeling **3)** ............................. (tire), so they decided to relax by the water's edge for a while. Joe was paddling towards the shore when he suddenly slipped, banged his head on the board and fell into the water.

**4)** ............................. (immediate), Jack dived bravely into the water and swam as deeply as he could. When he got to the bottom of the lake, he saw Joe, tangled in the weeds. Jack tore the weeds away and dragged him to the surface. Joe was struggling, but Jack held him tightly. "Try not to panic," he said as he pulled his friend to **5)** ............................. (safe) at the edge of the lake.

Everyone was incredibly relieved when the boys finally reached dry land. "Wow, you saved Joe's life," said Anna. Jack, however, couldn't respond; he just fell onto the grass. He was **6)** ............................. (exhaust)!

**7** Read the Writing Tip below. Then find an example in the story in Ex. 6.

---

 **Writing Tip**

**Expanding sentences**

We expand our sentences by adding specific information and descriptive details. We explain who was there, what happened, and when, where, how and why it happened. This gives the reader more information and makes the story more interesting. *She travelled to New Zealand.*

• **Who:** Olivia • **Where:** Auckland • **When:** Saturday
• **How:** by plane • **Why:** to go white-water rafting
*On Saturday, Olivia travelled by plane to Auckland, New Zealand to go white-water rafting.*

---

**8** Expand the following sentences using the information in the Writing Tip.

1 Kevin travelled to Kenya.
2 Ann went to a resort in Canada.
3 They were stuck in their hotel.
4 I saw an elephant.
5 He injured his leg.

## Writing (a short story)

**9** Read the task and underline the key words. Then answer the questions (1-5).

> You have decided to enter a short story competition for an English-language magazine for young people. Your story must begin with this sentence: *It was a beautiful January day, and Emma and her guide, Oliver, were out husky sledding.* Write your story (120-180 words).

1 What are you going to write?
2 Who is going to read it?
3 How must you start your piece of writing?
4 Should you use a first- or third-person narrative?
5 What tenses should you use?

**10** **LISTENING FOR IDEAS** 🎧 Listen to the story and put the events (A-H) in the order they happened (1-8).

A The sled got stuck in the snow.
B Oliver took Emma to hospital.
C Oliver suddenly had an idea.
D Emma and Oliver stopped for a break.
E The storm finally stopped.
F A snowstorm started.
G Emma twisted her ankle trying to move the sled.
H They dug a hole in the snow and climbed in.

**11** Use the events in Ex. 10 and the plan below to write your story.

**Plan**

**Para 1:** set the scene (characters, time, place, weather, feelings)
**Para 2:** events in the order they happened
**Para 3:** climax event
**Para 4:** ending; feelings

**VALUES**

**Boldness**
*Fortune favours the bold.*
**Latin proverb**

25

# 3  Culture

## Reading & Listening

**1** In one minute, write down as many outdoor activities as you can think of. Tell the class.

**2** Look at the text, the headings and the images. Which of these activities do you have to pay for? 🎧 Listen and read to find out.

**3** a) Read the text again and decide if the sentences are *T* (True), *F* (False) or *DS* (Doesn't Say).

1 The kite-buggying experience is not for beginners.
2 Kite-buggying takes place by the sea.
3 The Isle of Skye is a remote location.
4 Gorge walking guides can change the difficulty level of the activity.
5 You must have previous experience to go rock climbing in Llanberis Pass.
6 Rock climbing equipment is provided at no cost at Llanberis Pass.
7 Coasteering is a relaxing activity.
8 The Giant's Causeway is the most famous landmark in Northern Ireland.

b) Explain the words/phrases in bold. Then use them to talk about each of the activities.

## Speaking & Writing

**4** (THINK) Categorise activities A-D according to the level of difficulty, starting with the most difficult. Which one would you find too extreme to try? Why? Tell the class.

**5** 💬 ICT Find information about outdoor activity breaks in your country. Imagine you have experienced them. Prepare a review for an online magazine. You can use the text in Ex. 1 as model. Include: *places – level of difficulty – what you see/do – equipment (if necessary) – how much they cost.* Use present and past tenses. Present it to your class.

 ▶ VIDEO

# Outdoor Activity Breaks in the UK

Spring has finally arrived and it's time to get outdoors. Last week, we tried out some of the most exciting outdoor activities available across the UK. Here are our top four …

### A  Kite-buggying, East Sussex

Have you ever been go-carting? What about kite-flying? Imagine doing both at the same time: kite-buggying is just that! After a quick lesson to learn **the basics**, with only a kite, a three-wheeled cart and a good gust of wind, we were whizzing across a sandy beach at speeds of up to 50 mph! £59 per person for 2.5 hours.

### B  Gorge walking, Isle of Skye

We were particularly excited about this one because we had never been to the beautiful Isle of Skye before. Through a combination of walking, jumping, swimming, floating, splashing and sliding, we **squeezed** through narrow canyons and **crawled** up streams. The guides will tailor the experience to suit your needs, so if you want extra-scary, just ask! £47 per person for 4 hours.

### C  Rock climbing, Snowdonia National Park

Snowdonia National Park boasts some stunning scenery, but it is also a top destination for climbers. Llanberis Pass is ideal for rock climbing, as the challenges **range** in difficulty from beginner to expert. Naturally, as first-time climbers, we stuck to the easier climbs! Entry to the Park and access to the pass are both free of charge, but we had to **purchase** some climbing shoes and chalk for our hands in the nearby village of Llanberis.

### D  Coasteering, County Antrim

Visit the Giant's Causeway in Northern Ireland for an **adrenaline-filled** coasteering experience. We climbed, dived off cliffs, swam and more. By the end, we had worked every muscle in our bodies! It's certainly an **action-packed** day, during which you'll witness first-hand the beauty of this well-known coastline. £40 per person for 3 hours.

We hadn't been expecting to find so many adventures on our own doorstep! And that's just the tip of the iceberg. See our website for more exciting outdoor experiences in England, Scotland, Wales and Northern Ireland.

 ✓ **Check these words**

gust, whizz, tailor, stick to sth, access, on your doorstep, tip of the iceberg

## Vocabulary

**1** **Choose the correct word.**

**1** It was amazing to go diving at night and explore the **coral/sea/ocean** reef.

**2** John always feels a little **expectant/anxious/ extraordinary** when he flies.

**3** You've **twisted/bitten/stung** your ankle; you need to put an ice-pack on it.

**4** No one had ever visited the island before, and so it was in **low/perfect/active** condition.

**5** We were exhausted because we had **explored/ interacted/appreciated** the whole mountain.

*(5 x 3 = 15)*

**2** **Fill in:** *break, cruise, infection, spot, snap.*

**1** John got a bad .................................. in his finger.

**2** I can't go on a .................................. – I get seasick!

**3** A city .................................. in Paris would be great!

**4** Quick – .................................. a picture of that hippo!

**5** This is the country's leading .................................. for canyoning.

*(5 x 3 = 15)*

**3** **Choose the correct item.**

**1** There are trees **by/with/in** the centre of the square.

**2** I think I'll look **out/over/around** the flight details one more time before bed.

**3** People come from all **in/for/over** the world to see the canyon.

**4** He always looks **through/back on/out for** his time in India with happiness.

**5** The area is perfect **in/from/for** hiking.

*(5 x 2 = 10)*

## Grammar

**4** **Use the verbs in the list in the past perfect or past perfect continuous to complete the gaps.**

• reach • not bring • leave • hope • not search

**1** The last ferry .............................. by the time we arrived.

**2** I .................................................. online for long when I found the perfect guesthouse.

**3** They didn't let him on the plane because he ................. .................................... his passport with him.

**4** They .......................... the village by 10 in the morning.

**5** She ................................................ to go on a weekend break for months, but she had too much work.

*(5 x 4 = 20)*

**5** **Put the verbs in brackets into the correct past tense.**

**1** .................................................. **(Janet/hike)** when she tripped and banged her knee?

**2** How long ...................................................................... **(you/dream)** of a trip to Southeast Asia before you booked the tickets?

**3** Last year, we .......................................... **(visit)** some of the islands off the coast of New Zealand.

**4** I didn't call you back yesterday as I ................................. **(not/charge)** my phone and the battery ran out.

**5** Sheila .......................................... **(work)** as a guide for fifteen years before she opened her own tour company.

*(5 x 4 = 20)*

## Everyday English

**6** **Match the exchanges.**

**1** ☐ You won't believe what happened out there!

**2** ☐ What went wrong?

**3** ☐ My cousin got bitten by a snake.

**4** ☐ So what did you do?

**5** ☐ You got caught in a snowstorm? You're kidding!

**a** You haven't heard anything yet.

**b** I'm afraid I panicked at first.

**c** I broke my leg.

**d** Really? Tell me all about it.

**e** Oh dear! That's awful!

*(5 x 4 = 20)*

*Total 100*

## Competences

GOOD ✓

VERY GOOD ✓✓

EXCELLENT ✓✓✓

**Lexical Competence**
understand words/ phrases related to:
• adventure activities
• types of holidays & travel disasters

**Reading Competence**
• understand texts related to adventure travel (read for specific information – multiple matching; T/F/DS statements)

**Listening Competence**
• listen to & understand dialogues related to travel problems (listen for gist/specific information – multiple choice)

**Speaking Competence**
• describe an experience
• express interest & shock

**Writing Competence**
• write a review
• write a story in the third-person
• write a text about an imaginary adventurous experience

# Values: Curiosity

▶ VIDEO

# THE JOY OF CURIOSITY

One of the things we most **admire** about young children is their curiosity. They are always asking questions about the world around them – about how things work and why things happen. Later in life, though, for some reason, a lot of people lose that thirst for knowledge. But being curious is so important in all areas of life, in school, at work, and even in our **social lives.**

'I have no special talent. I am only **passionately** curious.'
Albert Einstein

## The benefits of curiosity

1 **Curiosity makes us more intelligent.** A curious person has a sense of **wonder** for the world and always wants to learn more. This means they are always building their knowledge and improving their skills.

2 **Curiosity brings excitement into our lives.** For curious people, the word 'boredom' doesn't exist. They're never **satisfied** with what they know or have experienced, and are always looking for the next adventure.

3 **Curiosity makes us better people.** When we feel curious about a person, who they are or how they're feeling, this often make us feel **empathy** for them. This helps us to become less selfish and more **likeable.**

4 **Curiosity makes us more successful.** A curious student or worker is always asking questions, learning from others, and trying to find ways to do things better. This greatly increases their chances of success in both school and the workplace.

## Tips to develop your curiosity

**Use technology.** Being curious means asking questions about the world around you, and these days, it's usually easy to find answers using the Internet. If you've got a smartphone, don't forget that you can even feed your curiosity **on the go.**

**Listen more.** When we have conversations, we're often more interested in sharing our opinions rather than learning about the opinions of others. But to grow your curiosity, try to listen and learn more when you're talking to people.

**Get inspired.** When we get older, we often forget there is a world outside our **daily routine.** A good way to fix this is through culture. Reading novels or looking at art, for example, can bring back that sense of wonder we had when we were children.

---

**1** Why is it important to be curious? What can we do to develop our curiosity?

🎧 Listen and read to find out.

**2** Read what six people say about curiosity (A-F). Which benefit of curiosity in the text (1-4) are they talking about?

A 'I had to find out what it would be like to live in a foreign country.' ..........

B 'Whenever I come across a flower I don't recognise, I always look it up on the Internet.' ..........

C 'I wondered what it must feel like to be homeless, and that inspired me to donate to the charity.' ..........

D 'If I hadn't researched new ways to increase sales, I wouldn't have got the promotion.' ..........

E 'When I thought about why Paul had lied to me, I stopped being angry with him'. ..........

F 'I had always wondered what it would feel like to go bungee jumping ... and now I know!' ..........

**3** Explain the words/phrases in bold.

**4** 👥 THINK Can you remember a time when you felt curious to learn more about something? What happened? How did the experience benefit you? Tell you partner.

**5** ICT THINK Read the list of questions and put a tick (✓) next to the one(s) you know the answer to. Then choose the un-ticked question that you are most curious to discover the answer to. Do some research to find the answer, then write a short text about why you were curious to find the answer, how you found the answer, and how you felt after you found it.

1 What is the most popular first name in the world? ........

2 Why do cats have whiskers? ........

3 How many steps are there in the Eiffel Tower? ........

4 What was the colour of the first car ever made? ........

5 Why are colds and flu most common in the winter? ........

# Public Speaking Skills

## 1 Read the task and answer the questions.

You are a careers adviser in a secondary school. Give a talk to students in their last year of school about the benefits of going on a gap year abroad.

1 Who are you going to speak to?
2 What is the talk going to be about?
3 What is the purpose of the talk?

### Study Skills

**Using a personal anecdote**

You can form a connection with your audience by including a personal anecdote. This is a very short story from your life. A funny or interesting personal anecdote that is relevant to your talk will make your audience more interested in listening to you.

## 2 🎧 Listen to and read the model. What personal anecdote has the speaker included? What effect do you think it had on the audience?

## 3 ICT Imagine you are the same careers advice teacher from the model. You have been asked to give a talk to those students who have decided to go on a gap year abroad. Give them some advice on what they should do to have a safe and enjoyable year. Include a personal anecdote.

Good morning, everyone. At this stage, I think I've spoken to all of you about your plans for next year. Some of you are planning to continue your education at university or college, while others want to head straight into the workplace. Today, I want to talk about an option for both groups – going on a gap year abroad.

It's actually something that I did when I finished secondary school – I volunteered as an English teacher in Thailand for a year. I can still remember my first day on the job – during break one of my students approached my desk and offered me a fried grasshopper. I think my scream was heard throughout the school! But, overall, my experience in Thailand was wonderful, and I actually learned to love fried insects in the end!

So, what are the benefits of going on a gap year abroad? Well, firstly, going on a gap year abroad is a great way to experience a different culture. And it's not the same as going on holiday. When you spend a long time in a foreign country, especially if you work there, you don't just see a different culture – you live it. This can really broaden your horizons, giving you a new way to see the world.

Another benefit is that a gap year gives you time to reflect. What do I mean by this? Well, right now, a lot of you are still trying to decide which subject to study or which career path to follow after school. Going on a gap year gives you time to sit back and think about your options. It sometimes even influences your decision – my experiences in Thailand inspired me to become a teacher. And even if you've already decided what you want to do after school, going on a gap year gives you the chance to think about your decision – is it really the right path for you?

Finally, going on a gap year will help you grow as a person. Soon, a lot of you will have to move out of your home to study or work in a different city. But if you're not ready for that – if you're not independent or mature enough – it can really ruin the experience. Going on a gap year gives you the chance to be completely responsible for yourself for the first time, and that really builds your character. It means you'll be more prepared for the next stage of your life after you return.

Of course, going on a gap year abroad isn't for everyone – it's definitely not something I encourage every one of you to do. But, if it's something that interests you, I think you should definitely think about it. As always, if anyone wants to chat about this, or any other issue, you're welcome to come to my office after school.

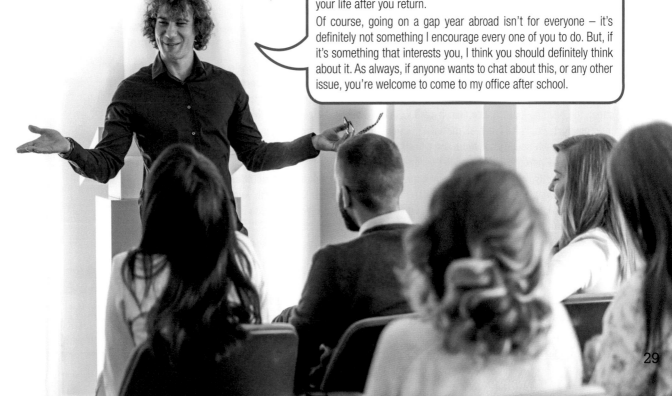

**4**

**Vocabulary:** types of houses; idioms with *house* & *home*; accommodation
**Grammar:** comparisons; impersonal sentences (*there – it*)
**Everyday English:** expressing satisfaction/ dissatisfaction
**Writing:** an advert for a home exchange

# There's no place like home!

## Vocabulary
### Types of houses

**1** Which of the following types of houses are the most common in your country? Which type of house do you live in?

- bungalow • mobile home • townhouse
- cottage • terraced house • farmhouse
- villa • detached house • flat • houseboat
- castle • semi-detached house

▶ **VIDEO**

# EXTRAORDINARY HOUSES

Bored with living in a place that's nothing to write home about? Wishing you could have a house that's exciting to be in? Then maybe you should think about moving into one of these unusual houses from around the world.

### Ⓐ Reversible Destiny Lofts, Mitaka, Japan

What exactly is a Reversible Destiny Loft? The architects of these homes in Japan – Shusaku Arakawa and Madeline Gins – believed that we can reverse, or turn back, our **fate** and live life differently! They wanted to **express** this idea through a building and the Reversible Destiny Loft was born. The whole point of these homes is to give each of its **residents** a physical challenge when they move in rather than allow them to live in total luxury! The floors are bumpy, not level, so you have to be more careful than usual when walking across them! There are no cupboards, so you have to **stretch** to hang clothes from hooks in the ceiling. Even in the study, a resident might be expected to use a children's swing as a desk! Fortunately, there are metal poles from floor to ceiling in these houses to help people get around and avoid an accident! There's never a **dull** moment in a Reversible Destiny Loft!

### Ⓑ The Cube Houses, Rotterdam, The Netherlands

These strange buildings look more like Rubik's Cube puzzles than homes. Architect Piet Blom was thinking of the countryside when he was designing them, and so they **remind** you of a forest of trees. It seems a bit **odd**, then, that they are **located** on top of a bridge above a busy road in Rotterdam city centre! Although their shape is unusual, Cube Houses are very simple and functional on the inside. The ground floor is a tiny entrance hall, with just enough room to hang your coat. Going up the narrow stairs you come to the first floor, where you'll find a surprisingly large kitchen with an oven, dishwasher and fridge. Next to the kitchen is a living/dining area with a dining table, chairs, a television and a big sofa for up to 6 people! Most Cube Houses have 3 floors, and some even have roof gardens with **stunning** views of Rotterdam. They are not as large as regular houses, but they are a great answer to **lack of** space in big cities!

### Ⓒ Habitat 67, Montreal, Canada

In 1967, architect Moshe Safdie designed and built Habitat 67, and for many it really is the most unusual building in Montreal. He built the block of flats using 354 concrete cubes. The result looks something like an **enormous** Lego house! Looking at it from the street, the building looks a little uninviting, but Safdie actually designed it for living in total **comfort**. Habitat 67 has all the latest devices! Noisy neighbours? No problem! Every flat is totally soundproof. Need some fresh air? Just go out on your private balcony for a while. The view of the river couldn't be lovelier. Habitat 67 gives you the peace and quiet of a country cottage while providing **convenient access** to modern city **facilities**. Talk about having the best of both worlds! The flats are modern inside, with large windows and lots of natural light, and the furniture is cleverly designed so it doesn't waste space. This is a luxury complex where you can really make yourself at home!

## Reading & Listening

**2** Read the title and look at the pictures. What do you think makes these houses unusual? What do you think they look like on the inside?

 Listen and read to find out.

✓ **Check these words**

physical challenge, bumpy, level, hang, hook, swing, pole, avoid, cube, functional, concrete uninviting, soundproof, complex

**6** COLLOCATIONS **Find and complete the words in the text that describe the following. Then use the phrases to make sentences.**

1 ..................... challenge     5 ..................... air
2 ..................... moment        6 ..................... balcony
3 ..................... road          7 ..................... light
4 ..................... stairs        8 ..................... complex

**7** WORDS EASILY CONFUSED **Choose the correct item. Check in your dictionary.**

1 He still lives at **home/house** with his parents.
2 We're **living/staying** in a hotel for a few days.
3 They turned their spare bedroom into a(n) **office/study**.
4 It's very **convenient/comfortable** living in a city.

**8** PHRASAL VERBS **Fill in the correct particle.**

**move in:** to begin to live somewhere as your home
**move into (a house):** to start living in a new house
**move on:** to progress; to go on
**move away:** to leave your area/town and go to live in another area/town
**move up:** to increase; to get a better job

1 A new family has just moved ................ next door!
2 After 10 years working in the same company, Jody decided she wanted to move ................ .
3 Ann moved ................ from town five years ago.
4 When are you moving ................ your new flat?
5 Ted's really moving ................ in his career; he's been promoted to Area Manager.

Idioms: *house* & *home*

**9** **Fill in** *house* **or** *home*. **Explain the idioms. Check in your dictionary.**

1 John and Sarah have only just met, but they're already getting on like a ..................... on fire.
2 Come in and make yourself at ..................... .
3 The flat I viewed was nothing to write ..................... about; I've seen 20 others like it.
4 Instead of criticising others all the time, you should put your own ..................... in order first!

## Speaking & Writing

**10** THINK **Imagine you are architects. Design an unusual home. What makes it unique? For how many people is it? What facilities does it have? Where is it located? Present it to the class. The class votes for the most creative home.**

**3** **Read the texts again and for questions 1-6, choose the correct text (A-C). The texts can be chosen more than once. Then explain the words/phrases in bold.**

Which house/building ...

1 has a safety feature?                         ........
2 makes you feel you're not living in a city?   ........
3 looks like a natural object?                  ........
4 is not designed for comfort?                  ........
5 has lots of room for visitors?                ........
6 doesn't look all that great from the outside? ........

**4** THINK **Which place would be the most expensive to buy? Why? Discuss.**

**5** PREPOSITIONS **Fill in:** *in, of, above, with, on (x2)*. **Which house from Ex. 2 is the advert about?**

These unusual flats **1)** ................. the city centre are worth checking out! Don't let the shape fool you! **2)** ................. the inside, each flat is very comfortable **3)** ................. modern furniture. **4)** ................. top of the ground floor entrance hall is the kitchen and living area, and **5)** ................. that there are two more floors with bedrooms. We guarantee great views **6)** ................. the city too!

**Phone us for a viewing**

31

# Grammar in Use

⭐⭐⭐⭐⭐

**A** I had one of the most enjoyable stays I've ever experienced in this lovely bungalow. It looks exactly like the pictures in the advert and Mandy was the perfect host! The flat was a lot nearer to the town centre than I'd expected, too. In fact, it was close enough to go sightseeing on foot, which was great! I'm definitely going there again!

Luke, USA

⭐⭐⭐⭐☆

**B** I had a temporary job in the town centre so I rented this cute bungalow so I could get to work more quickly in the mornings. The best thing about the bungalow is the garden. There are lots of flowers and you won't find a more relaxing place to sit! The rent is not as cheap as for some of the other accommodation in the area, but it's very charming nevertheless.

Mao, Japan

⭐⭐☆☆☆

**C** I'd hoped a bungalow would be quieter than staying in a flat, but it's amazing how wrong you can be! The next-door neighbours were the noisiest people ever with parties every night. But by far the biggest problem was the heating system; it just didn't work. The hosts will have to try harder if they want to attract guests!

Aksel, Norway

## Comparisons ▶ pp. GR6-7

**1** Read the reviews of a bungalow to stay (A-C). Underline all the comparative and superlative forms. How do we form them? How do we use them?

**2** Choose the correct item. Give reasons.

1 This is **the most fashionable/more fashionable** area of the city to live in.

2 Our new house is **the least modern/less modern** than our old one.

3 The estate agent says **the earliest/earlier** we can move in is January.

4 This summer is **hotter/the hottest** than last year so it's great to have a garden!

5 Your house will be **the most eco-friendly/more eco-friendly** if you plant a roof garden.

6 One-bedroomed flats sell **more frequently/the most frequently** of all our properties.

7 It would be **simpler/the simplest** for us to rent a flat than to buy one.

8 This is **busier/the busiest** street in the town centre.

**3** Put the adjectives/adverbs in brackets into the correct form.

1 A: Young James can make cupboards just as ................ **(well)** as his father.
B: Yes, he did our kitchen. I've never seen a .............. ................................... **(professional)** job than this!

2 A: Living on the edge of town is so peaceful. It's ............................... **(quiet)** than the town centre.
B: I agree, but living in a big city is ............................. ...................................................... **(stressful)** of all.

3 A: Your mum's living room isn't as ............................... **(big)** as ours.
B: I know, but hers is a lot ............................... **(cosy)**!

4 A: House prices are going up much ............................... **(fast)** than they have been for months.
B: Yes, it's much ........................................ **(sensible)** to sell now than ever before.

5 A: My daughter's just bought a house. She's ........................................... **(happy)** girl in the world!
B: And it's a lot ............................... **(good)** than paying rent!

6 A: Gas heats your home ........................................... **(efficiently)** than electricity.
B: That's true, but, it has become .................................. **(expensive)** than it used to be.

**4** Read the theory. Then choose the correct item. Find examples in the reviews in Ex. 1.

### Types of comparisons ▶ p. GR7

- *very* + adjective/adverb
  *House prices are going up **very quickly**.*
- *by far* + superlative forms of adjectives/adverbs
  *This is **by far the untidiest** garden in the street.*
- *even* + comparative forms of adjectives/adverbs
  *Your smart TV is **even more user-friendly** than mine!*
- *too* + adjective/adverb + *to*-infinitive
  *My old oven cooks **too slowly to prepare** a meal.*
- adjective/adverb + *enough* + *to*-infinitive
  *The garage is **big enough to take** two cars.*

1 This is **by far/very/much** the nicest house of all.

2 We're going to have to move house **even/as/very** sooner than we'd planned.

3 Rents aren't as cheap **as/than/to** they used to be.

4 The new bungalows are **very/much/a lot** expensive.

5 This house isn't big enough for us **live/to live/living** in.

6 The sofa is **too/enough/far** big for our living room.

7 Our old water heater worked just as effectively **as/more/most** the new one.

8 Pat's house is **very/by far/enough** warm.

9 We aren't rich **too/enough/much** to buy that villa.

10 This is **very/by far/too** the best flat.

**5** SPEAKING 👥 **Imagine your family wants to rent a house. Read the table below and use the information to compare the three buildings. Which one would you decide to rent?**

| | Villa | Semi-detached house | Flat |
|---|---|---|---|
| big | ✓✓✓ | ✓✓ | ✓ |
| bright | ✓✓✓ | ✓ | ✓✓ |
| quiet area | ✓✓✓ | ✓✓ | ✓ |
| modern | ✓✓ | ✓ | ✓✓✓ |
| reasonably priced | ✓ | ✓✓ | ✓✓✓ |
| economical to run | ✓ | ✓✓ | ✓✓✓ |

A: *The semi-detached house isn't as big as the villa, but it's bigger than the flat.*

B: *That's true, but the flat is brighter than the semi-detached house. etc*

**6** **Complete the second sentence so that it means the same as the first. Use two to five words, including the word in bold.**

1 I've never seen such a beautiful house! **THE**
This is ............................................ I've ever seen.

2 Her house is more expensive than mine. **AS**
My house ............................................. hers.

3 This flat is more attractive than the others. **MOST**
This flat is .................................................. all.

4 This sofa costs the same amount of money as that bed. **MUCH**
This sofa costs .................................. that bed.

5 The living room isn't as comfortable as the study. **MORE**
The study is ......................................................
the living room.

6 No room in the house is as big as the kitchen. **FAR**
The kitchen is ...............................................
room in the house.

7 The house we live in is too small for us. **ENOUGH**
The house we live in ........................... for us.

8 The thing I liked most about the house was the modern bathroom. **BEST**
To me, the .......................................... was the modern bathroom.

**7** **Read the theory. Find examples in the reviews on p. 32.**

### Impersonal sentences *(there – it)* ≫ pp. GR7-8

**Impersonal sentences** have no natural subject and the words **there** or **it** can be used in the subject position.
We use **there + be** to:
* say where or when sth is *There's a garage next to our house. There's a meeting at 10 am.*
* refer to a number or amount *There are 20 bedrooms in the castle. There are lots of skyscrapers in Dubai.*
* say that sth exists or happens *There is a problem. There's an argument going on.*
We use **it + be** to:
* refer to times/dates *It's six o'clock. It's a bank holiday next Monday.*
* talk about the weather/temperatures *It's raining. It's very cold today.*
* begin a sentence followed by an adjective *It's nice living here. It's easy to find my house.*

**8** **Fill in *there* or *it*.**

1 A: You'd better hurry up, ....................'s almost moving day!
B: I know, but ....................'s a lot of stuff to pack.

2 A: Come on! Let's not be late for our appointment with the estate agent.
B: Relax. ....................'s no rush. ....................'s only 3 o'clock.

3 A: ....................'s great living in the city! ....................'s so much to do!
B: Maybe, but ....................'s difficult to get any peace and quiet.

4 A: Phew! ....................'s really hot in here.
B: ....................'s a fan in the cupboard. I'll go and fetch it.

5 A: Wake up. I think ....................'s someone downstairs!
B: No, .................... isn't. ....................'s just the wind rattling the window.

6 A: I can't believe it! .................... are 15 people queueing to see the flat.
B: Yes, ....................'s amazing how many people are looking for homes to rent.

7 A: I'm so happy. ....................'s almost the weekend!
B: And ....................'s a party at Stewart's house on Saturday. Are you going?

**9** THINK **Continue the story. Use *there* or *it*.**

*It was very late when Bob left his office to go back home.*

# Skills in Action

## Vocabulary

### Accommodation

**1** Complete the gaps in the adverts with the words in the lists.

(A) • roof • heated • train • conditioning • central
• studio • en-suite

◄ ► ◯                    🔍 search text...

**Large 1) ......................... flat in town centre**

▪ near 2) ......................... station
▪ close to shops
▪ sleeps 4, large kitchen & living room
▪ 3) ......................... bathroom with walk-in shower
▪ access to 4) ......................... garden

**Amenities**

• TV • 5) ......................... towel rail • air 6) .........................
• 7) ......................... heating

(B) • solar • king-size • entrance • dryer • basement
• fireplace • open-plan

◄ ► ◯                    🔍 search text...

**1) ......................... flat in modern townhouse**

▪ private 2) .........................
▪ 3) ......................... kitchen & dining area
▪ 4) open ......................... in living room
▪ 2 5) ......................... beds
▪ convenient for sightseeing

**Amenities**

• 6) ......................... water heater • private parking
• free Wi-Fi • clothes 7) .........................

42 Reviews ★★★★★

🔍 Search Reviews

**2** 👥 (THINK) **Which flat would be best for a family of three for a weekend? Why?**

## Listening

**3** 🎧 Listen to an estate agent leaving a voicemail for her client Mr Davies and complete the gaps.

**Terraced House for Sale**

**Address: 1)** ..................... Barony Street, Bristol
**Location:** 15-minute **2)** ..................... away from city centre; also with **3)** ..................... service
**Accommodation:** open-plan **4)** ..................... and kitchen; double bedroom with en-suite bathroom; single bedroom; bathroom with bath & walk-in shower
**Amenities:** gas-fired **5)** .........................;
back & front **6)** .........................
**Price:** £250,000

## Everyday English

### Expressing satisfaction/dissatisfaction

**4** What does Mr Davies dislike about the house?
🎧 Listen to and read the dialogue to find out.

**A:** So glad you could make it for the viewing, Mr Davies. Please step this way. Just through here is the open-plan living and kitchen area.

**B:** Fantastic! There's lots of space here.

**A:** Indeed! The bedrooms are upstairs ... the master bedroom has got its own en-suite bathroom.

**B:** I like that ... I'm not sure about the colour scheme in here, though.

**A:** That's easy to fix. ... Here's the single bedroom.

**B:** Perfect! And the main bathroom?

**A:** Here we are. Look at this gorgeous walk-in shower!

**B:** That's lovely, but I'd prefer to have a bath.

**A:** There isn't a bath, but the house has solar panels so you always have hot water.

**B:** That's nice. And what was the price again?

**A:** Two hundred and fifty thousand pounds.

**B:** Right, well, I'll think about it and let you know.

**A:** Very good, I'll look forward to that.

**5** 👥 Use the ideas below and language from the box to act out a similar dialogue to the one in Ex. 4.

• modern hall & living room – bright & airy • double bedroom – built-in wardrobes – lots of storage space – not like light fittings • bathroom – big bath – no shower • heated towel rail • £120,000

| Expressing satisfaction | Expressing dissatisfaction |
|---|---|
| • Terrific! | • I don't really like ... |
| • Perfect! | • I'm not that impressed with ... |
| • How lovely! | • I'm not sure about ... |
| • That's a big advantage. | • I'd prefer (not) to have ... |

### Intonation: rising – falling

**6** a) 🎧 Listen and say how each speaker feels: *anxious, pleased, sarcastic, dissatisfied*. **In which sentences does the intonation rise?/ fall? Listen again and repeat.**

1 That's so kind of you!     3 We can't afford it!
2 I'm not that keen on it.   4 What a delightful flat.

b) 👥 Express the same feelings in sentences of your own. Use appropriate intonation. Your partner says how you feel.

## Reading & Writing

**7** Read the advert on a home exchange website and complete the gaps with words derived from the words in brackets.

**HolidayHomeExchange**

**Great house in central Edinburgh**

**Brendan**

2 Bedrooms | Sleeps 5 | 2 bathrooms

**About our home**

**1)** ............................... **(locate)** in the heart of Edinburgh city centre, this modern semi-detached house offers you the greatest opportunity to see the city sights. The Royal Mile and Edinburgh Castle are both within **2)** ............................ **(walk)** distance. 15-minute bus ride to Holyrood Palace, one of the British monarch's official residences.

House consists of two **3)** ......................... **(comfort)** bedrooms upstairs, (the bigger one with a king-size bed, the smaller with a single), and **4)** ............................. **(recent)** redecorated bathroom. Second bathroom downstairs – more convenient if **5)** ............................ **(visit)** come over! **6)** ............................. **(space)** living room with double sofa bed. Kitchen fully **7)** ....................... **(equip)** to the highest standards.

★★★★★ **5 Reviews**

**Features**

Cleaner

Garden

Wi-Fi

Cable TV

**8)** ......................... **(centre)** heating

Pets welcome

Show all ▼

**More about us**

My wife and I love travelling to **9)** .............................. **(differ)** parts of the world and seeing new places – and there's no better way to make new friends!
We like exploring big cities but also walking in the countryside. I do **10)** .................................. **(garden)** in my spare time and my wife makes pottery.

Read more ▼

 **Writing Tip**

**Advertising language**

We often omit pronouns, auxiliary verbs or articles when we write an advert. We can use adjectives to make our description more interesting to the reader.

**8** Read the advert in Ex. 7 again. Find examples of: **a)** *omission of pronouns, auxiliary verbs, articles;* **b)** *adjectives.*

**9** Shorten the sentences by omitting *pronouns, auxiliary verbs* or *articles*. **Change punctuation/ wording where necessary.**

**1** It is located near the city centre.
*Located near city centre, it ...*

**2** The roof of the house has a cool, shady garden.
............................................................................

**3** The basement has a spare bedroom.
............................................................................

**4** It is just a ten-minute train ride to the centre.
............................................................................

**5** A full English breakfast is provided.
............................................................................

**6** It is situated by the river.
............................................................................

## Writing (an advert for a home exchange)

**10** **a)** Imagine you want to take part in a holiday home exchange. Make notes about your home under the headings: *Type of house – Location – Description – Features – More about you.*

**b)** Use your notes to write an advert (120-180 words). Follow the plan. You can use the advert in Ex. 7 as a model.

**Plan**

**Main heading:** details of bedrooms/bathrooms/how many can be accommodated
**About our home**
**Para 1:** type of house; location
**Para 2:** description
**Features:** *(list with symbols)*
**More about us:** personal details of houseowners *(hobbies, likes, etc)*

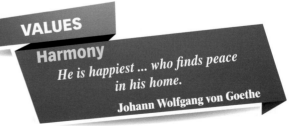

**VALUES**

**Harmony**

*He is happiest ... who finds peace in his home.*

**Johann Wolfgang von Goethe**

▶ VIDEO

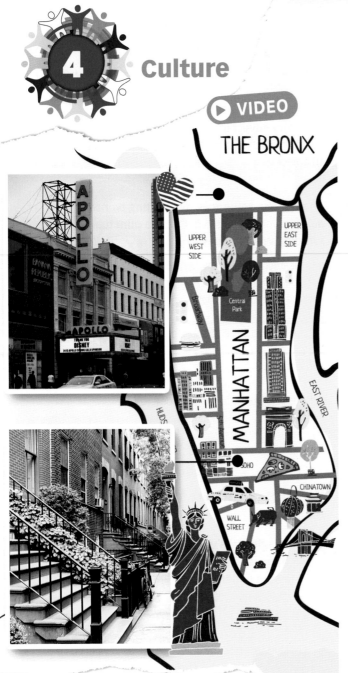

THE BRONX

# Neighbourhoods of New York

*New York City is home to many different kinds of people, all with different origins and all living completely different lives. Perhaps nowhere is this truer than in the Manhattan district **in the heart of** the city. Each of Manhattan's neighbourhoods has got its own **unique** atmosphere and culture. Let's take a look at two of them.*

### Ⓐ Greenwich Village

You'll find the downtown neighbourhood of Greenwich Village on the west side of Lower Manhattan. 'The Village', as it is known, has always attracted famous artists and writers. It became well known in the 1950s when it was home to writers like Allen Ginsberg and Jack Kerouac. These days, Greenwich Village is an extremely **well developed** and rich area. Along with the artists, there are now families, business people and even **celebrities**, making it one of the **trendiest** neighbourhoods in NYC. However, among the gourmet bistros, vegan kiosks, art studios and designer boutiques, you will still see the old 19th century brownstones. These four-storey townhouses are so called because of the ornate brown stone covering their fronts – and they are now the most fashionable homes in The Village!

### Ⓑ Harlem

For a less trendy neighbourhood, let's visit uptown Harlem at the other end of the island of Manhattan, just next to the Bronx. In many ways, the area is almost exactly as it was 50 years ago, with old-fashioned barbershops, family-owned restaurants and jazz cafés going back at least 40 years! But like Greenwich Village, Harlem **has got its share of** traditional brownstone houses – they're cheaper to buy here too! Nor is there a lack of the arts in Harlem. The neighbourhood is a **hotspot** for street artists and there are even organised graffiti tours. But perhaps the most famous landmark of all is the Apollo Theater. First opening its doors in 1914, it **featured** big names in African American music like Ella Fitzgerald and Billie Holiday and helped to make jazz, soul and R & B more popular. Now over 100 years old, the theatre is still going strong today!

## Listening & Reading

**1** **What do Greenwich Village and Harlem have in common?**

🎧 **Listen and read to find out.**

**2** **Read the text and complete the email extract. Use ONE word in each gap. Then explain the words/phrases in bold.**

### ✉ INBOX ⟳ ◈ ◈

Hi Frank!

Hope all is well. I had a great time in New York visiting Manhattan. It's got so many different **1)** ..........................! My favourite was Greenwich Village. Many famous **2)** .......................... lived there in the 1950s, but now it attracts all sorts of people. Maybe it's more modern now, but the old brownstone **3)** .......................... are still around. Harlem is more traditional with a lot of old family businesses. I took a(n) **4)** .......................... tour of the work of the **5)** .......................... artists there. Very impressive! But the best was the Apollo Theater, the cultural home of **6)** .......................... American music! How was your summer?

......

### ✓ Check these words

gourmet bistro, vegan kiosk, designer boutique, ornate, barbershop, graffiti, be going strong

## Speaking & Writing

**3** **THINK** **Compare the two neighbourhoods. Which one would you like to live in? Why?**

**4** **💬 ICT Collect information about two neighbourhoods in your town/city or your country's capital city. Make notes under the headings:** *Name – Location – Housing – Shops – Famous for.* **Use your notes to prepare a 2-minute video presenting them. Alternatively, give the class a digital presentation.**

## Vocabulary

**1** Choose the correct word.

1 You can move a **detached/mobile/simple** home around.
2 The windows let in **physical/narrow/natural** light.
3 Sean bought his new flat in that new **concrete/luxury/bumpy** complex.
4 What an ugly **block/cube/floor** of flats!
5 It's hot in here. Please turn on the **central/air/functional** conditioning.
6 Sue and Hal get on like a **house/home/villa** on fire.
7 We've got our own **private/convenient/comfortable** balcony all to ourselves!
8 Sue lives on a very **terraced/busy/level** road with lots of traffic.

*(8 x 2 = 16)*

**2** Fill in: *en-suite, open-plan, basement, roof, dryer, train, solar, king-size.*

1 We bought sheets for our ........................... bed.
2 A(n) ........................... garden makes your house cooler.
3 The master bedroom has its own ........................... bathroom.
4 I've always wanted a ........................... water heater!
5 The ........................... flat had steps leading down to it from the pavement.
6 Where's the nearest ........................... station? I need to go into the city.
7 Having a clothes ........................... means you don't have to worry if it rains!
8 We knocked down a wall and made a(n) ........................... kitchen and dining room.

*(8 x 3 = 24)*

**3** Choose the correct item.

1 Harry's rented a flat and he's moving **in/into** next week.
2 Outside, the house looked dirty, but **on/in** the inside it was sparkling clean.
3 We packed up our mobile home and moved **up/on**.
4 Mrs Richards asked for a room **of/with** a view.
5 When we moved **in/into** the flat, it needed repairs.

*(5 x 2 = 10)*

## Grammar

**4** Put the adjectives/adverbs in brackets into the correct form.

1 This is by far ........................... **(bad)** flat we've seen.
2 A houseboat isn't ........................... **(cheap)** to run as a mobile home.
3 This villa is ........................... **(expensive)** on our list – it's only €300,000.
4 Our new fridge is a lot ........................... **(modern)** than our old one.
5 Everyone admires Max's cottage; it's ........................... **(historic)** one in the village!

*(5 x 3 = 15)*

**5** Fill in: *it, very, too, there, enough.*

1 We weren't fast ................. to book the last hotel room.
2 Next to the house ................. is a big park.
3 ................. is impossible to find the perfect home!
4 I feel ................. tired to go house-hunting today.
5 The old castle has a(n) ................. long history.

*(5 x 3 = 15)*

## Everyday English

**6** Match the exchanges.

1 ☐ I'm not that impressed with the kitchen cupboards.
2 ☐ There's a heated towel rail in the bathroom.
3 ☐ I'll let you know next week.
4 ☐ And the bedroom?
5 ☐ Here is the kitchen and dining area.

a Here we are.
b I'll look forward to your call.
c I'd prefer it not to be open-plan.
d That sounds good!
e That can soon be fixed.

*(5 x 4 = 20)*

*Total 100*

## Competences

GOOD ✓
VERY GOOD ✓✓
EXCELLENT ✓✓✓

**Lexical Competence**
understand words/ phrases related to:
• types of houses
• idioms (house & home)
• accommodation

**Reading Competence**
• understand texts related to unusual homes & city neighbourhoods (multiple matching – text completion)

**Listening Competence**
• listen to and understand monologues related to selling a house (listen for specific information – gap fill)

**Speaking Competence**
• express satisfaction/ dissatisfaction

**Writing Competence**
• write about an unusual home
• write an advert for a home exchange

**5**

**Vocabulary:** ways to communicate; textspeak; body language; feelings
**Grammar:** future tenses; time clauses
**Everyday English:** agree/disagree, express doubt
**Writing:** a for-and-against essay

# Let's talk

▶ **VIDEO**

## A NEW KIND OF DIRECT MESSAGING

Hey there tech fans!
This week at Tech Magazine
we've been thinking about the future of communication.
In our lifetime, the invention of the Internet and the smartphone have
revolutionised the way we interact. But what's next?
Well, imagine a world where we don't need language
to communicate. This might sound like something from a sci-fi
movie, but brain-to-brain communication could become a reality
sooner than you think! Read on to find out more ...

Have you ever tried to tell someone something, only for them not to fully understand what you mean? **[1]** There are so many different **elements** involved in spoken communication, such as tone of voice and body language, it's not surprising we struggle to **get** our **message across** sometimes. But, if we can work out how to communicate directly, brain-to-brain, we won't need to worry about **communication breakdowns** ever again.

Believe it or not, brain-to-machine communication is already possible. A Brain Computer Interface (BCI) is a form of technology that allows people to control things using only their thoughts and a computer. **[2]** Clearly, this amazing technology is going to have a massive **impact** on the lives of people who are paralysed. Over the coming years, scientists will be developing this idea further in the hope that, one day, we'll be able to send mind-messages to people as well as computers.

So, how will brain-to-brain communication affect our lives? For one thing, it will be extremely helpful for people who are unable to talk. **[3]** It will also play an important role in education. In the future, we won't be spending hours studying

## Vocabulary
### Ways to communicate

**1** Copy and complete the mindmap with these **words:** *drawing, eye contact, facial expressions, gestures, speech, touch, text message, video chat, writing, TV & radio, newspapers/magazines.*

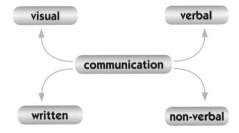

## Reading & Listening

**2** Read through the text quickly and decide if this idea about the future of communication seems interesting to you or not.

**3** Read again and complete the gaps (1-5) with the sentences (A-H). There are three extra sentences which you do not need to use.

🎧 Listen and check. Then explain the words/phrases in bold.

**A** They will be able to communicate their thoughts and feelings with others quickly and accurately, which will make their daily lives much easier and more enjoyable.

**B** This will make education a lot cheaper and available to everyone.

**C** An EEG cap is used to record the electrical activity of the brain.

**D** Despite these concerns, it's exciting to think what the future holds.

**E** Misunderstandings are a common part of everyday life.

**F** Many people don't believe that brain-to-brain communication will ever be possible.

**G** For example, experiments have shown that it is possible to move a robotic arm using a BCI.

**H** Do we really want to live in a world where anyone can access our private thoughts and feelings at any time?

because we'll be learning skills directly from other people's brains! Imagine you're training to become a doctor – what could be more useful than a few brain-to-brain **sessions** with an **expert**? And in the business world, brain-to-brain communication will also be extremely useful. More and more companies are becoming international these days, and communication issues such as language barriers are common. In the future, instead of travelling and using the Internet, we will be doing business across borders through our minds!

But what about the possible dangers? If we don't find a way to govern brain-to-brain communication, we will be **at risk** of things like mind control and unwelcome mind-reading. ⟨4⟩ This could put national security at risk and encourage spies and cheats to commit crimes. Hopefully, by the time this technology exists, we will have **come up with** a way to keep these things from happening. ⟨5⟩ The possibilities of brain-to-brain communication really are endless. Who knows – perhaps one day people will be reading each others' minds so much that spoken communication won't even exist anymore!

### ✓ Check these words

interact, tone of voice, paralysed, language barrier, govern, commit crimes

**4** **PREPOSITIONS** Fill in: *across*, *from*, *on*, *of*, *about*, *at*. Check in your dictionary.

1 It seems that lots of languages are ..................... risk of becoming extinct.
2 Communicating with other people is an important part ..................... everyday life.
3 International phone calls are expensive, but the Internet has made communicating ......... borders much cheaper.
4 Texting and emojis are having a negative effect ..................... children's spelling.
5 Brain-to-brain communication will allow us to send messages directly ..................... one brain to another.
6 Do you ever worry ..................... the dangers of social media?

**5** **COLLOCATIONS** Find the words in the text that describe the following. Then use the phrases to make sentences

1 ..................... language      4 ..................... control
2 ..................... impact       5 ..................... security
3 ..................... barrier       6 ..................... life

**6** **WORDS EASILY CONFUSED** Choose the correct word. Check in your dictionary. Make a sentence with the other option.

1 Instant messaging lets us **communicate/express** with people all over the world at the click of a button.
2 Can you **speak/say** louder please? I can't hear you.
3 I **talk/tell** to my cousin in America at least once a month on Skype.

**7** **PHRASAL VERBS** Fill in the correct particle.

> **keep down:** to make less noise
> **keep from:** to prevent sb from doing sth; to prevent sth from happening
> **keep on:** to continue to employ sb
> **keep out:** to prevent sb from entering
> **keep up:** to maintain sth

1 Her parents kept her .................. having a social media account until she was 13.
2 The IT company decided to keep Thomas .................. after his internship; he must have made a good impression.
3 Bob asked his neighbour to keep ................. the noise because they were being too loud.
4 Please keep ................ of the lab. Entrance isn't allowed.
5 Keep .................. the good work! Your French is really improving, you're almost fluent.

## Speaking & Writing

**8** **THINK** Think of the dangers this type of communication could cause in the future. Can you think of ways to prevent them?

**9** Imagine you are in a place where you don't understand the language. Suggest ways to communicate with the locals.

**10** **ICT** "Brain-to-brain communication will improve the way we communicate." Collect information and prepare your argument. Use your notes to have a class debate.

# Grammar in Use

## Future tenses ▶ pp. GR8-9

**1** Read the forum entry. Identify the tenses in bold. Which tense do we use for: *timetables; predictions based on what we think or imagine; predictions based on what we can see or know; fixed arrangements in the near future; action in progress at a definite time in the future; actions that will have finished before a stated time in the future?*

**▶ Student Advice Forum**   🔒 Log out

**James, 1 day ago**
End-of-year assessments **start** next week and I'**m giving** a presentation on Monday. Public speaking makes me really nervous, so I know I'**m going to fail**. I need to work on my communication skills, but I'm not sure how. Please help!

**Alan, 9 hours ago**
I think an online course in communication skills **will** really **help** you. Many of them are free and don't take long to complete, so you'**ll have finished** it <u>before</u> you give your presentation. Trust me, this time next week you'**ll be wondering** why you were so stressed.

**Sophie, 4 hours ago**
Alan is right. Don't worry, you **won't fail**! I did one of those courses and it really helped me. It taught me all about the importance of things like body language. <u>When will</u> you get your feedback? Let us know how it goes!

**2** Choose the correct tense. Give reasons.

**1** I don't think people **will ever get/are ever getting** bored of social media.

**2** On tomorrow's show, we'**ll be talking/will talk** about how technology is affecting our ability to communicate face-to-face.

**3** I **will/'m going to buy** a new smartphone once I've saved enough money.

**4** The workshop on body language **won't have finished/isn't finishing** before 5 pm.

**5** We **will have updated/will be updating** the app this evening, so the video call function will be temporarily disrupted.

**6** The company **launches/will have launched** the new smartphone at 9 am tomorrow.

**7** Initial sales figures suggest that this new instant translation device **is going to be/will have been** very popular.

**8** I'**m meeting/will meet** Rachel for a catch-up tomorrow.

**3** Fill in *will* or *am/is going to*.

**1** A: We are holding free sign language classes at lunch if anyone's interested.
   B: I ...................... sign up! I've always wanted to learn.

**2** A: Mark, I really need to talk to you.
   B: I'm busy right now, but I promise I .......................... call you this evening.

**3** A: I .......................... stop using social media so much. I know it's having a bad effect on me!
   B: I think that's a good idea; it's taking over your life!

**4** A: John thinks he .............................. get by in Vietnam without knowing the language.
   B: Really? He should at least try to learn a few words.

**5** A: Are you free this evening?
   B: Sorry, my sister .............................. call me tonight; she always calls me on Mondays.

**6** A: You .......................... make a bad impression if you keep frowning like that!
   B: I know, I need to relax and remember to smile.

**7** A: I don't think anyone .......................... use a landline in the future.
   B: Me neither. Almost everyone has a mobile phone these days.

**4** Put the verbs in brackets into the present simple or the present continuous. Give reasons.

**1** My plane ........................................... **(take off)** at 5 pm so you won't be able to reach me on the phone for a few hours.

**2** Lisa ........................................... **(start)** her new job at the local radio station next week. She's so happy!

**3** The tech shop ........................................... **(close)** at 6 pm every day so you'd better hurry if you want to get a new phone charger today.

**4** Uni ........................................... **(start)** next week. Have you finished preparing for your presentation yet?

**5** Tech companies in the area ........................................... **(hold)** a job fair on Saturday.

**6** He ........................................... **(attend)** a conference about translation this weekend.

**5** **SPEAKING** Expand the sentences, as in the example. Use *will*, *going to*, present simple or the present continuous (future meaning). Compare with your partner.

**1** What a terrible film! *When will it finish?*
**2** It's raining!
**3** The bus hasn't come yet.
**4** Can I borrow your jacket tonight?
**5** I can't come with you.
**6** Hurry up!
**7** Can you buy me some flour?
**8** I'm hungry.

**6** **Put the verbs in brackets into the future continuous or the future perfect. Give reasons.**

**1** Jake ......................................... **(have)** a seminar on digital communication at 5 o'clock tomorrow afternoon.

**2** Alison ................................... **(give)** her speech by 6 o'clock next Friday.

**3** It's Monday tomorrow, which means I ........................ ............................................ **(probably/reply)** to emails all morning.

**4** Jessica ........................................ **(learn)** sign language by the time she graduates.

**5** Melissa ....................................... **(record)** her first podcast on Thursday at 10 am. I can't wait to hear it!

**6** They ............................................. **(install)** the optical fibre by this time next week.

**7** They ...................................... **(speak)** to their manager by tomorrow afternoon.

**8** John ...................................... **(be)** online for three hours by noon.

**7** **SPEAKING** 🗣️🗣️ **Ask your partner questions using the sentences in Ex. 6. Your partner responds.**

A: *Will you be having a seminar on digital communication at 5 o'clock tomorrow afternoon?*

B: *Yes, I will. / No, I won't. I will be studying in the library.*

**8** **Use the verbs in the list in the correct future tense to complete the sentences.**

• call • read • not finish • chat • not answer • drop • fly

**1** A: This letter has just arrived for you, Mr Smith.
B: Thanks, I .......................................... it now.

**2** A: Excuse me, I have a few questions I'd like to ask.
B: The lecturer ............................................. any questions until the Q&A session at 3 pm.

**3** A: I haven't heard from Lucy since last Saturday.
B: Don't worry, I'm sure she ......................................... you soon.

**4** A: Get ready, we're leaving in ten minutes.
B: But I ................................................ writing my blog entry by then.

**5** A: Be careful! You ..................................... your phone.
B: Thanks, I really shouldn't put it in my pocket.

**6** A: Will Mary come with us tomorrow at noon?
B: No, she ................................................. to Rome at that time.

**7** A: How will you keep in touch with Paul while he's away?
B: We ................................................. online. I've already downloaded this new app.

**9** **Choose the correct item. Give reasons.**

**1** I ............. my mobile data plan next month – I've already chosen a new package.
A upgrade    C 'll have upgraded
B 'll upgrade    D 'm upgrading

**2** This time next week, she'll ............. the morning news!
A present    C be presenting
B presenting    D have presented

**3** I'm sure you ............. better once you talk about your problem.
A 'll feel    C 'll have felt
B 're feeling    D 'll be feeling

**4** Dont' worry! The technician ............. the Internet connection before 10 am.
A will have repaired    C will be repairing
B is going to repair    D will repair

**5** Joy ............. at the Technology and Communication conference tomorrow at 6 o'clock.
A speaks    C is speaking
B will speak    D will have spoken

## Time clauses ▸ p. GR9

**10** **Look at the highlighted verbs in the forum on p. 40. What tenses do we use after time words/phrases? Why have we used *will* after *when*?**

**11** **Choose the correct tense.**

**1** I **will call/call** you as soon as the plane **will have landed/lands**.

**2** We **send/will send** you an SMS before we **will leave/leave**.

**3** They **will have missed/miss** the beginning of the presentation by the time they **arrive/will arrive**.

**4** She **won't buy/doesn't buy** a new smartphone until her current one **will break/breaks**.

**5** **Do/Will** you call your grandma after you **finish/will finish** your homework?

**12** **SPEAKING** 🗣️🗣️ **Say a sentence. Your partner responds using future tenses. Try to keep the conversation going for as long as possible.**

A: *I'm not going to the cinema tonight.*
B: *Will you stay at home instead?*
A: *Yes, I will. I'm going to watch a film on TV. Why don't you come to my place and we can watch it together?*
B: *I'll be working on my project all afternoon. What time does the film start?*
A: *It starts at 7 pm.*
B: *I'm not sure I'll have finished by then. I'll give you a call later to let you know.*

# Skills in Action

## Vocabulary

### Textspeak

**1** a) **Match the abbreviations to their meanings.**

| | | | | |
|---|---|---|---|---|
| 1 | BB | **a** | away from keyboard |
| 2 | BRB | **b** | I don't know |
| 3 | CUL | **c** | thanks |
| 4 | IDK | **d** | at the moment |
| 5 | F2F | **e** | to be honest |
| 6 | ATM | **f** | bye-bye |
| 7 | AFK | **g** | call you later |
| 8 | BBS | **h** | face to face |
| 9 | tbh | **i** | be back soon |
| 10 | thx | **j** | be right back |

b) **Explain what the following mean. Check online.**

| 1 | NP | 4 | PLZ | 7 | HF |
|---|---|---|---|---|---|
| 2 | ASAP | 5 | JK | 8 | GR8 |
| 3 | WB | 6 | L8R | 9 | BTW |

**2** Do you use textspeak when you send messages? Why? Tell your partner.

## Listening

**3** a) 🎧 **You will hear four people talking about the pros and cons of textspeak. For questions 1-4, choose the best answer (A, B, or C).**

1 You will hear a teenage boy talking about textspeak. He likes it because
   A he can talk privately with his friends.
   B everyone can understand it.
   C he uses the Internet a lot.

2 You will hear a school teacher speaking about textspeak. She believes that it is
   A having a negative effect on the way kids talk.
   B the main reason why kids' spelling is getting worse.
   C only appropriate online.

3 You will hear a middle-aged man talking about textspeak. He uses it because it is
   A useful in certain situations.
   B not difficult to understand.
   C too simple and robotic.

4 You will hear a university student talking about textspeak. She thinks that it isn't as
   A effective as body language.
   B intelligent as people think.
   C simple as it seems.

b) 👥 THINK **How does textspeak affect language in your opinion? Discuss.**

## Everyday English

### Agree/disagree – Express doubt

**4** **Why is Jim confused about the message?**
🎧 **Listen and read to find out.**

**Max:** What's the matter, Jim? You look a bit confused.

**Jim:** I've just received this text message from my grandson, but I've got no idea what it says.

**Max:** He's used textspeak. It says: "Hi Granddad, how are you? Looking forward to seeing you later. Meet me at 6pm. See you."

**Jim:** Really? It looks like nonsense to me!

**Max:** I can see why you'd think that, but it's quite simple really. He's used letters, numbers and symbols that sound like words.

**Jim:** I see. But why is he writing like this?

**Max:** Well, I guess it saves time and space.

**Jim:** I don't know about that but this isn't proper English!

**Max:** Well, I guess it's OK but I'm sure it's affecting spelling.

> Hi Granddad, how R U?
> Looking fwd 2 seeing U l8r.
> Meet me @6. C U

**5** 👥 **Act out a dialogue between two parents about their son's hobby of podcasting similar to the one in Ex. 4. Use language from the box and the prompts below.**

| Agreeing | Disagreeing |
|---|---|
| • I completely agree. | • Not necessarily. |
| • That's for sure. | • I don't think so. |
| • You have a point. | • I know what you mean, but ... |
| **Expressing Doubt** | |
| • Really? | • I don't know about that. |

**pros** – develops research skills & chats with the viewer
**cons** – spends too much time in front of PC, doesn't socialise enough

## Intonation: expressing feelings

**6** a) 🎧 **Listen and match the speakers (1-4) with the feelings (a-d).**

| a | irritation ....... | c | uncertainty ....... |
|---|---|---|---|
| b | enthusiasm ....... | d | agreement ....... |

b) **Practise expressing different feelings using these words:** *Yeah!*, *Hey!*, *Right!*.

## Reading & Writing

**7** **a)** Read the essay and fill in the topic sentences (1-4). Two sentences do not match.

Face to Face Communication

**A** In today's modern world, there are many different ways in which we can communicate with each other. With videoconferencing, instant messaging and email, it has never been easier to keep in touch. But can technology ever replace talking face-to-face?

**B** .......... In the first place, we can see the person's facial expressions and body language. This makes it easier to know how someone is feeling. In addition, it is more personal. For instance, if someone is talking about a problem, we are better able to comfort them in person, as opposed to through an email or text message.

**C** .......... Firstly, it takes more time to meet someone in person. Sending a message is a lot quicker and easier. Secondly, it can sometimes be difficult or impossible to speak to someone face-to-face. For example, if they live far away you might not see them very often so other modes of communication are necessary.

**D** .......... In conclusion, I believe that face-to-face communication is highly effective. Despite the fact that it takes more time and can be difficult, it allows us to read non-verbal clues and better understand people.

1 It's impossible to say what kind of communication is the best.
2 There are many arguments in favour of communicating face-to-face.
3 Face-to-face communication is no longer necessary.
4 However, there are some negative aspects to face-to-face communication.

### Writing Tip

**Topic/Supporting sentences**

In essays, each main body paragraph should begin with a topic sentence that introduces or summarises its main idea. A topic sentence should be followed by supporting sentences, which further develop the main idea of the paragraph.

**b)** Think of other topic sentences to introduce the two main body paragraphs.

## Linkers

**8** Look at the underlined linkers in the essay in Ex. 7a. Which are used to: *express contrast*; *add points*; *list points*; *conclude*; *give examples*? **Can you think of other synonymous ones?**

### Writing (a for-and-against essay)

**9** **a)** Read the task and underline the key words. Answer the questions.

> You have had a class discussion about textspeak. Now, your teacher has asked you to write an essay presenting the pros and cons of using textspeak. Write your essay (120-180 words).

1 What are you going to write? Who for?
2 What are you going to write about?
3 What style should you write in?

**b)** Match the arguments (1-4) to their justifications/examples (a-d). Which are for/against the topic?

| Arguments | Justifications/Examples |
|---|---|
| 1 ☐ promotes misspelling | **a** faster and takes up less space |
| 2 ☐ convenient way to communicate | **b** older people might not understand it |
| 3 ☐ excludes and confuses people | **c** affect schoolwork |
| 4 ☐ fun and creative | **d** chat with friends and invent new abbreviations |

**10** Use the ideas in Ex. 9b as well as your own ideas to write your essay. Use appropriate linkers. Follow the plan.

### Plan

**Para 1:** state the topic
**Para 2:** arguments for (with justifications/examples)
**Para 3:** arguments against (with justifications/examples)
**Para 4:** summary of arguments; express opinion

### VALUES
**Communication**

*The most important thing in communication is hearing what isn't said.*

Peter Drucker

# British Body Language

Hey there globetrotters! Are you planning a trip to the UK? Not sure which gestures and greetings to use? Never fear – we've got you covered! Avoid **awkward** social situations or misunderstandings by reading our advice on British body language before you go ...

**A** As any seasoned traveller will know, body language and the way people greet each other varies from country to country. From a bow of the head to a handshake, a high-five, a hug and a kiss (or two!), we all have different **non-verbal** ways of communicating with one another. And while variety is the spice of life, sometimes all this variation can lead to confusion and misunderstandings. It can be difficult to read the body language of a person from another country, or to know which greeting is **appropriate** to use in which country.

**B** The type of greeting people use in the UK **tends** to differ depending on whether the situation is formal or informal. A handshake is an appropriate greeting for formal situations, such as business meetings or when meeting someone for the first time. When **greeting** a close friend or family member, however, a hug is more **typical**, although some people (usually men) are still traditional about physical contact and prefer to shake hands instead. Having said that, the European kiss on the cheek is now becoming more common in the UK among some friends and families.

**C** Making eye contact while you're talking to someone is important, but it can be tricky to get the balance just right. Too much eye contact can look like you're staring, which is rude, while no eye contact at all makes it seem as though you're not interested in what the person is saying. Try to look into a person's eyes most of the time while they're speaking, but **glance** away every so often so that it's not too uncomfortable. Smiling and nodding your head are also polite signs that you're listening to a person and that you understand what they're saying.

**D** Hand signals are a kind of body language that can differ **greatly** from place to place. For example, holding up your fingers to indicate a number when ordering food or drinks. In Britain if you do this with the back of your hand facing the other person it is extremely rude. So use your words not your hands.

**E** In the UK, people generally don't like it if you stand unnecessarily close to them. Of course, sometimes this can't be avoided, like on a busy bus or train. But in a large, comfortable environment such as an office, try not to stand or sit too close to someone, especially if you don't know them very well. If someone is **leaning** their body away from you, this might mean that they're uncomfortable with how close you are. Try to keep an arm's length of space between yourself and the person you're talking to.

Body language is a hugely important part of communication. Being able to read a person's non-verbal signals is almost as crucial as being able to understand the language they are speaking. So, even if you're a **fluent** English speaker, remember to pay attention to body language while you're in the UK!

✓ **Check these words**

globetrotter, seasoned, bow, variety is the spice of life, balance, stare, nod, crucial

## Listening & Reading

**1** Look at the pictures. What do you think each gesture means? When do the British use them? 🎧 Listen and read to find out.

**2** Read the text and match the paragraphs (A-E) to the headings (1-6). One heading is extra. Then explain the words in bold.

1 Conversation
2 Personal Space
3 Cultural Differences
4 Hidden Meaning
5 Saying Hello
6 Gestures

## Speaking & Writing

**3** 💬 THINK Compare body language in the UK to body language in your country. Can you mention some gestures that are different?

**4** 💬 ICT Collect information about gestures and body language that people in your country use. Use your notes to prepare and give a presentation to a group of foreign people visiting your country.

# Review 5

## Vocabulary

**1** **Choose the correct word.**

1 We would like to **communicate/express/speak** our deepest gratitude to everyone who called in with information about the incident.
2 Mr Jones is great at public speaking, look how expressive his **body/business/mind** language is!
3 Did you **say/talk/tell** Mark that we're having a team meeting this afternoon?
4 There was a communication **barrier/impact/ breakdown** at the office and the project wasn't finished on time.
5 I can tell when Bob is annoyed by the **tone/impact/ session** of his voice – he sounds so serious when he's angry.

*(5 x 2 = 10)*

**2** **Fill in:** *get, commit, access, come, interact.*

1 We've ........................ up with an amazing new app to help tourists overcome language barriers.
2 Do you really want anyone to ..................... our private thoughts?
3 When you're giving a presentation, visual aids can help to ........................ your message across.
4 It is clear that animals ........................ with each other, even though they don't have language like humans.
5 Technology could help more criminals ........................ crimes.

*(5 x 3 = 15)*

**3** **Fill in:** *at, about, from, on, down.*

1 Please keep the noise ....................! I need to make an important phone call.
2 Loss of signal kept me ................... phoning home while I was camping.
3 Looking at your phone screen late at night can have a negative effect ................... your ability to sleep.
4 Some languages are ................... risk of disappearing.
5 Do you worry ................. the effect that textspeak is having on your children's spelling?

*(5 x 3 = 15)*

## Grammar

**4** **Choose the correct tense.**

1 She **is meeting/will have met** John for lunch tomorrow – they arranged it last night.
2 The Italian course for beginners **begins/will begin** next week.
3 I **buy/am going to buy** a new smartphone now that I have enough money.
4 Listen to that person shouting! He **will/is going to lose** his voice!
5 Jane **will be working/will have worked** this time tomorrow afternoon.

*(5 x 4 = 20)*

**5** **Put the verbs in brackets into the correct future tense.**

1 Textspeak ................................... **(change)** completely by the time my kids are teenagers.
2 Gemma ................................... **(drive)** home between 3 and 4 pm this afternoon so don't call her then.
3 This translation device looks really cool. I ........................ ........................... **(take)** it!
4 I hope someone ................................... **(invent)** a universal language in the future.
5 Beth ........................................... **(learn)** sign language. She starts lessons next month.

*(5 x 4 = 20)*

## Everyday English

**6** **Match the exchanges.**

1 ☐ It's textspeak. It says "See you tomorrow".
2 ☐ Why is he doing this?
3 ☐ It's very convenient.
4 ☐ What's the matter? You look confused.

a Really? I don't think so.
b I think he enjoys it.
c I've got no idea what this message says.
d Are you sure? It looks like nonsense to me!

*(4 x 5 = 20)*

*Total 100*

## Competences

GOOD ✓

VERY GOOD ✓ ✓

EXCELLENT ✓ ✓ ✓

**Lexical Competence**
understand words/ phrases related to:
• ways to communicate
• textspeak
• body language
• feelings

**Reading Competence**
• understand texts related to communication (read for cohesion and coherence – gapped text; read for gist – match headings to paragraphs)

**Listening Competence**
• listen and understand dialogues about textspeak (listen for specific information – multiple choice)

**Speaking Competence**
• agree-disagree/express doubt
• have a debate

**Writing Competence**
• write a for-and-against essay

# 6

## Challenges

Vocabulary: jobs; work values
Grammar: modal verbs; modals of deduction

Everyday English: congratulating
Writing: an email of congratulations

## Vocabulary

### Jobs

**1** Match the words to form jobs. Which ones require a vocational school/university degree?

| | | | | |
|---|---|---|---|---|
| 1 | supermarket | **a** | reporter |
| 2 | sales | **b** | developer |
| 3 | art | **c** | guide |
| 4 | bank | **d** | director |
| 5 | weather | **e** | star |
| 6 | fitness | **f** | artist |
| 7 | flight | **g** | manager |
| 8 | marketing | **h** | cashier |
| 9 | multimedia | **i** | attendant |
| 10 | rock | **j** | clerk |
| 11 | street | **k** | assistant |
| 12 | tour | **l** | trainer |

### Listening & Reading

**2** 🎧 Listen to and read the three people's profiles. Who is *enthusiastic*? *sociable*? *artistic*?

Fran has a high-powered job at one of the city's most successful companies. She's the youngest marketing manager they've ever had! She makes good money, but it's very stressful, and the only time she gets a break is when she works out. Exercise makes her feel alive – she just wishes she could do more of it, and have time to socialise a little more, too. She's a people person and she doesn't enjoy being in front of a screen all day.

①

Max is a bank clerk. It's a steady job that pays the bills, but his true passion is art. He studied it at college and people say he should use his talent. He has created some great murals on the walls of his friends' homes, but he'd love to try a public space. He thinks it would be amazing to get his work noticed by a wider audience, but there are lots of rules about where you can and can't create art, and he doesn't know where to start.

②

Jess has always been fascinated with technology. She studied Programming and Film Technology at university and she loved it. She's got a good job in IT now, but really it's just fixing hardware problems. She'd prefer something more creative and exciting. She doesn't fancy designing apps or software – she thinks it would get boring after a while. She needs something fast-paced and fun!

③

▶ VIDEO

# SWAP LIVES

*Have you ever **wondered** what it's like to be someone else? With us, you can get a taste of another home, neighbourhood, family and job without leaving your own. It's like taking a holiday for a week in someone else's life! Let's fill you in on our latest listings and find a life that **suits** you.*

**A** | **Multimedia Developer,**
*Auckland, New Zealand*

This life is for you if you're hard-working, imaginative and believe that 'variety is the spice of life'. You'll work at a small **independent** company and spend your days **hanging out** with a team of young, talented people. You'll be designing graphics and animations for websites, social media and TV, so you have to have a good knowledge of code, plus filming and editing techniques. Every day is different, and you'll need **creativity**, time management skills and a lot of coffee to meet all those **deadlines**!

**3** The young people in Ex. 2 want to change their lives for a week. Read the text. Decide which life (A-E) would be the most suitable for each person. There are two extra options that you do not need to use. Then explain the words in bold.

**4** **COLLOCATIONS** Find the words in the text that describe the following. Use them to make sentences of your own.

| | | | |
|---|---|---|---|
| 1 | ............................. media | 5 | ............................. designers |
| 2 | ............................. management | 6 | ............................. blogs |
| 3 | ............................. time | 7 | ............................. image |
| 4 | ............................. restaurants | 8 | ............................. life |

46

### B Tour Guide,
**Venice, Italy**

Are you great with people? Do you love art, history and culture? Then this life is for you! Spend every day seeing the sights of one of the most famous destinations in Europe, and **share** it all with a new group of people every day. Walking tours, boat tours, food tours and night tours – you'll never be bored because no day will ever be the same. In your free time, you can **explore** the city on your own and discover Venice as the **locals** see it.

### C Art Director,
**New York City, USA**

You needn't know anything about producing artwork to **step into** this person's life. All you need is a good eye for detail. You'll meet with **clients** at stylish restaurants to discuss the look of their new product, website or TV advert, and then you'll delegate tasks to graphic designers, animators and artists. The main **requirement** of the job and lifestyle is that you're sociable and are able to communicate with a variety of people in a variety of situations.

### D Fitness Trainer,
**Gold Coast, Australia**

To live this life, you should definitely be **passionate** about keeping fit! It involves long hours of meeting with clients, **designing** programmes for them and writing articles for fitness blogs. You may even have to give interviews on podcasts or radio shows. And don't forget to squeeze your own workout in! The upside is that you get to be your own boss while helping others to improve their health and body image. It's a great feeling to watch others achieving their **goals** while achieving yours!

### E Street Artist,
**London, UK**

Have you ever wanted to lead a double life? Try working at London's famous Borough Market selling vegetables by day, while moonlighting as an artist! When the sun goes down, you'll meet your crew somewhere in the city and fill the **blank**, grey walls with something inspirational for the **citizens** to see when they wake up. Don't worry about breaking the law – your crew has contacts and they always ask for permission first.

 **Check these words**

listings, spice, code, delegate, podcast, squeeze in, crew, inspirational, contacts

## 5 PREPOSITIONS Choose the correct preposition. Check in your dictionary.

1 You've got too many tasks to do. You should delegate some **for/to** your team.
2 My dad is a builder **by/in** day, but he paints beautiful pictures in the evenings.
3 Jack worked hard to get his project noticed **from/by** the senior manager.
4 Do you think Lucy will be able to manage that account **on/by** her own?
5 You need to ask **for/from** permission to access those files.

## 6 WORDS EASILY CONFUSED Choose the correct word. Check in your dictionary.

1 I feel **live/alive** when I'm under pressure to meet a deadline.
2 We're doing a(n) **live/alive** demonstration of our latest product tomorrow.
3 The **audience/spectators** at the football match seemed to love our new advert.
4 When you finish your presentation, don't forget to ask the **audience/spectators** if they have any questions.
5 You're very disorganised. You should make a **list/listing** of all your projects.
6 I saw a **list/listing** in the paper yesterday for a job at your company.

## 7 PHRASAL VERBS Fill in the correct particle.

**fill in: 1)** to complete a form or document (also: fill out); **2)** to give details to sb about sth
**fill out:** to gain weight
**fill up: 1)** to put sth in a container so that there's no more space; **2)** to eat enough so that you don't feel hungry

1 Don't worry about missing the meeting; I'll fill you .......... on what was discussed.
2 My nephew used to be quite thin, but he really filled .......... during the summer.
3 I won't leave the office for lunch; I filled .......... on a sandwich I ate earlier.
4 To apply for the job, you have to fill .......... this form with your personal details.
5 Stephen always fills .......... a bottle with water before he goes to work.

## Speaking & Writing

## 8 THINK Listen to and read the 'Swap Lives' text again. Which of these lives would you like to live for a week? Why? Discuss.

## 9 Write a short text describing your life for the life swap webpage. **Write:** *job, place, qualities/skills needed, duties, advantages.* **Read your text. Find someone in the class who wants to swap with you for a week.**

# Grammar in Use

## Modals ▶pp. GR9-10

Home | About | Features | FAQ | Contacts    search.......

### Travel and Work in New Zealand

*Living and working in another country gives you a much richer cultural understanding than just visiting. With a working holiday visa, you really get to experience New Zealand.*

- **How long is the working holiday visa valid?**
  If you are from Canada or the UK, you **may** stay for up to 23 months. People from other countries can stay for up to a year.

- **Can anyone apply?**
  Applicants **must** be aged 18-30. For some nationalities, you can be as old as 35.

- **Do I need a job offer before I apply?**
  No, you **don't have to** have a job offer to get your visa. You **should** do some research before you arrive, however, to see if the jobs you **can** do are available.

- **How do I apply?**
  You **need to** fill in an application form on the Immigration New Zealand website.

- **I am a UK citizen under 30, but I wasn't able to obtain a visa. Why is this?**
  You might not have submitted the correct supporting evidence for your application. We **may** also decline your application if you're not in good health.

**1** Read the FAQs. Match the modal verbs in bold to their uses: *possibility, permission, absence of necessity, obligation, advice, necessity, ability*.

**2** Choose the correct item.

1 A: Shall I wear this outfit to my interview next week?
   B: No, don't. You **don't have to/shouldn't** wear casual clothes to a job interview.
2 A: **Must/Can** I apply for a work visa?
   B: Are you over 18 years of age?
3 A: Is cleaning the office kitchen part of my duties?
   B: Yes, but you **can't/don't have to** clean the corridors and stairs – another cleaner does those areas.
4 A: Have you completed the project yet?
   B: No, but we **can/would** finish it by Friday.
5 A: They're advertising for a new manager at the clothes shop.
   B: I think you **must/ought to** apply for the job.
6 A: I've never worked in retail before.
   B: That's OK. You **needn't/shouldn't** have previous experience to apply.
7 A: Are there any office rules?
   B: Yes. You can have drinks at your desk, but you **mustn't/shouldn't** eat food in the office.
8 A: Can you give the presentation on Wednesday?
   B: I **have to/may** have a meeting then. Let me check my schedule.

**3** Fill in: *must, mustn't/can't, have to, don't have to.*

1 All employees ........................... arrive at the office between 8 and 10 am.
2 You ........................... stay later than 8 pm because the office insurance doesn't cover you after this time.
3 You ........................... carry your pass card with you because you need it to enter and leave the building.
4 You ........................... wear formal clothes to the office, but please be presentable.
5 All new employees choose passwords for their computers. They ........................... be unique or the system won't accept them.
6 You ........................... tell anyone else your password.
7 You ........................... keep your desk neat and tidy.
8 Employees ........................... give their managers a daily progress report, but most do.

**4** Read the situations. Write sentences, as in the example. Use the verbs in the list.

- may • would • shall • can

1 You see an old lady carrying heavy bags.
*Shall I help you?*
2 You want to ask your boss for a day off on Friday.
.................................................................
3 You tell your colleague it's possible you'll be late tomorrow.
.................................................................
4 You offer to make your colleague a cup of coffee.
.................................................................
5 You ask your colleague to email you the files.
.................................................................
6 It's possible you'll finish work early today.
.................................................................

**5** Rewrite the sentences using an appropriate modal verb.

1 **She was obliged** to deliver the project on Tuesday.
.................................................................
2 **I advise you** to talk to the manager.
.................................................................
3 **It is possible** Steve will get a promotion.
.................................................................
4 **It's forbidden** to enter this lab.
.................................................................
5 **Is it OK if** I take my break now?
.................................................................
6 **They are able to** work under pressure.
.................................................................
7 **Do you want** to meet on Tuesday?
.................................................................
8 **It's necessary** for Ben to pick up the group at 8:30.
.................................................................

**6** SPEAKING 👥 Discuss what kind of rules a company might have regarding their staff. **Think about:** *health and safety, dress, appearance, behaviour.* **Do these rules apply to all companies or particular companies?**

## Modals in the past ⟫ pp. GR9-10

**Obligation** *(had to)*
*They **had to** clock out at 5 yesterday. (They were obliged to.)*
**Necessity/Lack of necessity** *(had to – didn't have/ need to)*
*We **had to** wear formal clothes at the meeting yesterday.* (It was necessary.)
*Max **didn't have/need to** send the emails.* (It wasn't necessary.)
**Ability/Lack of ability** *(could/was able to – couldn't/ wasn't able to)*
*Paul **could** type very fast when he was 15.* (general ability in the past – repeatedly)
*I **was able to** meet last week's deadline.* (specific ability in the past – in a particular situation – I managed to)

**7** Read the theory. Find an example in the text in Ex. 1. Then, fill in the gaps with the correct past modal from the list below.

• was able to • could • had to • didn't have to
• couldn't • wasn't able to

**1** A: Did you cancel your computer class this afternoon?
B: No, I .............................. . John volunteered to teach it for me.
**2** A: Have you always been a good singer?
B: No. There's a video of me when I was three years old, and I .............................. sing at all!
**3** A: I heard you stayed in the office until 10 pm last night!
B: Yes, but at least I .............................. finish preparing my presentation.
**4** A: Why didn't you come to the yoga class yesterday?
B: I .............................. take an important client out to dinner.
**5** A: I'm afraid I .............................. recover the files from your hard drive.
B: That's OK. Luckily, I had saved them on the cloud before my computer crashed.
**6** A: I'm not surprised that Ross became a programmer.
B: Me neither. He .............................. work our home computer better than I could when he was a child!

**8** SPEAKING What rules did you have when you were in primary school? Tell your partner, using past modals. Your partner responds.

*A: I had to wear a uniform when I was in primary school.*
*B: I didn't have to. etc*

## Modals of deduction ⟫pp. GR10-11

• **I'm sure** he **is** at work. → He **must be** at work.
• **I'm sure** he **isn't** at the café . → He **can't/couldn't be** at the café .
• **Maybe** he **is working** on the report. → He **may/ might/could be working** on the report.
• **I'm sure** he **has sent** the emails. → He **must have sent** the emails.
• **I'm sure** he **didn't meet** Mr Harris yesterday. → He **can't/couldn't have met** Mr Harris yesterday.
• **I think** he **was working** when I left. → He **may/ might/could have been working** when I left.
**NOTE:** *Can* can be used in questions to express possibility. Where **can** they be? Where **can** he have put the flash drive?

**9** Study the table. Find an example in the text in Ex. 1. Which modal verb(s) do we use to express *possibility*? *positive logical assumption*? *negative logical assumption*? How do infinitive forms change in modals of deduction?

**10** Choose the correct item.

**1** Daniel's definitely in today. If he's not at his desk, he **must/can** be in a meeting.
**2** Ellen **can't/must** have taken the file – she hasn't been here all week.
**3** I don't know what the meeting was about – they **can/ might** have been discussing your case.
**4** Luke **could/must** be having his interview today but I'm not sure.
**5** Mr Jason **must/can** have seen the report yesterday. I left it on his desk at 9 am.
**6** They **may/can't** be at the office – I saw them going into a restaurant 20 minutes ago.

**11** SPEAKING
Look at the pictures. Make deductions.

49

# Skills in Action

## Vocabulary
### Work values

**1** **Fill in:** *punctual, respectful, autonomous, cooperative, creative, responsible.*

# HEREFORD
## Nursing Home

*We're looking for a qualified caregiver with at least two years' experience. Applicants should also match our work values. Read below to see if this job suits you.*

To be a carer at Hereford Nursing Home, you need to be:

- 1) ................................., so that you can work well with our other caregivers, nurses and doctors.
- 2) ................................., especially when giving the correct medication to residents.
- 3) ................................., as you may need to make important decisions on your own.
- 4) ................................. to others, both other staff and our residents, so that we can all live in harmony.
- 5) ................................., as you may need to come up with ways to entertain residents.
- 6) ................................., so that you can replace another caregiver at the end of their shift.

*Does this sound like you? Then send your CV to*
jobs@hereford.nh.com
*We look forward to hearing from you.*

**2** **THINK** **What are your top three work values? Why are they important to you? Discuss. You can use your own ideas.**

## Listening

**3** **You will hear five short extracts in which people are talking about work values. For questions 1-5, choose from the list (A-H) what each speaker says about it. Use the letters only once. There are three extra letters which you do not need to use.**

| | |
|---|---|
| **Speaker 1** | |
| **Speaker 2** | |
| **Speaker 3** | |
| **Speaker 4** | |
| **Speaker 5** | |

**A** My employer allows staff to be autonomous.

**B** My work values were the reason why I got my current job.

**C** I don't agree with the work values my boss expects.

**D** The values I have at work have changed over time.

**E** I tried to change my colleagues' work values.

**F** I try to have a positive outlook where I work.

**G** I don't believe that teamwork is important in a workplace.

**H** My colleagues don't have the same work values as I do.

## Everyday English
### Congratulating

**4** **Read the first exchange. What good news does Paul have?**

**Listen and read to find out.**

| **Anna:** | Paul, you should have told me about your good news! Well done! |
|---|---|
| **Paul:** | Thanks, Anna. Actually, I just found out this morning. |
| **Anna:** | Well, I knew you would get it. You were definitely the best candidate to become head manager after Debby Rodgers retired. |
| **Paul:** | Maybe, but I did terribly in the interview. I was so nervous I wasn't able to speak properly! |
| **Anna:** | It can't have been so bad! And anyway, you are the most hard-working junior manager in the company. When do you start? |
| **Paul:** | Well, all next week, I have to go to training seminars. Then the following week, I'll be the official department head. I can't believe it! |
| **Anna:** | You really deserve it. I wish you all the best in your new position, Paul! |
| **Paul:** | Thanks a lot, Anna. I really appreciate it. |

**5** **You have just learned that a colleague has become the head teacher in the school where you work. Use the dialogue in Ex. 4 as a model and language from the box to act out your dialogue.**

| Congratulating | Wishing |
|---|---|
| • Well done!<br>• Congratulations (on your new job/success etc.)<br>• You (really) deserve it! | • Good luck/Best of luck (in your new job, etc.)!<br>• Wish you (all) the best (for the future, etc.)! |
| **Expressing thanks** | |
| • Thank you (very much).<br>• Thanks (a lot/a million). | • That's (so/very) kind of you.<br>• I (really) appreciate it. |

## Pronunciation: reduced pronunciation

**6** **a)** **Listen and repeat.**

1 Could you help me with this report?
2 Would he mind if I borrowed his laptop?
3 Should you call him now?
4 They ought to work harder.
5 We have to stay in the office late

**b)** **Use the modal verbs in the sentences in Ex. 6a to form sentences. Read your sentences aloud.**

*Would you mind opening the door for me?*

## Reading & Writing

**7** Read the email and complete the gaps with the word derived from the word in brackets.

---

**New message** ⊖ ⊘ ⊗

From   Dave          ▾ Cc Bcc
To      Kate
Subject   Congrats!

🖉 ✉ 🖼   A̅ T̅ ⌀   ☰ ☰ ☰     🗑 ⚙

Hi Kate,

It's been months since we were last in touch, but I wanted to congratulate you on your good news! I was **1)** ............................ **(delight)** to read about it on your career profile page: Kate Simmons – Head Accountant at Hayes and Burns!

I remember when we worked together at Milford Department Store ten years ago. You were always so hard-working and **2)** ............................ **(rely)**, so it's not **3)** ............................ **(surprise)** that you've become so successful in your career. I imagine that your new position will be quite **4)** ............................ **(demand)**, but I'm sure you'll be able to rise to the challenge. After all, you definitely have the **5)** ............................ **(able)** and the work values required. Just remember to eat and sleep well, and get some daily exercise, too.

Well, that's all from me. Once again, congratulations on your **6)** ............................ **(achieve)** and best of luck with everything.

All the best,

Dave

                                    Send

---

 **Writing Tip**

**Emails congratulating a person**

Emails expressing congratulations are written in response to some good news (a new job, a promotion, an anniversary, etc.). They are usually written in informal or semi-formal style and also contain wishes for the future.

**8** **a)** What style is the email in Ex. 8 written in? Why? Does it contain a wish for the future?

**b)** Replace the underlined phrases in the email with the ones in the list below.

- you'll need
- I guess your new job
- good luck
- well done
- done so well
- I haven't talked to you in ages
- manage fine

## Writing (an email of congratulations)

**9** Read the rubric, underline the key words and answer the questions.

> Imagine an ex-colleague of yours has got a new job as the manager in a electronics shop. Write an email to congratulate the person, mentioning their skills and work values, and wishing them well for the future (120-180 words).

**1** What are you going to write? Who for?
**2** What are you going to write about?
**3** What style should you write in?

**10** 👥 THINK Which of the following skills and work values should a manager in an electronics shop have? Decide in pairs.

**Skills**

– good communication skills     ........
– good leadership skills     ........
– able to work under pressure     ........
– able to meet customers' needs     ........
– able to make right decisions     ........

**Work values**

| | | | |
|---|---|---|---|
| – hard-working | ........ | – influential | ........ |
| – reliable | ........ | – punctual | ........ |
| – responsible | ........ | – polite | ........ |
| – flexible | ........ | – creative | ........ |
| – cooperative | ........ | – tolerant | ........ |

**11** Use the ideas in Ex. 10 to write your email of congratulations for Ex. 9. Follow the plan.

**Plan**

*Hi (person's first name),*
**Para 1:** opening remarks, congratulate person
**Para 2:** discuss person's skills and work values
**Para 3:** discuss challenges of future job
**Para 4:** repeat congratulations, closing remarks
*All the best,*
*(your first name),*

**VALUES**

**Challenge**
*Don't limit your challenges.*
*Challenge your limits.*
**Jerry Dunn**

▶ VIDEO

# Working Stateside

*Business etiquette is not the same in each country. In Italy, you shouldn't feel insulted if a colleague or client arrives a little late for a meeting. In Japan, you must offer and accept business cards with both hands. What about the USA? What are the dos and don'ts from East to West Coast?*

**1** The handshake is still the standard greeting when meeting someone for the first time or after a period of time (though you don't have to shake hands with your colleagues every morning). It's important not to do it too softly or too hard. A **bone-crushing** grip just makes the person whose hand you are crushing uncomfortable, whereas a soft handshake makes you seem uncertain or lacking in self-confidence.

**2** And speaking of introductions, you should always give your full name – first name and surname – when introduced to someone for the first time. After all, you want people to hear it, remember it, and know you as someone more than just Maria or John. After that, things are pretty informal in the US workplace, with most managers quite happy to be on first name terms with their teams.

**3** Americans like to smile and expect you to smile back. At the very least, have a **receptive** and welcoming look on your face, rather than a frown or a blank gaze. Keep eye contact when you are talking to someone (without staring, of course). Someone who can't look an American in the eye is not considered trustworthy by them.

**4** Mostly, American offices run on **business casual**, which generally means trousers, shirt and jacket, but not necessarily a suit and not always a tie. However, most businesses will have a code of conduct for you to read, and what they expect you to wear will be in there. A warning: even the 'casual Friday' that many offices enjoy doesn't mean you can rock up in shorts, vest and flip-flops!

**5** Most US offices these days are **open plan**, which means you could find yourself in a room full of cubicles, with only a chest-high divider separating you from your colleagues. This needn't be a problem as long as you respect their right to work in peace. This means no long chats at people's desks, no talking on your phone to arrange your social life and no eating at your desk.

**6** Americans value **punctuality**, so turning up late to a meeting is considered very disrespectful. They value their time, which is why meetings are short and for business only, not catching up on people's personal news. You are also expected to contribute at a meeting and to show interest.

*All in all, however, you will be valued in a US company as long as you work hard. And if in doubt, ask someone – as a nation of immigrants, Americans are happy to help someone fit into the culture.*

## Listening & Reading

**1** From the TV shows and films about American companies you have seen, what do you think American office etiquette is like?

🎧 Listen and read to find out.

**2** Read the text again and match headings A-H to paragraphs 1-6. There are two extra headings. Then explain the words/phrases in bold.

A  Show me respect
B  What's in a name?
C  Dress code
D  The right balance
E  Short and sweet
F  Expressions of interest
G  Watching the clock
H  Shared space

✓ **Check these words**

stateside, etiquette, crush, first name terms, gaze, code of conduct, rock up, flip-flop, divider, immigrant

## Speaking & Writing

**3** 👥 THINK How does office etiquette in your country compare to the USA? With a partner, come up with two similarities and two differences.

**4** ICT Research office etiquette in another English-speaking country. Prepare and give a presentation about it to the class.

## Vocabulary

### 1 Choose the correct item.

1 Mike works as a flight **clerk/reporter/attendant**.
2 John's a great manager; he is always kind and **flexible/polite/influential** to the customers.
3 Beth is a **multimedia/art/marketing** developer.
4 Brian is meeting an important **citizen/client/spectator** for lunch.
5 His project was late again. He needs to work on his time **editing/detail/management**.
6 Singing on stage really makes me feel **live/life/alive**!
7 She works as a weather **guide/cashier/reporter**.
8 He wants to become a famous rock **artist/star/designer**.
9 What are the main **contacts/requirements/blanks** of the job?
10 I'm sure this job **wonders/shares/suits** you.

*(10 x 2 = 20)*

### 2 Fill in: *cooperative, creative, autonomous, punctual, responsible, respectful.*

1 Chris is ........................ and can make his own decisions.
2 She's never late – she's always ................................. .
3 Please be polite and ............................. towards our visiting colleagues.
4 You're ............................., so I think you would do well in a career in art or design.
5 A(n) ..................................... person can work well with others.
6 You need to be .............................. to do this job, as you will be in charge of 20 children under five.

*(6 x 2 = 12)*

### 3 Choose the correct item.

1 Fill **in/up** this form to register for the scheme.
2 He delegated this project **to/for** Emma.
3 Ask **from/for** permission to take a break.
4 Can you fill **up/out** the printer tray with paper, please?
5 The problem was noticed **from/by** the accounting department.
6 She's very skinny, but she'll fill **out/in** as she gets older.

*(6 x 2 = 12)*

## Grammar

### 4 Fill in: *must, mustn't, don't have to, wasn't able to, ought to, shall, can, may.*

1 Max tried, but he ................................. fix the problem.
2 You .................................. print the document – you can just email it to me.
3 Mr Jenson ................................. see you this afternoon.
4 You .................................. remove these files from the building. It's against the company rules.
5 ................................. we ask Mr Perk to join us?
6 ............................. I use Meeting Room 6 this afternoon, please?
7 I .................................. get a promotion this year. I've promised myself.
8 If you want my advice, you ................................. look for a morning job.

*(8 x 3 = 24)*

### 5 Complete the gaps with modals of deduction and the verbs in brackets in the correct form.

1 Ben .......................................... **(go)** to his interview yesterday. He was with me all day.
2 I'm not sure what she was doing here. She ................................................ **(wait)** for Mrs Reed.
3 Ross ............................................. **(be)** in the meeting – I just saw him by the photocopier.
4 Mr White ....................................... **(work)** near Prince's Square. I see him get off the bus there every morning.

*(4 x 3 = 12)*

## Everyday English

### 6 Match the exchanges.

1 ☐ My interview was terrible!
2 ☐ When do you start?
3 ☐ I can't believe I got the job!
4 ☐ I wish you all the best for the future.
5 ☐ Congratulations! Great job!

a That's very kind of you.
b You really deserve it.
c It can't have been so bad!
d Thank you very much.
e Next Friday.

*(5 x 4 = 20)*

*Total 100*

---

## Competences

GOOD ✓
VERY GOOD ✓✓
EXCELLENT ✓✓✓

**Lexical Competence**
understand words/phrases related to:
• jobs
• work values

**Reading Competence**
• understand texts related to jobs, business etiquette & work values (read for specific information – multiple matching; match headings to paragraphs)

**Listening Competence**
• listen to and understand monologues related to work values (listen for specific information – match speakers to sentences)

**Speaking Competence**
• congratulate

**Writing Competence**
• write an email of congratulations
• prepare a presentation about the office etiquette in another country

# B

## Values: Productivity

◀ ▶ ↻   SEARCH 🔍

HOME | ABOUT | BLOG | CONTACT |

# Getting things done
**Seven tips to increase your productivity**

*Productivity is one of the most important values in the modern workplace. But being productive won't just get you a promotion at work   it'll also help you get better marks in your studies, reach your fitness goals ... in fact, productivity is a key to success in every area of life! So, here's seven tips to help you get more things done!*

**1**

A great idea is to write down the tasks you want to complete each day. This can include tasks that you want to do on a daily basis or one-off tasks for a **specific** day. Then, tick off the tasks as you complete them. You'll get a great feeling of satisfaction as you tick off each task, and you'll feel **motivated** to complete the whole list.

**2**

There's no point in setting yourself a list of tasks, however, if you don't have the energy to get them done. And the best way to get it isn't by drinking coffee – it's by eating well, sleeping well and exercising regularly. If you take care of your body, you'll be amazed by how much more you can do in a day!

**3**

Another way to keep productive is to promise yourself a **treat** when you've completed a task. For example, you could treat yourself to a pizza delivered to your door or an evening out at the cinema – whatever you enjoy! You'll feel more enthusiastic about a task when you know there is a prize at the end!

**4**

Getting things done sometimes means you have to be a little bit selfish. Of course, it's important to be helpful and thoughtful, but, from time to time, don't feel **guilty** about finding a quiet place to focus on your tasks.

**5**

When deciding on what you want to achieve, don't aim too high. It's OK to set yourself **challenging** tasks, but remember that the more difficult the task is, the more likely it is that you will give up. Instead, divide big tasks into smaller ones – it'll help you stay on track.

**6**

Do you ever feel like there aren't enough hours in the day? Find the periods in your day when you do very little, and try to make them more productive. One of the worst time wasters is the **commute** to college or work, but instead of looking out the bus or train window, why not tick a task or two off your list?

**7**

Research any successful person and, more often than not, you'll discover that they begin their day early. For one, the early morning is a great time to focus on your tasks in peace and quiet. And if you tick off some tasks early, you feel more **capable** of finishing your list by the end of the day.

---

**1** Read the title and the introductory paragraph quickly. What are the benefits of being productive?

**2** Read the article and match headings A-G to tips 1-7.
🎧 Listen and check, then explain the words/phrases in bold.

A  Find some hidden time
B  Don't always be available
C  Make a good start
D  Set yourself reasonable goals
E  Reward yourself
F  Have a healthy lifestyle
G  Make a to-do list

**3** 👥👥 THINK Which two methods in the text do you think are the most effective for increasing productivity? Why? Tell your partner.

**4** ICT Research a successful person (e.g. businessperson, inventor, etc) online. What do they do in their daily life to increase their productivity? Write a short text to read to the class.

# Public Speaking Skills

**1** Read the task. Who are you? Who will you be speaking to? What is the purpose of the speech? What will you be talking about?

You are running for election to become mayor of your city. Give a speech to local citizens about the problems the city faces and what you would do as mayor to fix them.

---

### Study Skills

**Using questions**

A question in public speaking always makes the audience pay attention. There are three kinds of questions commonly used in speeches.

**1 Hook questions** are interesting questions that the audience will want to know the answer to, e.g. *What makes a city great?*

**2 Rhetorical questions** are questions that do not need an answer, because it is so obvious, e.g. *Who wouldn't want a change like this to happen?*

**3 Hypophora** is a question that the speaker presents as if coming from the audience, which he/she then immediately answers, e.g. *Why do we need this? Let me tell you ...*

---

**2** 🎧 Listen to and read the model. Match the underlined questions with the question types in the *Study Skills* box.

**3** **ICT** Imagine you are standing against Callum Forrest to become mayor of Winford. You feel the biggest problems the city faces are litter, a lack of housing and the need for high-speed Internet. Make notes about ways these problems could be solved. Then use your notes to give a speech to a group of local citizens.

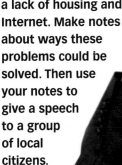

Good afternoon everyone. Thank you all for coming today. My name is Callum Forrest and I'm running for mayor of Winford. Now, what does it take to be a great mayor? A person who knows their city, loves it, and wants to make it better. I was born and raised in Winford, and I've been elected as a city councillor for the last five years. I have a good understanding of the problems our city faces today, and I'm passionate about fixing them.

We all know that one of the major problems in our city is unemployment. Unfortunately, over 20% of our city's working population is unemployed. It's one of my key aims to lower this number. How do I plan to do this? By attracting new companies to the area, first of all. Also, I will set up unemployment centres in the neighbourhoods, not just in the city centre. By doing this, we save unemployed people a 45-minute journey before they even see what jobs are available!

Another problem our city suffers from is a lack of green spaces. Compared to neighbouring cities, our city has a very small number of parks. Why is this an important issue for me? Well, I believe that green spaces are very important for the happiness of a city's citizens. If we had more parks, then more people would get out of their homes, meet each other and get fresh air and exercise. Wouldn't this make a huge difference to our city? As mayor, I plan to create more parks in the city, and I think that this will make us feel healthier and bring our community together.

Lastly, another problem that I would like to highlight is the air pollution in our city. Do you know where this city stands for air quality compared to others in this region? Last, that's where. Now, I'm not talking about banning cars, but one thing I will do is lower fares for public transport and make buses and trains more frequent. This will encourage people to use public transport, and it will eventually reduce the pollution in our city. Do you want a city suitable for the 21st century? Then vote Callum Forrest for mayor on 26th March. I won't let you down!

**Vocabulary:** technology; apps
**Grammar:** the passive; personal – impersonal constructions; the causative; reflexive/emphatic pronouns
**Everyday English:** expressing opinion – agreement/disagreement
**Writing:** an opinion essay

# High-tech

## Vocabulary

### Technology

**1** **a)** Match the words to form compound nouns.

| | | | |
|---|---|---|---|
| **1** ☐ artificial | **a** | reality |
| **2** ☐ virtual | **b** | Things (IoT) |
| **3** ☐ smart | **c** | assistant |
| **4** ☐ high-speed | **d** | intelligence |
| **5** ☐ the Internet of | **e** | broadband |
| **6** ☐ digital | **f** | devices |

**b)** Use the compound nouns to complete the sentences below.

**1** It is said that ............................................. is the future of gaming – it's like you're actually there.

**2** ....................................... are able to communicate between themselves.

**3** My new ................................................. is so sensitive that it can hear me when I whisper.

**4** We've just had ........................................... installed that delivers 1GB a second.

**5** Machines with .......................................... are able to think for themselves.

**2** Make a list of the latest technology and share it with the rest of the class. How much tech do you use every day? What for?

## Reading & Listening

**3** Read the title. What technology from Ex. 1a do you think you are going to read about?

🎧 Listen and read to find out.

✔ **Check these words**

access, device, lightbulb, go off, run out of, manage, industrial equipment, wearable, offender, remotely

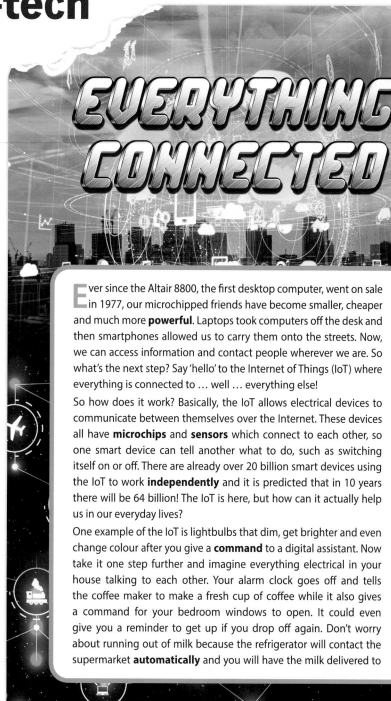

# EVERYTHING CONNECTED

Ever since the Altair 8800, the first desktop computer, went on sale in 1977, our microchipped friends have become smaller, cheaper and much more **powerful**. Laptops took computers off the desk and then smartphones allowed us to carry them onto the streets. Now, we can access information and contact people wherever we are. So what's the next step? Say 'hello' to the Internet of Things (IoT) where everything is connected to … well … everything else!

So how does it work? Basically, the IoT allows electrical devices to communicate between themselves over the Internet. These devices all have **microchips** and **sensors** which connect to each other, so one smart device can tell another what to do, such as switching itself on or off. There are already over 20 billion smart devices using the IoT to work **independently** and it is predicted that in 10 years there will be 64 billion! The IoT is here, but how can it actually help us in our everyday lives?

One example of the IoT is lightbulbs that dim, get brighter and even change colour after you give a **command** to a digital assistant. Now take it one step further and imagine everything electrical in your house talking to each other. Your alarm clock goes off and tells the coffee maker to make a fresh cup of coffee while it also gives a command for your bedroom windows to open. It could even give you a reminder to get up if you drop off again. Don't worry about running out of milk because the refrigerator will contact the supermarket **automatically** and you will have the milk delivered to

**4** Read the text again and, for questions 1-4, choose the correct answer (A, B, C or D). Then explain the words/phrases in bold.

**1** Why does the writer mention the Altair 8800?
**A** to encourage readers to buy a laptop
**B** to show how computers have changed
**C** to inform readers about new technology
**D** to tell readers about the first smartphone

**2** What do we learn about the IoT?
**A** It needs chips and sensors to work.
**B** It can send email and text messages.
**C** It does not need an Internet connection.
**D** It is not ready to be used at the moment.

▶ VIDEO

your house. And when it arrives, it is already paid for as the money has been taken out your bank account **straightaway**.

The IoT is not just for the home, though. It helps companies manage stock more efficiently by collecting data that can be used to predict **customer behaviour**. And it's not just about the amount of paper in the stationery cupboard, either. Factories are able to **maintain** industrial equipment better because machines can speak up when they need repairing or replacing.

Also, medical information can be sent by wearables to our doctors to **monitor** us 24/7. This data can also be used to track crowds across the city to inform us of traffic jams and cut air pollution. That's not the only way the IoT can help the environment, though. Sensors have already been installed in some trees in the Amazon Rainforest, so when one is cut down illegally, **the authorities** track it and catch the offenders.

In 1956, the first wireless remote control **revolutionised** TV; viewers could change channels without getting up off the sofa. Now, the IoT is making it possible for almost all the devices in the modern home to be activated remotely. Sit back and enjoy the Internet of Things – life just got a little bit easier.

**3** How is the IoT affecting the environment?
  **A** It causes air pollution.
  **B** It reduces deforestation.
  **C** It saves electricity in the home.
  **D** It helps us to cut down on rubbish.

**4** What does the writer say about the first remote control?
  **A** It was not originally used for TVs.
  **B** It was invented before the television.
  **C** It was connected to the TV with wires.
  **D** It changed the way audiences watched TV.

**5** COLLOCATIONS **Find the words in the text that complete the following phrases. Then use the completed phrases to make sentences.**

**1** ..................... computer    **4** ................... account
**2** ..................... clock        **5** ................... equipment
**3** ..................... maker        **6** ................... control

**6** PREPOSITIONS **Fill in**: *to, on, with, out, about*. **Check in your dictionary.**

**1** Some people worry ................ the development of AI.
**2** I use cards, so I don't need to take money ................ of the bank.
**3** Harry can't get his tablet connected ................ the Internet.
**4** The very first smartphone went ................ sale in 1994.
**5** Can I have a word ................ you about installing IoT devices?

**7** WORDS EASILY CONFUSED **Choose the correct word. Check in your dictionary.**

**1** I gave Kate a **memory/reminder** about the science fair.
**2** Our IoT system **consists/composes** of hundreds of devices.
**3** All the cars were **stationary/stationery** in the traffic jam.
**4** These earbuds are **in the sale/for sale** – they're 50% cheaper!

**8** PHRASAL VERBS **Fill in the correct particle.**

> **drop by:** to visit sb informally
> **drop off: 1)** to fall asleep; **2)** to decrease
> **drop out:** to leave a college/university course without having finished it

**1** Amy got a job in IT and dropped .......... of her course.
**2** I dropped .......... on the sofa just before the TV show about the IoT came on.
**3** Tom dropped ........ to show me his new smartphone.
**4** Sales of desktop computers have dropped ....... recently.

## Speaking & Writing

**9** 💬 THINK **Think of three things you would like the IoT to do. Tell the class.**

**10** 💬 ICT **Is the IoT going to make our lives easier or not? Do some research online and make notes. Write a short text, giving your opinion. Have a class debate and defend your opinion.**

# Grammar in Use

## The passive ▶pp. GR11-12

# Step into Tomorrow!

**W**hich tech fair was awarded the best in the industry three times in a row by *Tech Magazine*? Bright Sparks Tech Fair, of course, and it's back this May! From Thursday 5th to Sunday 8th, travel into tomorrow and get a glimpse of next year's tech. Last year's fair was considered the most successful in its seven-year history and this year's is expected to be even better. Hot new designs from all the biggest tech companies are being displayed across 10 halls. This year's theme is the Internet of Things. Demonstrations will be held with all the latest IoT tech. The fair is going to be opened by Kelly Carlton, presenter of the TV show *Tomorrow Today*, and a live episode of the show will be broadcast from the fair itself. Tickets cost £15 and are available on the door. They can also be ordered online to avoid queues. Book early and you will have your tickets delivered to your door at no extra charge!

**1** Read the announcement. Identify the passive forms. What tense is each?

**2** Read the sentences and decide which of them are *T* (True) or *F* (False).

1 We form the passive with the verb *to be* in the appropriate form and the past tense of the main verb. ........

2 We use the passive when the agent is more important than the action. ........

3 We can omit the agent when it is not important. ........

4 We use the passive to make statements more formal. ........

5 Only verbs that take an object can be changed into the passive. ........

6 In passive questions with *who*, *whom* or *which* we omit *by*. ........

**3** Choose the correct item. Give reasons.

1 Joe's password **is wrote/is written** on his monitor for everyone to see!

2 Have phone screens that don't crack **been invented/ be invented** yet?

3 Can wearables **be cleaned/have been cleaned** in the washing machine?

4 The latest phones **to be displayed/are being displayed** at the tech fair.

5 Used batteries shouldn't **be thrown/threw** in the rubbish bin.

6 The mouse broke when it **knocked/was knocked** off the desk.

7 Everyone **has been shown/are shown** how to install the new software.

8 The headphones **can be returned/were able to be returned** if they're faulty.

**4** Fill in *with* or *by*.

1 The office lights are activated ........... staff telling them to switch on.

2 Can the name of any piece of music be found ........... this app?

3 Was the app installed ........... you or did it come with the phone?

4 The term 'IoT' was first used in 1999 ......... Kevin Ashton.

5 I haven't cleaned my laptop in ages and it's covered ........... dust.

6 The back of the laptop needs to be opened carefully ........... a screwdriver.

**5** Rewrite the sentences in the passive voice in your notebook.

1 Electricians have installed IoT devices at work.

2 The IT department is updating the computer system this evening.

3 The organisers called off the science fair last Monday.

4 The creators won't release the app until later this year.

5 Who installed the new computers in the office?

6 Can I stream films and TV series using this device?

7 How have you updated your anti-virus software?

8 You must read the instructions before installing the router.

**6** SPEAKING 💬 ICT Collect information, then prepare a quiz for your classmates. Play in two teams.

*A: Who was the World Wide Web invented by?*

*B: Tim Berners-Lee.*

## Personal – Impersonal constructions
▶ p. GR12

We can have personal and impersonal constructions with verbs such as *say*, *believe*, *consider*, *expect*, etc.
**Active:** *People* **say** *that Steve Jobs was a genius.*
**Passive:**
- **Personal (subject of *that*-clause + passive form of main verb + *to*-inf)** *Steve Jobs is said to have been a genius.*
- **Impersonal (It + passive form of main verb + *that*-clause)** *It is said that Steve Jobs was a genius.*

**7** Study the theory. Then complete the sentences.

1 Everyone says that Tyler is an expert at fixing laptops.
It .................................................................

2 People believe that Internet crime is increasing.
Internet crime .................................................

3 People say that Claire crashed the computer system.
It .................................................................

4 They expect the new phone to come out soon.
The new phone .................................................

5 The IT department thought the email contained a virus.
The email .......................................................

6 They claim that the IoT will change the way we work.
It .................................................................

**8** Rewrite the text in the passive voice in your notebook.

.ıll ●      10:30 AM      100% ▬▶

New **App** for the **Blind**

Programmers released an amazing new app at Hereford Tech Fair last week. They have created an app to help blind people in their everyday lives. When a blind person needs help, they open the app on their smartphone. They can do this with an audio command. Then, the app starts a video call with a volunteer. The volunteer can see live video footage from the smartphone's camera. The volunteer helps blind people read things or find things. People say millions of people will download the app.

## The causative ▶ p. GR12

**9** Study the examples. Which sentence suggests that someone else did the action for Max? How is the causative formed? When do we use it? Find an example in the text on p. 58.

*Max **fixed** his laptop.*
*Max **had** his laptop **fixed**.*

**10** Rewrite the sentences using the causative and the words in brackets.

1 An IT technician is checking Sue's Internet connection. **(having)**
Sue ................................................................

2 Medical wearables monitor our health. **(monitored)**
We .................................................................

3 They asked a programmer to develop an app. **(had)**
They ...............................................................

4 *Tech Magazine* will present the company's new education software. **(have)**
The company ....................................................

5 Pete has upgraded my computer. **(had)**
I ...................................................................

**11** SPEAKING 💬 Your school will be holding a tech fair. Use the prompts and the causative to discuss details of the fair's organisation.

- book venue • advertise in local press • design posters
- print flyers • invite speakers • set up equipment

## Reflexive/Emphatic pronouns
▶ pp. GR12-13

**12** Read the examples. Which of the pronouns in bold is reflexive? Which is emphatic? Find examples in the text on p. 58.

*The mayor **himself** opened the new technology museum.*
*Jane bought **herself** a state-of-the-art smartphone*

**13** Fill in the correct pronoun. Which is reflexive? Which is emphatic?

1 Tom hurt ................................. removing his phone's battery.

2 Did you repair the smartphone .................................?

3 This phone scans ................................. and gets rid of any viruses.

4 It was Bill Gates ................................. who created the software.

5 Did Mike and Fran enjoy ................................. at the tech fair?

6 I did all the coding for the new app ................................. .

**14** SPEAKING Imagine you have attended a science fair. Report what you saw. Use the passive and reflexive/emphatic pronouns.

# Skills in Action

## Vocabulary

### Apps

**1** **Fill in:** *upload, browse, chat, monitor, share, order, get, book, create, stream.* **Then do the quiz. Compare with your partner.**

**Apptastic!**

would love to know what apps you use every day.
Complete this short questionnaire and send it to our website.

**Do you ever use an app to . . .**

1) .................... a taxi? ☐
2) .................... how much exercise you have done? ☐
3) .................... and **4)** .................... short videos with music? ☐
5) .................... a stay at a hotel? ☐
6) .................... films, TV series or music? ☐
7) .................... for something interesting to buy? ☐
8) .................... a video for everyone to see? ☐
9) .................... with your friends? ☐
10) .................... food and have it delivered at home or at work? ☐

**2** **THINK** **Design your own app. Give it a name and explain what people can use it for. The class votes for the best idea.**

## Listening

**3** 🎧 **Listen and, for each question, choose the best answer (A, B or C).**

1 What kind of app is the man using?
  **A** a taxi app
  **B** a fitness app
  **C** a music streaming app
2 Where did the woman get her laptop?
  **A** online
  **B** from a friend
  **C** in an electrical shop
3 What is the problem with the tablet?
  **A** It won't switch on.
  **B** It has not been charged.
  **C** It won't connect to the Wi-Fi.
4 Why doesn't the woman like the app?
  **A** It was very expensive.
  **B** She is not getting fitter.
  **C** It makes her exercise a lot.

## Everyday English

### Expressing opinion – agreement/ disagreement

**4** **Read the first exchange. What is Alesha's opinion of the app?**

🎧 **Listen and read to find out.**

**Alesha:** How are you getting home, Oliver?
**Oliver:** I think I'll get a taxi. I've got one of those taxi apps on my phone. I just tell it where I want to go and a taxi usually arrives quite quickly. If you ask me, these sorts of apps are fantastic!
**Alesha:** I'm not so sure about that. For one thing, they collect data on you. They know where you've been and when.
**Oliver:** Well, in my opinion, they're really useful. For example, I don't need to carry cash to pay, as the money is taken out of my bank account.
**Alesha:** That's another thing. You can't be sure how much you'll spend, because the app raises prices when it gets busy.
**Oliver:** That's not true. The app tells you how much the journey is going to cost before you book. Anyway, here's the taxi. Do you want a lift? I can drop you off at your house.
**Alesha:** Thanks Oliver, but I think I'll take the bus.

**5** 👥 **Use the language box and the ideas below to act out a similar dialogue about fitness apps.**

• monitors how much exercise you do • causes anxiety about your fitness • sets targets • not always accurate

| Expressing opinion | Expressing agreement |
|---|---|
| • In my opinion, ... | • You're right. |
| • I think/believe (that) ... | • I couldn't agree more. |
| • It seems to me (that) ... | • You took the words right out of my mouth. |
| • If you ask me, ... | |
| • In my view, ... • As I see it, ... | |
| **Expressing disagreement** | |
| • I'm not (too/so) sure about that. | |
| • (No,) I don't agree with that. • That's not how I see it. | |

## Pronunciation: word junctures (vowel to vowel)

**6** 🎧 **Listen and pay attention to the underlined parts. What sound is inserted at the beginning of the second word?**

1 I'm sure he'd <u>be amazed</u>.
2 It might <u>be a</u> bit expensive.
3 <u>You all</u> need to be here by 10.00 am.
4 My grandad says he's <u>too old</u> to use a smartphone.

## Reading & Writing

**7** **a)** Read the essay and complete the gaps with words derived from the words in bold.

**A** If you have ever had an online chat with a company, you might not have been speaking to a human, but to a chatbot. A chatbot is a program designed to mimic humans. I believe chatbots are **1)** ............................ **(excel)** for several reasons.

**B** Firstly, chatbots provide **2)** ............................ **(effect)** customer service. This is because they have a huge amount of possible answers programmed into them. Furthermore, they are online 24 hours a day, which sometimes is not the case with human customer care.

**C** Moreover, they can save companies money. A company will not need as many **3)** ............................ **(employ)** with chatbots to do the work. Perhaps the only extra member of staff that will be needed is an IT technician to set up and maintain the chatbot.

**D** On the other hand, customers do not always like having **4)** ............................ **(converse)** with chatbots. It is often assumed that a computer will not be able to help them with their problem. In addition, people sometimes prefer something more personal than an impersonal program.

**E** All in all, I think that chatbots are a great way for companies to provide **5)** ............................ **(assist)** to their customers. They may not be liked by some people, but they are going to become the main way that we communicate with companies online.

**b)** What is each paragraph about?

**8** Copy and complete the table in your notebook. Which viewpoint is the opposing one?

| | Viewpoints | Reasons/Examples |
|---|---|---|
| 1 | faster customer service | • has programmed answers<br>• **1)** ........................... |
| 2 | **2)** ........................... | • fewer members of staff<br>• needs just one IT technician |
| 3 | customers do not always like talking to chatbots | • **3)** ........................... |

### Writing Tip

**Formal style – Linking ideas**
Essays are written in formal style, that is, long complex sentences, no contractions, use of the passive voice and formal linking words/phrases. Formal linking words/phrases include: *Firstly*, *Secondly* (listing points); *In addition*, *Moreover* (adding points), *On the other hand*, *However* (expressing contrast); *for example*, *for instance*, *such as* (giving examples/reasons); *All in all*, *In conclusion* (concluding). They link ideas and help the reader follow the piece of writing.

**9** **a)** What style is the essay in Ex. 7a written in? Give examples.

**b)** Find examples of linking words/phrases in the essay in Ex. 7a. What does each express?

## Writing (an opinion essay)

**10** **a)** Read the task. What are you going to write? Who for? What style should you write in?

> You have had a class discussion about gaming apps. Your teacher has asked you to write an essay about gaming apps giving your opinion (120-180 words).

**b)** 🎧 Listen to two people expressing their opinion about gaming apps. List their viewpoints and the examples/reasons they use to support their points.

**11** Use your notes from Ex. 10b as well as your own ideas to write your essay. Follow the plan.

**Plan**

**Para 1:** state the topic; give your opinion
**Para 2:** first viewpoint & reasons/examples
**Para 3:** second viewpoint & reasons/examples
**Para 4:** opposing viewpoint & reasons/examples
**Para 5:** restate your opinion

**VALUES**

**Creativity**
*Creativity is intelligence having fun.*
**Albert Einstein**

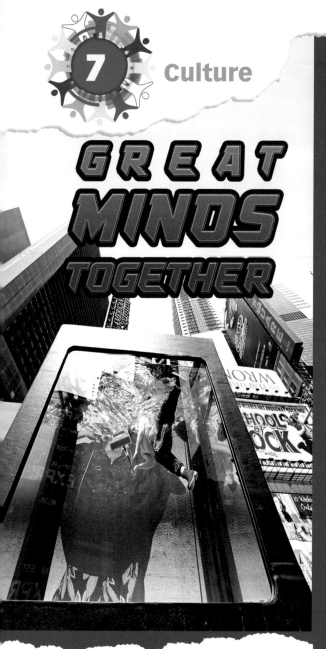

# GREAT MINDS TOGETHER

Held every year, the World Science Festival is not just a huge celebration of STEM subjects (science, technology, engineering and mathematics), it is also a live spectacular that can also be accessed online. Its **mission** is to make science come alive in a way that **the public** can easily understand. Located in New York, this week-long festival is usually in May and has, from the very start, attracted Nobel Prize winners from the world of science as well as famous names from the arts. **Founded** In 2008 by physicist Brian Greene and his wife, TV presenter Tracey Day, the festival's events take place in a variety of New York **venues**: art galleries, museums, parks and even the streets. There are talks, debates, theatrical productions and music performances, all of which aim to show the power of science and the imagination. Events have ranged from talks about the future of AI and colonising other planets to orchestral works that feature dancers moving through **CGI** representations of time and space.

One thing that makes the festival so special is the stunning stage shows **combining** the latest special effects, music and even dance, and featuring famous names from the world of science and technology. 'Icarus at the Edge of Time' is a **multimedia** work featuring music from the **renowned** composer Philip Glass to retell the myth of Icarus in the age of black holes. It is **narrated** by Brian Greene himself and based on his own book. 'Light Falls' is a visual explanation of Einstein's work that uses **state-of-the-art** animation to **depict** his ideas and his intellectual journey. The World Science Festival is incredibly successful and tickets are usually sold out well **in advance**. It is so popular that the very first World Science Festival Brisbane was held in Australia in 2016. It also started the World Science U – an online resource for everyone to dive deep into the wonders of science. The World Science Festival is now an important date on the science and technology calendar, **spreading the word** about how science plays such a vital role in our lives, and exciting the public's imagination.

## Listening & Reading

**1** Read the title of the article and look at the picture. What do you think it is about?

🎧 Listen and read to find out.

**2** Read again and use words from the text to complete the email. Then explain the words/phrases in bold.

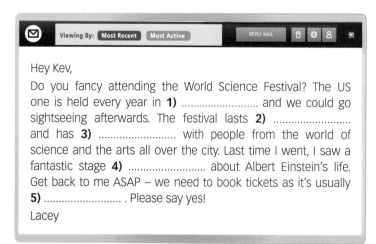

Hey Kev,
Do you fancy attending the World Science Festival? The US one is held every year in **1)** ........................ and we could go sightseeing afterwards. The festival lasts **2)** ........................ and has **3)** ........................ with people from the world of science and the arts all over the city. Last time I went, I saw a fantastic stage **4)** ........................ about Albert Einstein's life. Get back to me ASAP – we need to book tickets as it's usually **5)** ........................ . Please say yes!
Lacey

▶ **VIDEO**

✓ **Check these words**

colonise, intellectual, resource, play a role, vital

## Speaking & Writing

**3** THINK What topic from science and technology would you like to see on stage? How would it be presented? Think about: *famous presenters*, *music*, *special effects*.

**4** ICT Research similar events in your country or in another country. Imagine you are holding a press conference to talk about it. Present the event in English or in your own language.

## Vocabulary

**1 Choose the correct word.**

1 You can **monitor/share/upload** your health using wearable devices.

2 Janet **booked/ordered/created** her accommodation on a mobile app.

3 I think my digital assistant just ignored my **career/innovation/command**!

4 We stayed in last night and **maintained/streamed/browsed** a film.

5 This desktop computer **comprises/contacts/consists** of a monitor, a keyboard and a tower.

6 Tom realised **independently/automatically/straightaway** why the tablet wasn't working.

7 Fran has an app that **dims/tracks/revolutionises** her daughter's mobile phone.

*(7 x 2 = 14)*

**2 Fill in:** *artificial, reality, account, behaviour, share, sensors, control, high-speed, reminder, command.*

1 Pass me the remote ..............................., will you?

2 Tom has bought a virtual .............................. headset.

3 We get .................................. broadband here.

4 Companies predict customer .............................. from their data.

5 A(n) .............................. about the delivery popped up.

6 All my devices at home have .............................. to connect to each other.

7 You can give a .............................. to the robot to wash the dishes.

8 How much money is in our bank ..............................?

9 Scientists are already developing .............................. intelligence.

10 Can you .............................. that video with everyone?

*(10 x 2 = 20)*

**3 Choose the correct item.**

1 When does the new games console go **for/on** sale?

2 Can I have a word **to/with** you in my office, please?

3 Sales of tablets have dropped **out/off** recently.

4 I can't connect my phone **at/to** the speaker.

5 Beth dropped **out/by** of her Science course last month.

*(5 x 2 = 10)*

## Grammar

**4 Rewrite the sentences using the passive, the causative or an impersonal construction.**

1 They are repairing the office computer system now.
The office's ..................................................

2 Steve asked Bob to fix his computer.
Steve ..................................................

3 You should return the phone to the shop.
The phone ..................................................

4 Which company did Bill Gates found in 1975?
Which company ..................................................

5 I'll ask Max to download the app for me.
I ..................................................

6 They say that the science fair is cancelled this year.
The science fair ..................................................

7 You can ask Mark to check your connection.
You ..................................................

8 They expect the new games console to be popular.
It ..................................................

*(8 x 2 = 16)*

**5 Complete with the correct reflexive/emphatic pronoun. Then decide whether they are R (Reflexive) or E (Emphatic).**

1 Professor Mike Caine .................. gave the presentation. ......

2 Make sure you keep your password to .................. . ......

3 Kate set up the printer .................. . ......

4 Smart devices can tell .................. what to do. ......

5 I'm sure I can repair the laptop .................. . ......

*(5 x 4 = 20)*

## Everyday English

**6 Match the exchanges.**

1 ☐ How are you getting home?

2 ☐ The taxi can drop you off.

3 ☐ In my view, it's a fantastic app.

4 ☐ The app always finds the cheapest tickets.

a I couldn't agree more.

b I think I'll take the bus.

c That's not true.

d OK, if you're paying.

*(4 x 5 = 20)*

*Total 100*

## Competences

| | | |
|---|---|---|
| GOOD ✓ | | |
| VERY GOOD ✓✓ | | |
| EXCELLENT ✓✓✓ | | |

**Lexical Competence**
understand words/phrases related to:
• technology
• apps

**Reading Competence**
• understand texts related to technology & apps (read for specific information – multiple choice; text completion)

**Listening Competence**
• listen to and understand dialogues related to technology (listen for specific information –

multiple choice)

**Speaking Competence**
• express opinion – agreement/disagreement

**Writing Competence**
• write a short text about the IoT
• write an opinion essay about gaming apps

# 8

**Vocabulary:** world problems; social problems
**Grammar:** conditionals; wishes; question tags
**Everyday English:** making suggestions – agreeing/disagreeing
**Writing:** an article suggesting solutions to a problem

# Better societies

## Vocabulary

### World problems

**1** Which of these problems do you think are the most serious in your country? Can you think of more problems? Discuss, then tell the class.

| 1 overpopulation | 2 homelessness |
|---|---|

| 3 child labour | 4 climate change |
|---|---|

| 5 poverty | 6 famine |
|---|---|

| 7 refugees | 8 inequality |
|---|---|

| 9 wars | 10 illiteracy |
|---|---|

## Reading & Listening

**2** Read the title of the text and look at the picture. Which problem from Ex. 1 do you think you are going to read about?

🎧 Listen and read to check.

# A Warm Welcome in Ethiopia

▶ VIDEO

Ethiopia is one of the poorest countries in the world. An **estimated** 44% of its population lives in poverty, but refugees from **neighbouring** countries still continue to arrive because it's **relatively** peaceful. The result is that there are now nearly a million refugees in Ethiopia. At first, they were living in camps and not allowed to work, just waiting to move on to their next destination. Then, in January 2019, the government passed a new law that gave refugees **access** to free education and financial services, and the right to work. They reasoned that, instead of keeping refugees in camps, why not let them become productive members of society? Now, as employees and business owners, refugees can give back to the Ethiopian economy and, more importantly, become part of its society. We spoke to Aisha Dualeh, a student at Nefas Silk College in the country's capital, Addis Ababa, to find out how the new law has **affected** her.

**WV:** *You're from Somalia, aren't you? How did you end up in Ethiopia?*

**AD:** I grew up in Somalia's capital, Mogadishu, in a beautiful big house. We hardly ever went outside because of the war, but I always felt happy and safe. Then everything fell apart. One night, when I was 12 years old, my parents woke me and my sisters up and told us we were leaving. We travelled in the back of a lorry and crossed the border into Ethiopia. My father stayed behind in Somalia. I haven't seen him since then.

**WV:** *How awful. Where did you live when you arrived in Ethiopia?*

**AD:** We were in a refugee camp for years. It was crowded and many people were sick. We spent our days looking for wood to build fires for cooking, and waiting for bags of rice and flour to be handed out so that we could eat. I was **miserable**. I wished I could go to school. I thought if I got an education, I would have a future. Without school, I didn't see a future for myself in Ethiopia.

**3** Read the text. For questions 1 to 5, decide which option (A, B or C) best answers each question. Then explain the words in bold.

**1** In comparison to its neighbours, Ethiopia is
  A wealthier.  B safer.  C larger.

**2** What does the January 2019 law allow refugees to do?
  A open businesses  B use money  C work legally

**3** Where was Aisha's first home in Ethiopia?
  A in a camp  B in the capital city  C in a large house

**4** Aisha now runs a business with
  A a friend from the camp.  B a student from college.
  C her mother and sisters.

**5** According to Melese Yigzaw, training refugees means they will
  A always have a way to make money.
  B be able to go back to their own countries.
  C become legal citizens of Ethiopia.

**WV:** *What happened next?*

**AD:** Well, after seven years, an international NGO came to our camp. They offered us free group therapy to help us deal with the stress of being refugees. I went along and it really helped me. The organisers there told me about Nefas Silk College and they helped me **apply**.

**WV:** *What did you study?*

**AD:** I took a cookery course. I learnt a lot and made lots of friends, too. I passed last year and set up a business with another woman from my course, Mazaa. She's Ethiopian, from Addis Ababa, and she's my best friend.

**WV:** *So what's your business?*

**AD:** We make and sell **healthy** food. People working in shops and offices buy it during their lunch breaks. We are quite successful. A few months ago, I moved my family out of the camp and into a flat in the city. My mother helps with the business, and my sisters go to school. Our life is so different now, and all because of my time at Nefas Silk College.

The courses at Nefas Silk College have changed many lives, just like Aisha's. It is not only the lessons, however, as the dean of the college, Melese Yigzaw, said, "We don't have special treatment for the refugees … we treat them as citizens. If someone is skilled and can change the gears of a vehicle or cook, they can generate income. If you train them, they can create jobs wherever they go." Ethiopia is a great example of a country that has taken action to make a difference to the refugee crisis.

 **Check these words**

reason, border, NGO, dean, gear, generate, income

**4** **COLLOCATIONS** **Find and complete the words in the text that describe the following. Then use the phrases to make sentences.**

1 ............... of society
2 ................. owner
3 ..................... camp
4 ..................... NGO
5 ................. therapy
6 ............... treatment

**5** **PREPOSITIONS** **Fill in:** *as, to, in, with.*

1 Over 70 million refugees live ............... poverty.
2 They don't have access ............... basic medical care.
3 He can't deal ............... stressful situations.
4 The refugees in the camp treat me ............... a friend.

**6** **WORDS EASILY CONFUSED** **Choose the correct word. Check in your dictionary.**

1 I admire the Ethiopian government for taking **action/activity** to help refugees.
2 It was another **common/ordinary** day at the refugee camp when the new doctor arrived.
3 Eating food from her country **remembers/reminds** Aisha of home.
4 The situation looks bad on TV, but it is much worse in **real/true** life.
5 Refugees aren't asking for **special/specialised** treatment – just a chance to live normal lives.

**7** **PHRASAL VERBS** **Fill in the correct particle(s).**

**fall apart: 1)** to break into pieces; **2)** to be unable to think calmly; **3)** to stop functioning successfully
**fall behind:** to make no progress
**fall in with: 1)** to accept (an idea/plan, etc); **2)** to become friends with someone
**fall out:** to have an argument
**fall through:** to fail to happen

1 They wanted to volunteer at a refugee camp last summer, but their plans fell ..................... .
2 I fell ..................... with Katie when she started making rude comments about the new employee in our office.
3 Her coat was so old that it was falling ..................... .
4 When his family moved to the UK, he didn't speak the language and he fell ..................... in his studies.
5 Julia just fell ..................... when she heard the awful news.
6 He was lucky that he fell ..................... a nice group of people at college.

## Speaking & Writing

**8** **Suggest other ways the Ethiopian government could improve refugees' conditions. Have a class discussion.**

**9** **THINK** **Imagine you are a refugee. Write a diary entry describing your day and expressing your hopes and dreams. Read it to the class.**

# Grammar in Use

## Conditionals Types 0-3  ▶ p. GR13

▶ p. GR13

Home | About | Contact                    SEARCH 🔍

**@martin97** 01/01 Happy New Year, everyone! Who made a wish at midnight last night? I always do, and I always wish for the same thing: an end to climate change. If we carry on polluting the planet like this, there won't be many more New Year's Days left! What are you wishing for?

**@carrie.marsh** 01/01 I wish child labour didn't exist. When children work, they don't go to school and illiteracy rates rise. Unless children receive an education, they won't break free from their lives of poverty, will they?

**@amy.g** 02/01 I'm not just making a wish this year – I'm acting! I've become a volunteer at an animal shelter. If more of us volunteered, we could solve many of the world's problems. I just wish I'd done it sooner!

**@d.turner** 02/01 Most of the refugees in my country are escaping wars. If the wars had never started, they wouldn't have had to leave their homes. I wish people would stop fighting each other, and I'm going to donate money to a charity that promotes peace. If I were you, I'd do the same.

Read more

### 1 Read the messages. Which of the underlined sentences expresses:

– a general truth/scientific fact? (Conditional Type 0)

– a situation that is likely to happen in the present/future? (Conditional Type 1)

– a situation that is unlikely to happen in the present/future/advice? (Conditional Type 2)

– an unreal situation in the past? (Conditional Type 3)

**How do we form each type of conditional?**

### 2 Choose the correct tense. Identify the type of conditional. When do we use a comma to separate the two clauses?

1 If the world's population **would keep/keeps** growing, there will soon be 10 billion people on Earth.

2 Sea levels rise when the ice at the poles **melts/will melt**.

3 If I had known you were collecting money for charity, I **would make/would have made** a donation.

4 I **would volunteer/will volunteer** at the refugee camp if I had more free time.

5 The famine **won't happen/wouldn't have happened** if it had rained like it usually does.

6 Unless we **deal/will deal** with the problem of homelessness soon, it will get worse.

### 3 Put the verbs in brackets into the correct tense. Give reasons. Add commas where necessary.

1 A: My colleagues are rude to me because they think I'm different.
   B: I ........................................... **(report)** their behaviour to the manager if I were you.

2 A: How is the Education Programme for Refugees going?
   B: Not well. It's popular, but unless we ........................................... **(get)** more volunteer teachers we'll have to shut it down.

3 A: I was at the camp yesterday teaching the children.
   B: Really? If I had known you were going I ........................................... **(give)** you a lift.

4 A: If you drive an electric car it ........................................... **(not/pollute)** the air.
   B: That's why I'd like to buy an electric car one day.

5 A: If climate change continues coastal cities and islands ........................................... **(disappear)**.
   B: Yes, sea levels will rise and they will be under water.

6 A: Did you hear about the factory? They've been accused of using child labour!
   B: It's shocking. I'm sure the owner would have done something if he ........................................... **(realise)** there were children working there.

7 A: The river always ........................................... **(flood)** when it rains.
   B: It didn't use to. It started after they made the channel narrower.

8 A: If everyone shared the world's resources overpopulation ........................................... **(not/be)** a problem.
   B: It would help, but there'd still be the problem of overcrowding in big cities.

### 4 Use the verbs in the list in the correct tense to complete the sentences. Identify the type of conditional.

• donate • tell • finish • vaccinate • die • give

1 If they ........................................... the shelter, the homeless in our town would have had somewhere to sleep.

2 Unless we stop polluting the river, all the fish ........................................... .

3 When we ........................................... children against measles, the number of cases goes down.

4 If I were you, I ........................................... those clothes to charity.

5 The council ........................................... free houses to refugees if they had had the money to build them.

6 Chris would have come with you if you ........................................... him where you were going.

## 5 SPEAKING 💬 Start a sentence. Another group member completes it. Use conditionals types 0-3.

A: *We wouldn't have missed the bus ...*
B: *if we had left on time. If I were you, ….*
C: *I'd call them. If we are late, ...*
D: *they will be angry with us.*

## Wishes ▶p. GR14

### 6 Look at the highlighted sentences in the group chat messages on p. 66. Which expresses:

– a desire for a present situation to be different?
– a desire for something to change?
– regret that something didn't happen in the past?

**What words do we use to introduce wishes?**

### 7 Put the verbs in brackets into the correct tense.

1 A: I can't believe you made £200 for charity by selling cakes!
B: I could have collected even more money. If only I ............................................... **(bake)** more cakes!

2 A: I wish I ............................................... **(know)** how to help the homeless in our city.
B: There's a charity called Helping Hands. Why don't you check out their webpage?

3 A: If only I .................................................... **(not/drive)** my car to work all those years. Think of all the pollution!
B: It's OK. At least you use public transport now.

4 A: We should volunteer to help.
B: I know. I just wish I ............................................... **(not/be)** so busy at the moment.

5 A: If only the refugees ............................... **(have)** proper houses to live in.
B: Yes, they only have tents at the camp and they must be cold in winter.

6 A: Climate change will affect us all.
B: I know. I wish previous generations ........................... ........................... **(take)** better care of the planet.

7 A: I wish Zoe ............................................... **(not/lose)** the paperwork.
B: She didn't mean to. Look, let's fill the forms out again.

8 A: I give 10% of my wages to charity.
B: Me too. If only I ............................................... **(earn)** more money – then I could donate more.

## 8 SPEAKING 👤👤 Say a sentence. Your partner expresses a wish.

A: *There are so many homeless people.*
B: *I wish there were homes for all of them.*

## Question tags ▶p. GR14

### 9 What are question tags? When do we use them? How are they formed? Find an example in the group chat messages on p. 66.

### 10 Complete with the correct question tag. 🎧 Listen and tick the correct box.

| | | ↘ | ↗ |
|---|---|---|---|
| 1 | Let's leave now, ...................................? | ☐ | ☐ |
| 2 | I've got an appointment later, ...................................? | ☐ | ☐ |
| 3 | Don't forget the tickets, .............................? | ☐ | ☐ |
| 4 | He's speaking at the conference, ...................................? | ☐ | ☐ |
| 5 | We had a great time, ...................................? | ☐ | ☐ |
| 6 | Everyone appreciated the food, ...................................? | ☐ | ☐ |
| 7 | That's the refugee camp, .............................? | ☐ | ☐ |
| 8 | Emma has a van, ...................................? | ☐ | ☐ |
| 9 | No one came to the therapy session, ...................................? | ☐ | ☐ |
| 10 | You don't know where Daniel is, ...................................? | ☐ | ☐ |

## 11 SPEAKING 👤👤 Say a sentence. Your partner replies using question tags depending on whether they think the sentence is true or false.

A: *I went to the animal shelter last Saturday.*
B: *You didn't adopt another animal, did you?*
*My brother doesn't walk to work.*
A: *He takes the bus, doesn't he?*

# Skills in Action

## Vocabulary
### Social problems

**1** 🗣️🗣️ **Match what the people say (1-8) to the problems in the list.**

**A** depression **B** animal abuse **C** unemployment
**D** racism **E** obesity **F** stress **G** addiction **H** bullying

1. ☐ "I'd say about half of the children in my daughter's class are overweight."
2. ☐ "She was the perfect candidate, but they didn't give her the job because of her nationality."
3. ☐ "My symptoms include trouble sleeping, inability to concentrate and lack of interest in everyday life."
4. ☐ "I saw him kicking his dog. It was awful. I called the police."
5. ☐ "A lot of people from my class struggled to find a job after we finished college."
6. ☐ "I've given up smoking recently, but it's so hard sometimes!"
7. ☐ "Her high-pressure job causes her to feel anxious almost constantly."
8. ☐ "He was picked on at school because of his accent."

**2** (THINK) **Which of the problems in Ex. 1 are social? socio-economic?**

## Listening

**3** 🎧 **You will hear an interview with a woman called Claire Franklin, who runs her own business. For each question, choose the correct answer (A, B or C).**

1. When Claire left college, she
   **A** worked at the weekends.
   **B** lost her job.
   **C** found a job at the supermarket.
2. Claire and her mother had to survive on
   **A** money from the government.
   **B** her mother's wages.
   **C** money Claire collected from rent.
3. What did Claire's doctor tell her to do?
   **A** take medication for her symptoms
   **B** apply to do an online course
   **C** see a therapist
4. Claire thinks unemployment is a problem because young people lack
   **A** qualifications.
   **B** opportunities.
   **C** intelligence.

## Everyday English
### Making suggestions

**4** **Read the first exchange. What suggestion do you think Dan makes to solve the problem?**
🎧 **Listen and read to check.**

> **Dan:** You wouldn't believe the state of a dog they brought in today to the animal shelter! Its owner had locked it in the kitchen and gone on holiday!
> **Max:** You should publish pictures of people who abuse their pets. That way, they would get publicly embarrassed. People hate that!
> **Dan:** I'm not so sure about that. After all, it's too late for the animal, isn't it?
> **Max:** I see what you mean. What do you suggest?
> **Dan:** How about free education? If you want to own a pet, there could be a course you can take. It would mean every pet owner gets basic knowledge of animal care.
> **Max:** Good thinking. Let's suggest your idea to the manager of the animal shelter.
> **Dan:** Yes, let's.

**5** 🗣️🗣️🎧 **Listen to the interview in Ex. 3 again and make notes. Use your notes, as well as your own ideas, to act out a dialogue similar to the one in Ex. 4 about youth unemployment. Use sentences/phrases from the language box.**

| Suggesting | Agreeing |
|---|---|
| • What/How about ...? | • You're right about that. |
| • We could ... • Let's ... | • Good thinking. |
| **Disagreeing** | |
| • I don't think so. | • I don't see how that'd help. |
| • I'm not sure about that. | • I totally disagree. |

## Pronunciation: diphthongs
(/ɪə/, /eə/, /ʊə/, /eɪ/, /aɪ/, /ɔɪ/, /əʊ/, /aʊ/)

**6 a)** 🎧 **There are 8 diphthongs in English. Listen and identify the diphthongs in the sentences below.**

1. Are you sure he didn't know about the animal abuse?
2. It's not fair that the puppies have nowhere to play.
3. There is a real need in the camp for children's toys.
4. Let's try volunteering. How about helping out at the animal shelter?

**b)** 🗣️🗣️ **Say a sentence. Your partner identifies the diphthongs you have used.**

## Reading & Writing

**7** **a)** Read the article and fill in the gaps with the word derived from the words in brackets.

**Calories in, Calories out**

**A** 1) ........................................ (obese) is a serious problem in modern society. Worldwide, over 380 million children and teenagers are 2) ........................................ (weight), and 1.9 billion adults. Many people are uninformed about how to eat properly and others are simply careless. This leads to an increase in the risk of disease and a 3) ........................................ (reduce) in quality of life. So what can we do about this problem?

**B** One possible solution is to decrease food intake. In other words, both children and adults can regulate the size of their portions. In this way, people don't consume more food than their bodies need, and 4) ........................................ (consequence) don't put on weight.

**C** Another useful suggestion is to exercise. This can be taking up a sport, or simply walking short distances. This means that people burn the energy from the food they eat, rather than let it turn into fat in their bodies.

**D** In conclusion, reducing food intake and exercising are both good ways to reduce body fat. I believe, by making 5) ........................................ (sense) lifestyle choices, we can 6) .................................... (sure) that we are a healthy weight and be happy in our bodies, too.

**b)** What is each paragraph about?

### Writing Tip

**Supporting suggestions**
Always support your suggestions with explanations/ examples and expected results. This helps the reader understand your suggestions more easily.

**8** What are the writer's suggestions in the article in Ex. 7? What explanations/examples and expected results are given to support each suggestion? What words/phrases are used to introduce them?

**9** Read the conclusion to the article in Ex. 7. Which of the following does it include?

**a** summary of suggestions
**b** opposing argument
**c** writer's opinion

## Writing (an article suggesting solutions to a problem)

**10** Read the task and answer the questions.

A local newspaper has asked its readers to send in articles about animal abuse in our modern society. They will publish the best ones. Write an article for the newspaper (120-180 words) suggesting ways of solving the problem.

**1** What are you going to write? Who for?
**2** What should you write about? How many words should your piece of writing be?

**11** **BRAINSTORMING** Copy and complete the table in your notebook. You can use ideas from Ex. 4 as well as your own ideas.

| Suggestions | Explanations / Examples | Expected results |
|---|---|---|
|  |  |  |

**12** Use your notes in Ex. 11 to write your article. Give it a title. Follow the plan.

### Plan

**Introduction**
**Para 1:** state topic & cause
**Main body**
**Para 2:** first suggestion – explanation/example – expected result
**Para 3:** second suggestion – explanation/example – expected result
**Conclusion**
**Para 4:** summarise points; state your opinion

**VALUES**

**Kindness**
*Be kind whenever possible. It is always possible.*
Dalai Lama

69

▶ VIDEO

# The Borgen Project

**1** The World Bank defines extreme poverty as living on less than $1.90 a day, but it's not just about money; people living in extreme poverty also lack **clean** drinking water, enough food, access to healthcare or education, and they often work in dangerous conditions.

**2** The Borgen Project is a non-governmental organisation with one mission: to end extreme poverty. They are sure it is possible, if only the governments of the world would use their power to help. For example, members of the Borgen Project believe it would take $265 billion a year to end world hunger by 2030. This is less than half the amount of money the USA spends on defence every year.

**3** The story behind the Borgen Project is the story of one man: Clint Borgen. As an American student, he travelled to Europe to volunteer at a refugee camp. The extreme poverty he saw there changed his life forever. He returned to the States, determined to do something so that no one had to live that way any longer. Clint graduated from university and, after working as an intern at the United Nations, he took a job on a ship in Alaska to raise money to fund his idea. In 2003, from his laptop on board the cold, dark ship, he launched the Borgen Project.

**4** The Borgen Project now has volunteers working in over 900 US cities and in many other places around the world. The aim of the organisation is to **spread** the word about extreme poverty. They educate people about how to demand change from their governments, and **regularly** meet with politicians to discuss how laws can be changed to help and protect those in need.

**5** Extreme poverty is still a **major** issue in our modern world, but the good news is – thanks to campaigning by organisations like the Borgen Project – the situation is **improving**. In 1990, 1.9 billion people were living in extreme poverty worldwide. Today, that figure is 702 million. Let's hope, in the years to come, we can **reduce** that number to zero.

## ✓ Check these words

define, mission, power, intern, launch, campaign

## Listening & Reading

**1** Look at the pictures. What is the Borgen Project? What problem does it address? Read through to find out.

**2** Match the headings (A-G) to the paragraphs (1-5). Two are extra. Then explain the words in bold. 🎧 Listen and check.

A The origins of the organisation
B No hope for the future
C Actions and activities
D What's the issue?
E Success so far
F Why join the organisation?
G What's the solution?

**3** Match the words in bold to their opposites. Check in your dictionary.

• minor • rarely • contain • increase • polluted • worsening

## Speaking & Writing

**4** THINK Think of a motto that reflects the aim of the Borgen Project. Present your idea to the class. Explain how your motto represents the aims of the organisation.

**5** ICT Collect information about a non-profit organisation in your country. Use the headings in the text in Ex. 2. Prepare a digital presentation for the class.

# Review

## Vocabulary

**1 Read the sentences and write the problem.**

1 There are over 37 million people in the city of Tokyo.
o _ _ _ _ _ _ _ _ _ _ _ _ _

2 He sleeps on the streets every night.
h _ _ _ _ _ _ _ _ _ _ _

3 No one has enough to eat because of the drought.
f _ _ _ _ _

4 Over 700 million people are living on less than $1.90 a day. p _ _ _ _ _ _

5 She's 53, but she doesn't know how to read or write.
i _ _ _ _ _ _ _ _ _

6 39.8% of adults in the USA are seriously overweight.
o _ _ _ _ _ _

7 Millions are looking for work. u _ _ _ _ _ _ _ _ _ _ _

8 I feel unhappy all the time. d _ _ _ _ _ _ _ _ _
*(8 x 2 = 16)*

**2 Fill in:** *animal, racism, real, child, refugee, climate, group, stress.*

1 She suffers from ............................... at exam time.

2 It's hard to experience war in ............................... life.

3 ............................... labour is illegal in the USA.

4 ............................... change is turning some countries into deserts.

5 They arrested him for ............................... abuse.

6 ............................... therapy can help the survivors of war.

7 ............................... doesn't make sense – we're all the same underneath.

8 The war started a(n) ............................... crisis.
*(8 x 2 = 16)*

**3 Choose the correct item.**

1 When she heard the news, she fell **through/apart**.

2 They treat the refugees **as/for** members of their own family.

3 Jack and I fell **apart/out** because he wouldn't do anything to stop the bullying.

4 We didn't have access **in/to** the Internet at the camp.

5 It's awful how many children live **at/in** poverty.

6 We tried to start a non-governmental organisation, but unfortunately it fell **behind/through**.
*(6 x 2 = 12)*

## Grammar

**4 Put the verbs in brackets into the correct form. Write the type of conditional (0, 1, 2 or 3) in the box.**

1 If I had a pet, I ............................. **(treat)** it very well. ☐

2 Unless we stop climate change, environmental problems ............................. **(increase)**. ☐

3 Extreme poverty rises when people ............................. **(not/have)** access to free education. ☐

4 If I had saved more money, I ............................. **(go)** on the volunteer trip to Ethiopia. ☐
*(4 x 4 = 16)*

**5 Put the verbs in brackets into the correct tense.**

1 If only the refugees ............................... **(have)** access to better healthcare.

2 Jane wishes she ...................................... **(not/ignore)** the homeless woman's request for help yesterday.

3 I wish Tim ...................................... **(not/be)** so unkind.

4 I wish I ...................................... **(volunteer)** at the animal shelter with you last summer.
*(4 x 2 = 8)*

**6 Complete with the correct question tag.**

1 You volunteer at the refugee camp, .............................?

2 You've set up a kitchen there, .............................?

3 The refugees aren't paying for food, .............................?

4 You won't stop working there, .............................?
*(4 x 3 = 12)*

## Everyday English

**7 Match the exchanges.**

1 ☐ Have you heard about the famine?

2 ☐ I totally disagree.

3 ☐ What can we do?

4 ☐ Refugees deserve our help.

5 ☐ How about holding a competition?

a That's a good idea.

b We could raise some money.

c You're right about that.

d OK, let's collect food, then.

e It's awful, isn't it?
*(5 x 4 = 20)*

*Total 100*

---

## Competences

**GOOD ✓**

**VERY GOOD ✓ ✓**

**EXCELLENT ✓ ✓ ✓**

**Lexical Competence**
understand words/phrases related to:
• world problems
• social problems

**Reading Competence**
• understand texts related to world problems & social problems (read for specific information – multiple choice; read for gist – matching headings to paragraphs)

**Listening Competence**
• listen to and understand dialogues related to social problems (listen for specific information – multiple choice)

**Speaking Competence**
• make suggestions & agree/disagree

**Writing Competence**
• write a diary entry
• write an article suggesting solutions to a problem

# 9

# Live & Learn

▶ VIDEO

# AUGMENTED ACADEMIA
## The Future of UNIVERSITY Education Today!

Over the past few decades, university education has changed a lot, mainly through advances in technology. On modern campuses, the days of chalk and blackboards are long gone – now, many lecture halls use interactive whiteboards. Most undergraduates have **abandoned** paper, using tablets and laptops to take notes instead. Today's students use technology a lot in their everyday life, so naturally using it in teaching encourages them to learn. [1] And the next big technology to check off the list? It's augmented reality, or AR.

By now, most people have heard of virtual reality. Using VR headsets, we can dive into completely digital worlds, and **experience** places as if we were really there. [2] This could be because the world it surrounds the student with is too overpowering, too stimulating. AR, however, lays digital images (called auras) on top of the physical world so they see the real world – through the screen of their smartphone or tablet – but with a digital layer above it. [3]

For most people, their first experience of AR is probably adding effects like a rabbit's nose and ears to their face during a video chat, or the 2016 smartphone game which sent players around their neighbourhood looking for virtual **creatures**. [4] Medical students can use AR apps to see a 3D human heart **beating** in their professor's chest, even as he gives the lecture about it! Drama students can see how a stage will look on opening night, in order to try out different set designs. Nutritionists can have the facts on any food item at their fingertips.

Students can also use AR without any help from professors. Lots of educational AR apps are available that allow students to learn independently, and outside their narrow course of study. [5] You simply point your phone camera towards the night sky and the app recognises stars and planets, giving you information about them. It also lays the shapes of the constellations on top of the stars, allowing easy **identification**. In this way, the use of AR makes for a broader educational experience.

It seems that AR comes with a great deal of benefits. It brings courses to life, making them more interactive and enjoyable. It makes difficult concepts easier to understand for visual learners, who have always been at a disadvantage in the traditional education system. Maybe the best thing about AR, though, is that it gives students a new way to use their smartphones. [6] AR helps students become individual learners and active users of the technology, instead of **passive** consumers of content.

✓ **Check these words**

overpowering, stimulating, effect, nutritionist, constellation, interactive, concept, visual learner

## Vocabulary

### University

**1** **a)** Match the university vocabulary (a-b) with its school equivalent (1-7).

| | | | |
|---|---|---|---|
| 1 | ☐ school grounds | **a** | lecture |
| 2 | ☐ classroom | **b** | lecture hall |
| 3 | ☐ teacher | **c** | professor |
| 4 | ☐ lesson | **d** | undergraduate |
| 5 | ☐ pupil | **e** | notes |
| 6 | ☐ subject | **f** | course |
| 7 | ☐ textbook | **g** | campus |

**b)** How is university education different from school education? Discuss with your partner.

## Listening & Reading

**2** Read the definition. How can AR be used in university education? Skim the text to find out.

**augmented reality (AR)** /ɔːɡˌmentɪd riˈæləti/ (n): computer-generated images appearing on top of real world images

**3** **a)** Read the text again and fill in the gaps (1-6) with the correct sentence (A-G). One sentence is extra.

**A** So, it 'augments' (or adds) images on top of what we can see with the naked eye.

**B** It's a technology that nobody could have imagined just a few years ago.

**C** AR teaches students that they aren't just for socialising and gaming – they're also really useful learning tools.

**D** But research has shown that VR can sometimes lead to lower marks.

**E** In fact, one study found that technology in the lecture hall makes students 72% more likely to participate.

**F** On campus, the same technique can be used in nearly every course universities offer.

**G** For example, there are apps that act like a hand-held planetarium.

**b)** 🎧 Listen and check. Then explain the words in bold.

**4** **COLLOCATIONS** Find and complete the words in the text that describe the following. Then use the phrases to make sentences.

| | | | |
|---|---|---|---|
| 1 | .................... whiteboard | 4 | .................... images |
| 2 | .................... reality | 5 | .................... chat |
| 3 | .................... headset | 6 | .................... heart |

**5** **PREPOSITIONS** Choose the correct preposition. Check in your dictionary.

1 The app lets you write **at/on** top of the photo.
2 Students unfamiliar with technology are **on/at** a disadvantage.
3 Young people today have so much technology **at/in** their fingertips!
4 AR has become huge **over/above** the past decade.
5 The Microbiology Department website brings the world **for/to** life.

**6** **WORDS EASILY CONFUSED** Choose the correct word(s). Check in your dictionary.

1 Mike was sick and couldn't **attend/follow** the lecture, so he borrowed Cecilia's notes.
2 The best way to **revise/review** for the test is to read your notes from the lectures.
3 Mandy **is doing/is making** a course in digital marketing.
4 Tony was happy with his essay **score/mark** – he got a B.

**7** **PHRASAL VERBS** Fill in the correct particle(s). Then try to make up a story using the phrasal verbs.

**check in: 1)** to report your arrival (at a hotel, clinic, etc) (**Opp:** check out); **2)** to arrive at an airport and show your ticket before getting on a plane
**check off:** to tick off items on a list
**check out:** to look at sth to see if you like it
**check up on sb/sth: 1)** to find out if sth is true or correct; **2)** to find out if sb is doing what they're supposed to be doing

1 They checked .................... a few schools in the area before they decided on one for their children.
2 The professor checked .................... the names of the students as they entered the lab.
3 When you get to the hostel, you need to check .................... at reception.
4 Don checked .................... Lucy to make sure she was doing the job properly.
5 After we check .................... and drop our bags off, you can buy a book to read on the plane.

## Speaking & Writing

**8** 👥 **THINK** Why are AR apps a must for students? In pairs, think of three reasons. Tell the class.

**9** 💬 Design an educational AR app that you think would help students in their studies. Present your app to the class.

# Grammar in Use

## The Growth Mindset

One of the most popular ideas in education today is the 'growth mindset'. It was created by the American psychologist Carol Dweck. Our mindset is the way we think about our talents and abilities. Students have a fixed mindset or a growth mindset, or something in between. Having a fixed mindset means believing you can't change your abilities. For example, many students with a fixed mindset who have difficulty learning a foreign language believe they have no talent in languages. Some even quit learning languages when they get the chance. Having a growth mindset, though, means that you believe you can always improve your abilities. In other words, growth mindset students are always eager to improve and don't let failure stop them learning. So, a student with this mindset will continue working hard until they get better at a subject. It's very important to have a growth mindset at university, because the course material is designed to challenge students.

## Infinitive/-ing form  pp. GR14-16

**1** Read the text. Find the words/phrases that take *to*-infinitive, infinitive without *to*, or the *-ing* form. List them in a table.

| *to*-infinitive | infinitive without *to* | *-ing* form |
|---|---|---|
|  |  |  |
|  |  |  |
|  |  |  |

**2** Choose the correct form of the verbs in bold. Give reasons.

1 Sharon sometimes has trouble **finding/to find** a quiet place to study at home.
2 Joe sat down in the exam hall only **discover/to discover** that the exam had already finished!
3 You can't **bring/to bring** your smartphones into the final exams.
4 In addition to **be/being** an excellent student, Ken is the captain of the rugby team.
5 The student refused **to participate/participating** in the research.
6 Frank spends a lot of time **read/reading** novels.
7 Henry is very eager **start/to start** college in September.
8 Professor Rodgers makes us **send/to send** our assignments via email.
9 Peter wastes a lot of time **to play/playing** video games instead of studying.
10 The students were delighted **hear/to hear** that they had all passed the exam.

**3** Put the verbs in brackets into the *(to)* infinitive or the *-ing* form.

1 A: It was kind of you ................................. **(lend)** me your notes for the Ancient Greek History exam.
  B: No problem. I was glad ................................. **(help)**.
2 A: Do you plan ................................. **(study)** for the Russian Literature exam until midnight?
  B: No, I always avoid ................................. **(go)** to bed late on the night before an exam.
3 A: I can't stand people ................................. **(talk)** on their phones in the library.
  B: Me, too. I think we should ................................. **(say)** something to the person.
4 A: Would you like ................................. **(watch)** a film at the cinema on Sunday, Bill?
  B: Sorry, but I'll be busy ................................. **(do)** assignments all weekend.
5 A: You'd better ................................. **(finish)** your essay. It's due tomorrow, isn't it?
  B: No, my professor agreed ................................. **(give)** me more time, so it's not due until next Monday.
6 A: Why are you so late? ................................. **(be)** honest, I was starting to get worried!
  B: We were made ................................. **(stay)** behind to finish a report.

---

**Forms of the infinitive/-ing form** ▶ p. GR15
corresponding to verb tenses:
present simple/*will* → **present infinitive/-ing form**
present continuous/future continuous → **present continuous infinitive**
past simple/present perfect/past perfect/future perfect → **perfect infinitive/-ing form**
past continuous/present perfect continuous/past perfect continuous/future perfect continuous → **perfect continuous infinitive**

---

**4** Complete the sentences, as in the example.

1 They believe that the fire started in the lab.
  The fire is believed *to have started in the lab*.
2 It seems that they're doing their homework.
  They seem ................................................................. .
3 They think that she cheated in her finals.
  She is thought ................................................................. .
4 People expect that she will get a place at Oxford University.
  She is expected ................................................................. .
5 It appears that Peter has been studying all morning.
  Peter appears ................................................................. .
6 Everyone thinks that the professor is too strict.
  The professor is thought ................................................................. .

**5** Put the verbs in brackets into the *to*-infinitive or *-ing* form. Give reasons for your answers.

1 Being a professor means .................................. **(work)** both inside and outside the lecture hall.
2 If you can't think of ideas for your essay, try ..................................... **(look)** online.
3 I regret ......................................... **(announce)** that the campus summer festival has been cancelled.
4 Did you remember ........................................ **(submit)** your assignment today?
5 I'll never forget ........................................ **(meet)** my university roommate for the first time.
6 James stopped ..................................... **(drink)** some water in the middle of his presentation.

**6** Correct the sentences. Give reasons.

1 We heard Lisa giving a lecture – she was great from start to finish!
2 I hate Jim interrupt me all the time.
3 The student was seen to walk through the campus by five different people.
4 He is too tired to going on the excursion.
5 I saw Frank walk to the science building, but I'm not sure if he arrived there.
6 I'd like Max deliver the speech.

**7** **SPEAKING** 🗣🗣 Use these words and *(to-)* infinitive or *-ing* form to ask your partner questions about themselves. Your partner replies.

promise – avoid – decide – would love – hate – look forward to – regret – like – remember

A: *What was the last thing you promised to do for someone?*
B: *I promised to help my sister move house last month – and I did it!*

## Relative clauses 〉 pp. GR16-17

**8** Read the sentences. Which contains a defining relative clause/a non-defining relative clause? Which clause can be omitted because it is not essential to the main meaning of the sentence? Which of the relative pronouns can be replaced with 'that'? Find an example in the text on p. 74. Is it defining or non-defining?

*Steve,* **who** *has been teaching for over 40 years, will officially retire next week.*
*The novel* **which** *we're reading in my 18th Century English Literature module is quite interesting.*

**9** Choose the correct item. Decide which clauses are defining *(D)* and which are non-defining *(ND)*. Put commas where necessary. Which of the relatives can be omitted?

1 Do you know the reason **why/when** Peter left the lecture early today? ..........
2 Jane **who's/whose** son goes to an expensive college in the USA earns a high wage. ..........
3 Advanced Logic is the module **that/why** I find the most challenging. ..........
4 Mr Richards **whose/who** inspired me to become a teacher has recently retired. ..........
5 The gym **where/which** we work out is not far from the college. ..........
6 Do you remember the day **when/where** Professor Rodgers came to the lecture in costume? ..........
7 Lisa, **who's/whose** agreed to help me with my essay, has a degree in Philosophy. ..........
8 Is that book **which/who** you're reading any good? ..........

**10** Join the sentences using the relative pronoun or adverb in brackets. Write in your notebook.

1 The professor is talking to the students. They won an engineering competition. **(who)**
*The professor is talking to the students* **who** *won an engineering competition.*
2 I'll never forget the day. My daughter graduated from university. **(when)**
3 This is the reason. James should go to a private college. **(why)**
4 Alice reads a lot of novels. She borrows them from the library. **(which)**
5 The university has 200 foreign students. Many of them are from Asia. **(whom)**
6 Steve studies Marketing. His father is a celebrity chef. **(whose)**
7 This is the town. I went to college there. **(where)**
8 Paul did a study on volcanoes. It was impressive. **(that)**

**11** **SPEAKING** 💬 Work in groups of four. Three members of the group secretly think of a person or a place. Each says a sentence about it using a different relative pronoun or adverb. The fourth member of the group has to guess who the person or what the place is.

S1: *It's a town which is in the West Midlands in England.*
S2: *It's the town where you can visit a famous writer's house.*
S3: *The playwright who wrote 'King Lear' lived in this town.*
S4: *It's Stratford-upon-Avon!*

# Skills in Action

## Vocabulary

### Education

**1** Complete the gaps in the advert with the words in the list.

- register • fees • study • labs • certificate
- part-time • mature • description

**Sart** College

1) ............................ now for our new Introduction to Computer Science 2) ............................ evening course! This course has been designed for 3) ............................ students with little or no experience of computer science. 4) .................... sessions include coding and website design. Students will have access to all of the college's facilities, including its computer 5) ............................ .

**Course dates:** 15th September – 15th March

6) ............................: £800. Students who complete the course will receive an official 7) ............................ .

For more information and a full course 8) ............................, visit www.sart_college.com/evening

**2** **THINK** What do you think are the pros and cons of taking evening classes? Discuss in groups.

## Listening

**3** You will hear people talking in four different situations. For questions 1-4, choose the best answer (A, B or C).

**1** You hear two friends talking about a summer course. How does Bill feel?
- **A** worried that he will feel lonely
- **B** excited about meeting new people
- **C** concerned that it will be too difficult

**2** You overhear a woman telling her friend about an online course. Why did she decide to do the course online rather than in a college?
- **A** because it costs less
- **B** because it is more flexible
- **C** because it is more interesting

**3** You hear a professor talking to students. Why is she talking to them?
- **A** to encourage them to study more
- **B** to remind them about an upcoming exam
- **C** to inform them about a new school facility

**4** You hear two friends talking about a new professor. What do they agree about?
- **A** The professor is very strict.
- **B** The professor is difficult to understand.
- **C** The professor has interesting methods.

## Everyday English

### Asking for information

**4** Read the first exchange. What questions do you think Peter will ask about the course? Listen and read to find out.

> **A:** Hello, Milltown College of Art. How can I help you?
>
> **B:** Good morning. My name's Peter Phillips. I'm interested in attending the summer photography course, but I'd like to ask you some questions first.
>
> **A:** Yes, of course. What would you like to know?
>
> **B:** Well, could you tell me the fee for the course?
>
> **A:** Yes, it is £200.
>
> **B:** Thank you. Do you organise accommodation for students living outside Milltown? I live in Chester, so it would be too far for me to drive each day.
>
> **A:** No, unfortunately, we don't. But we can recommend some hotels or hostels where you could stay.
>
> **B:** Thank you for your help.
>
> **A:** My pleasure. I hope to see you in the summer!

**5** You have read the advert in Ex. 1 and are interested in attending the course. Act out a dialogue asking for information similar to the one in Ex. 4. Use sentences/phrases from the language box.

| Asking for information | Giving information |
|---|---|
| • I'd like to know ... . | • Sure. We/It… |
| • I was wondering if you could ... | • Of course we do. |
| • Could/Can you tell me ...? | • I'm afraid not. But ... |
| • I wonder if you could tell me ...? | • Not really. We could ... . |

### Intonation: follow-up questions

**6** **a)** Listen to and read the examples. What are follow-up questions? How do we form them? What intonation does the speaker use to show: *interest*? *surprise*?

A: *I went to Green College.*

B: *Did you? (falling intonation)*

A: *Becky's going to study Astrophysics!*

B: *Is she? (rising intonation)*

**b)** Make a statement. Your partner replies using a follow-up question. Identify whether they are expressing *interest* or *surprise*.

A: *My mum started taking an evening class!*

B: *Did she? (surprise)*

## Reading & Writing

**7** Read the task, then read the email and fill in the gaps with words derived from the words in brackets.

> You have read this advert in an international music magazine.

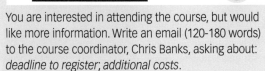

**BOURNEMOUTH**
*College of Music*

SUMMER ADVANCED PIANO COURSE
**(28 JULY – 15 AUGUST)** £800

> You are interested in attending the course, but would like more information. Write an email (120-180 words) to the course coordinator, Chris Banks, asking about: *deadline to register; additional costs.*

Dear Mr Banks,

**A** ▶ I am writing in **1)** ........................... (**connect**) with your advertisement in *Tunes Magazine* about your summer advanced piano course. I am 19 years of age and will be going to university in October to study Music, so I would like my piano-playing to be excellent. I have been learning the piano since I was 8 and I would now consider myself an advanced player. I am interested in attending your course, but I would like to ask you some questions.

**B** ▶ Firstly, I would like to know if there is a deadline for **2)** ........................... (**register**) for the course. Although it is likely that I will be free on the dates of the course, I am still not **3)** ........................... (**complete**) certain, so I would be interested to know the latest day possible when I could register.

**C** ▶ Secondly, could you tell me if there will be any **4)** ........................... (**addition**) costs during the course? For example, I imagine that the course will include some concerts. However, will the ticket price be covered by the £800, or will I have to pay extra? The same goes for the cost of **5)** ........................... (**equip**) during the course.

**D** ▶ I would be **6)** ........................... (**deep**) grateful for your help. I look forward to your reply.

Yours sincerely,
Maggie Smith

**8** Read the email in Ex. 7 again and answer the questions.

1 What is each paragraph about?
2 Does the email cover all the points in the task?
3 How does the sender start/end his email? Why?

 **Writing Tip**

**Formal style**
Emails/Letters asking for information are normally formal in style. Characteristics of formal style include: full verb forms, the passive, complex sentences, formal linkers, no emotive punctuation e.g. exclamation marks, ellipsis etc.

**9** a) Find examples of formal style in the email in Ex. 7.

b) Match the informal phrases (1-5) to the highlighted phrases in the email in Ex. 7.

1 have you any idea if I'll have to pay for more stuff
2 I'm thinking about coming on the course
3 I guess we'll be going to a concert or two on the course
4 I can't say for sure yet
5 I think I'm pretty good at it now

## Writing (an email asking for information)

**10** a) Read the task and answer the questions.

> You have read this advert in an international magazine.

**FLINT SUMMER SCHOOL**
**Summer English Course**
**25 JUNE – 9 JULY** £800
Register online at flintss/roboticsmusic.com or email jane.kemp@flintss.com for more information

> You are interested in attending the course, but would like more information. Write an email (120-180 words) to the course coordinator, Jane Kemp, asking about: *student accommodation; meals.*

1 What are you going to write? Who to?
2 Should your piece of writing be formal or informal?
3 What questions do you need to ask?
4 How many words should your piece of writing be?

b) Use your answers in Ex. 10a to write your email. Follow the plan.

**Plan**

*Dear Ms Kemp,*
**Para 1:** reason for writing
**Paras 2-3:** questions you have about the course
**Para 4:** closing remarks
*Yours sincerely,*
*(your full name)*

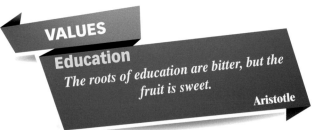

**VALUES**

**Education**
*The roots of education are bitter, but the fruit is sweet.*
**Aristotle**

▶ VIDEO

# I PROMISE

There are very few people who haven't heard of LeBron James. King James, as he is nicknamed, has played for some of the NBA's most successful teams, and is considered one of the greatest ever basketball players. But the work LeBron does off the court is just as **impressive** and important.

In 2004, LeBron set up the LeBron James Family Foundation (LJFF), an organisation that promotes education among young Americans. In many communities in the USA, it's normal for teens to drop out of high school when they **reach** 16 – the age in most states when this is legally allowed. In fact, **nationally**, up to 15% of Americans never finish secondary level education. This happens for a number of reasons – some students leave school because of financial problems, while others quit because of a lack of family support. The LJFF's chief aim is to change young people's attitudes towards education, so that they can see it is a path towards a brighter future.

The LJFF **runs** most of its programmes in Akron, Ohio, LeBron's hometown. And its main **focus** is on the I Promise Program. Through this programme, the foundation helps around 1,400 Akron students from poor **backgrounds** with their education. It matches students with mentors who support and motivate them, and also pays for local students to study at the University of Akron – but only if they **achieve** some academic goals.

Also, in July, 2018, the LJFF officially opened the I Promise School (IPS) in Akron. At the moment, the school only has 3rd and 4th grade students (aged 7-9), but it plans to become a full elementary school in the near future. The IPS opens for **longer** hours than most schools, from 8 am to 5 pm, and organises a lot of family events to get parents involved in their children's education. All of this gives students the chance to succeed, both at school and at home. But LeBron always **points out** that his foundation can't do everything. The young people he helps have to make a promise to themselves to work hard and achieve their goals. As LeBron says, "Nothing is given. Everything is earned."

✓ **Check these words**

promote, drop out (of), financial, attitude, mentor

## Listening & Reading

**1** Look at the pictures and read the title of the text. Who is LeBron James? What is *I Promise*?
🎧 Listen and read to find out.

**2** Read the text and answer the questions. Then explain the words in bold.

1 In most parts of the USA, at what age can you decide to leave school?
2 What is the main goal of LeBron James' foundation?
3 Why is Akron a significant city for LeBron James?
4 How do mentors help students in the I Promise Program?
5 In what way is the IPS different from other schools in the USA?

## Speaking & Writing

**3** THINK Imagine you want to start a foundation to help young people in your area/country with their education. What would you call it? What would it offer? How would it help students? Present your ideas to the class.

**4** ICT Collect information about an educational foundation in your country or another country. Make notes under the headings: *name of foundation – main aim of foundation – who foundation helps – success of the foundation*. **Use your notes to write a short article about it for a school magazine.**

## Vocabulary

**1** **Choose the correct item.**

**1** The teacher shows students a video on the interactive **creature/whiteboard/headset**.

**2** She tried to **encourage/augment/participate** her students to study harder.

**3** Paul decided to **register/follow/attend** for an evening course in graphic design.

**4** This course is suitable for **individual/mature/official** students with full-time jobs.

**5** Owen decided to **drop/abandon/quit** school when he was just 16.

**6** Kate was told her to change her **concept/attitude/description** and start turning in her assignments.

*(6 x 2 = 12)*

**2** **Fill in:** *campus, experience, identify, promote, beating, run.*

**1** This app lets people ......................... a virtual world.

**2** Peter was so nervous that he could hear his heart ......................... .

**3** Jane lives near the university ......................... .

**4** This AR app is able to ......................... and name different types of trees.

**5** The foundation decided to ......................... an education programme in the city centre.

**6** The aim of the foundation is to ......................... science subjects in schools.

*(6 x 2 = 12)*

**3** **Choose the correct item.**

**1** I've changed courses three times **above/over** the past year.

**2** Check **out/on** this tablet – I think you might like it.

**3** We checked **in/off** and went to our rooms.

**4** The head teacher checked **up/off** on the student studying in the library.

**5** With this new smartphone, the world is **on/at** my fingertips.

**6** You'll be **to/at** a disadvantage in a German university because of the language.

*(6 x 3 = 18)*

## Grammar

**4** **Put the verbs in brackets into the correct infinitive or -ing form.**

**1** Fred had better ......................... **(finish)** now.

**2** Ken's used to ......................... **(work)** on a laptop.

**3** He let me ......................... **(leave)** at 4:00.

**4** All students must ......................... **(go)** to the main hall.

**5** Kate agreed ......................... **(help)** her friend.

**6** The college considered ......................... **(buy)** IWBs.

**7** It's important ......................... **(exercise)** more.

**8** He continued ......................... **(study)** despite the noise.

**9** Paul wastes a lot of time ......................... **(play)** games on his phone.

**10** James was the first person in his family ......................... **(graduate)** from college.

*(10 x 2 = 20)*

**5** **Fill in:** *who, which, whose, when, where* **or** *why.* **Add commas where necessary.**

**1** Do you know the name of the person ............. invented the light bulb?

**2** I'll never forget the day ................... Professor Logan entered our lecture hall.

**3** Do you know the reason ................... Ken left?

**4** Our Maths test ................... I haven't prepared for is going to be really difficult.

**5** Phil ................... used to be an actor agreed to teach drama at the college.

**6** That's the library ................... I used to study when I was in secondary school.

*(6 x 3 = 18)*

## Everyday English

**6** **Match the exchanges.**

**1** ☐ Could I ask a few questions?
**2** ☐ What would you like to know?
**3** ☐ Have you any idea what the course fees are?
**4** ☐ Will you supply tablets?

**a** I'd like to know the course fees.
**b** No, we won't.
**c** £500.
**d** Yes, of course you can.

*(4 x 5 = 20)*

*Total 100*

# Values: Compassion

 ▶ **VIDEO**

Home | Posts | Food | Fashion | Archives | Features | Contact ✉ 🐦 f 📌

SEARCH 🔍

# Five ways to show compassion
## by Felix Dunn

*From time to time, everyone needs a helping hand or a shoulder to cry on. Compassion is the ability to recognise this need in others, and the **desire** to offer them comfort. It's a strong feeling that shows we really care about the person. But how can we show compassion? It depends on the situation, but compassion always comes from the heart.*

### ❶ Be all ears
Sometimes, showing compassion involves very little. In fact, often the best way is to simply listen. When someone comes to you with a problem, don't always give them advice, or offer to do something for them – they might just want to talk to you. Talking about problems out loud with another person helps us think about them in a different way. So, a good way to show compassion is to be a good listener.

### ❷ Share some positive thinking
When a person is suffering, the world can be a dark place. So, a great way to show compassion is by encouraging people. For example, if your friend has failed an exam, you could remind them about other subjects they are good at, or advise them to focus on the next one. Sometimes, a few **supportive** words can really help a person change their **mindset** and deal with their problems.

### ❸ Actions not words
When we notice that a person close to us is suffering, the first thing we usually do is speak to them. We give them advice and tell them that we are there for them. But sometimes this isn't enough. Sometimes, you have to take the next step and actually do something for the person. This might mean giving up some free time, but compassion is more than just **comforting** words.

### ❹ The power of touch
Sometimes, there is nothing more powerful than physical contact. A hug or just a gentle touch on the shoulder can mean a lot to a person who is suffering. These **gestures** connect you with the person physically and emotionally, showing you are with them. Of course, you should only show compassion in this way when you are sure it will be welcome.

### ❺ Compassion for all
It's natural to care more about the people close to us, but we shouldn't just show compassion to family and friends. We never know what problems the strangers we meet are experiencing, and for that reason they **deserve** our compassion too. Obviously, it's not usually **appropriate** to give strangers a hug or sit down with them for a chat, but simply being cheerful, polite and respectful is another powerful way to show compassion.

**1** In what situations do you show compassion? How do you show compassion?

🎧 Listen to and read the article to find out if your ideas are mentioned.

**2** Read the article again. Which ways of showing compassion (1-5) are the situations (A-E) examples of?

A Helen didn't just sympathise with me – she also helped me update my CV, so I could start looking for a new job. ........

B Tim helped me realise that losing the cup final wasn't the end of the world, telling me we'd win it next year. ........

C When my mum opened her arms and gave me a warm hug, I knew everything would be OK. ........

D I didn't even know the woman, but the bright smile she gave me really cheered me up. ........

E Paul didn't need to say anything – just talking to him about my problems really helped. ........

**3** Explain the words/phrases in bold.

**4** (THINK) Which of the ways of showing compassion described in the text do you appreciate most when you're feeling down? Why? Tell your partner.

**5** 👥 Read the four situations. How would you show compassion? Discuss with your partner.

- Your younger sister is having trouble with a subject at school.
- Your best friend's pet passed away.
- Your friend can't find a job.
- A stranger lost his phone.

# Public Speaking Skills

**1** Read the task. What type of speech does it ask for: *informative*, *persuasive* or *ceremonial*?

You are the president of a national homeless charity and are hosting an awards ceremony for volunteers. Give a speech presenting the winner of the 'Volunteer of the Year' Award.

---

**Study Skills**

**Emphasising key moments**

Sometimes people lose their concentration, so it's important to focus their attention again at key moments. We can do this by:

- taking a pause
- using key phrases (we've come to the highlight, it's finally time to, without further ado, what we've all been waiting for, etc.)
- changing your volume (speaking louder or quieter)

---

**2** 🎧 Listen to and read the model. What techniques has the speaker used in the three underlined key moments in the speech?

---

Good evening, everyone. My name is Keith Bates and I'm the President of Sheltered. Let me just start by saying how proud I am of the amazing work our charity has done this year! I think we should all give ourselves a pat on the back! <u>Now, we've come to the highlight of the evening. That's right, it's my great honour to present the Volunteer of the Year Award.</u>

The Volunteer of the Year Award, now in its 12th year, honours a volunteer in our organisation who has done incredible work to help the homeless in their area. It's important to remember, though, that this award isn't for the volunteer who has worked the most hours or raised the most money. As I always say, volunteering is about doing as much as you can. Many of our volunteers have jobs and families, so they can't volunteer for hours every day – <u>but the important thing to remember is: everything helps</u>. Every hour you volunteer and every penny you collect, no matter how little, helps in our fight against homelessness in the UK.

The winner of this year's award is a woman in a position exactly like this. She has a full-time job and two children, but even in her limited free time, she has achieved so much for our charity. She has been working in our Leeds team for six years now, and has been the team's leader for the past two years. And thanks mostly to her efforts, our Leeds team now raises more money and has more volunteers than any other in the country! This has made a huge difference in programmes to help the homeless in Leeds. But we can't talk about this person's achievements without also mentioning her character. Everyone who I've spoken to in Leeds has talked about her wide smile and cheerful attitude – in both good and bad times. And this has made her a very popular member of her team.

So, without further ado, it's finally time to invite this person onto the stage to collect her award. <u>The winner of this year's Sheltered Volunteer of the Year Award is, of course, ... Ayesha Abad.</u> Congratulations Ayesha!

---

**3** **ICT** Read the task and brainstorm for ideas. Prepare your speech and use techniques to emphasise three key moments in it. Present your speech to the class.

You are the president of a national education organisation and are hosting an awards ceremony for teachers. Give a speech presenting the winner of the 'National Teacher of the Year' Award.

**Vocabulary:** environmental problems; waste; carbon footprints
**Grammar:** reported speech; special introductory verbs
**Everyday English:** making proposals – agreeing/disagreeing
**Writing:** a proposal

# 10 Green minds

▶ VIDEO

## Vocabulary

### Environmental problems

**1 a) Complete the collocations. Use:** *change, production, pollution, growth, species, warming, rain.*

1 air/light/noise/water ........................
2 acid ........................
3 climate ........................
4 global ........................
5 population ........................
6 waste ........................
7 endangered ........................

**b) Which of these problems are the most serious in your country?**

### Waste

**2 Put the items into the correct bin. Which cannot go in any of the bins? Compare with your partner. Think of more items to put in each bin.**

- newspapers • vegetable peelings • plastic packaging
- leaflets and delivery menus • tree leaves
- cardboard boxes • eggshells • batteries • food tins
- mobile phones • tea leaves and coffee grounds
- drink cans • paper egg cartons • cut grass
- glass bottles • tin foil • jars • disposable water bottles

GLASS ................ ................
................ ................

PAPER ................ ................
................ ................

PLASTIC ................ ................
................ ................

ORGANIC ................ ................
................ ................

METAL ................ ................
................ ................

## Reading & Listening

**3 Can you name the animals/organisms in the pictures? How do you think the writer of the article feels about them?**

🎧 **Listen and read to check.**

# With a Little Help from our Friends

**L**ife on Earth is **under threat**. Animals and plants alike are at risk, with 150 to 200 species becoming extinct every day as a result of human activity. There is enough plastic waste in the Pacific to make an island the size of Europe, India and Mexico combined. Even in the EU, where there has been a huge recycling push, only 48% of household waste is presently recycled. Our factories, power stations and vehicles still pollute the air with fumes and raise the level of carbon dioxide in our atmosphere. Yet the very living organisms we are killing quietly spend their days cleaning up the **mess** on our planet.

We often think of bacteria as the bad guys. They cause infections and illnesses, after all, from cholera to anthrax and tuberculosis. But some bacteria also perform a vital role in breaking down the waste we and other animals and plants produce. Without them, the ground would soon be covered in deep layers of biological waste. Environmentalist Stewart Brand once said that if you didn't like bacteria, you were on the wrong planet! And bacteria might even save the planet from our waste. Scientists recently discovered a type of bacteria that 'eats' plastic, and are researching the possibility of using them to break down our mountains of plastic waste.

**Scavengers** are the animals that feed on the bodies of dead animals. They include hyenas, jackals, vultures and many more, and they all share one thing – strong stomachs! The turkey vulture, for example, has stomach acid so strong that

**4 Read the article again and decide if statements 1-10 are** *T* **(True),** *F* **(False) or** *DS* **(doesn't say). Correct the false statements. Then explain the words/phrases in bold.**

1 Up to 200 species die out each year. ........
2 Most rubbish in the European Union is recycled. ........
3 Bacterial diseases kill millions of people each year. ........
4 A newly found kind of bacteria may solve an environmental problem. ........

82

it kills any harmful bacteria that has grown on the rotting meat. The bird's droppings, therefore, are completely clear of bacteria, and actually very good for the soil. Scavengers are like the street cleaners of the natural world, and without them the plains and forests would be covered in dead bodies.

But that's on land – who's at work underwater? Well, the sea cucumber might sound like something you put in a salad, but some species of this strange-looking sea creature can grow to up to three metres in length. And they work a little like a vacuum cleaner. In just one year, some sea cucumbers can suck up 45 kg of sand from the seabed and coral reefs, removing any organic waste from it and making it clean again. Halima Zidane, a marine biologist who has studied them for many years, said of them: "They're like a **purifying** species for the ocean."

These are just a few of the eco-friends we have. There are many more that wander around, quietly tidying up the planet. But they can't head off environmental disaster alone. We need to learn from them, and start doing our bit to clean up the world that we all share. Little by little, it could stop being a planet in danger and again become a place we are proud to live in.

## ✔ Check these words

push, bacteria, infection, break down, hyena, jackal, vulture, turkey vulture, stomach acid, rotting, plain, sea cucumber, suck up, wander

5 Scavengers eat the meat of animals that have died. .........
6 The acid in the turkey vulture's stomach is the strongest we know. .........
7 Sea cucumbers are plants that grow on the bottom of the sea. .........
8 Coral reefs always have large populations of sea cucumbers. .........
9 There are other species with a positive effect on the planet. .........
10 The writer says the animals can save the planet on their own. .........

5 **COLLOCATIONS** Find and complete the words in the text that describe the following. Then use the phrases to make sentences based on the text.

1 ........................ stations
2 ........................ role
3 ........................ layers
4 ........................ acid
5 ........................ meat
6 ........................ world
7 ........................ reef
8 ........................ biologist

6 **PREPOSITIONS** Fill in: *at, in (x2), under, on*.

1 Rhinos in Africa are ................. threat from poachers.
2 The Amazon Rainforest is ............... risk of deforestation.
3 The largest bacteria are just 0.3 mm ............... length.
4 How many animals live ................. land?
5 Polar bears are ............... danger due to global warming.

7 **WORDS EASILY CONFUSED** Choose the correct word. Check in your dictionary. Then write sentences in your notebook using the other words.

1 Is the water in the lake **clear/clean** enough to drink?
2 There are **signs/signals** that deforestation is increasing.
3 Vultures eat animals that are already **dead/deadly**.
4 Good intentions **alone/lonely** won't save the planet – we have to act!

8 **PHRASAL VERBS** Fill in the correct particle.

> **head for:** to move or travel towards a place or a situation
> **head off: 1)** to stop sb/sth and make them change direction; **2)** to prevent sth bad from happening; **3)** to leave and go somewhere else
> **head out:** to go out
> **head up:** to be in charge of sth

1 It may be too late to head ............. some species' extinction.
2 Simon heads ................. the local branch of Greenpeace.
3 As soon as the sun came up, we headed ................ .
4 The wolf tried to head ............. the deer, but it got away.
5 We picked up litter on the beach and then headed ................ the park.

## Speaking & Writing

9 **THINK** Which of the organisms described in the text do you think is the most important? Discuss in groups.

10 **ICT** Collect information about another species that helps the environment. Prepare a digital presentation for the class.

# Grammar in Use

## Reported speech ▶ pp. GR17-18

The environmentalist Annie Leonard warned that there was no such thing as 'away', and that when we threw something 'away', it had to go somewhere. Zero waste, in other words, had to be the target. Michael Reynolds, an architect, took up the challenge. He said that what was going to get us through the future was radical change. The earthship was his solution. Made out of recycled materials and using solar and wind power, the earthship is a building that needs no cooling or heating system, collects and reuses rainwater and radically reduces the waste it produces. It is designed to be built anywhere, even by those with little knowledge of construction. Before he began the project Reynolds said that he was embarrassed to be a human and certainly was embarrassed to be an architect. With the earthship, he can now be proud, having designed a home that creates a better future.

**1** Read the article, then read the sentences below. Find the sentences in the article that report them. How do tenses and pronouns change in statements?

**A** "There is no such thing as 'away'. When we throw something 'away', it must go somewhere."

**B** "What's going to get us through the future is radical change."

**C** "I am embarrassed to be a human and certainly am embarrassed to be an architect."

**2** Choose the correct item. Give reasons.

1 "I planted a tree in the park yesterday," Paul said.
Paul **said/told** that he **planted/had planted** a tree in the park the **previous/following** day.

2 Kate said, "I need to buy some rechargeable batteries."
Kate **said/told** that **I/she needed/was needing** to buy some rechargeable batteries.

3 "24 species become extinct every day," Ken said to us.
Ken **said/told** us that 24 species **become/had become** extinct **that/every** day.

4 "I can install your solar panels," David said to me.
David **said/told him/me** that **I/he** could install **my/your** solar panels.

5 "We were picking up litter yesterday," Jo said to Jake.
Jo told Jake that **she/they** had **picked/been picking** up litter the day **before/previous**.

6 "I'm working at the health food shop this weekend," said Molly to Amy.
Molly **said/told** Amy that she **works/was working** at the health food shop **this/that** weekend.

**3** Rewrite the sentences in reported speech.

1 "The company is going to reduce its waste by 50%," said Dr Jones.
......................................................................................

2 "I may need some help with the recycling today," Harry told Ann.
......................................................................................

3 "We have installed a rainwater collector in our house," Brooke said.
......................................................................................

4 "I've been growing my own food for the past two years," said Jack.
......................................................................................

5 "We saw some signs of new growth in the forest last week," said the scientist.
......................................................................................

6 "Dan was volunteering at the bird sanctuary last summer," Lily told Max.
......................................................................................

**4** Study the examples. How do we report: *wh-* questions? *Yes/No* questions?

*"When did you join Greenpeace?" asked Niall.*
*Niall asked (me) when I had joined Greenpeace.*
*"Are you only eating organic food these days, Max?" asked Sara.*
*Sara asked Max if/whether he was only eating organic food those days.*

**5** Report Jamila's questions.

Am I doing enough to help the environment?

Where can I get rid of used batteries?

How much water does my bath use?

Do electric cars cost a lot of money?

Which colour bin do milk cartons go in?

When did the organic food shop open?

1 ......................................................................................
2 ......................................................................................
3 ......................................................................................
4 ......................................................................................
5 ......................................................................................
6 ......................................................................................

**6** **Read the examples. How do we report orders?**

*"Turn off the light," said Mario to me.*
*Mario told me to turn off the light.*

*"Don't leave the tap running," Mum said.*
*Mum told me not to leave the tap running.*

**7** **You and your friend have volunteered for a beach clean-up. Danny is the organiser and has sent you the email below. Report his orders to your friend, as in the example.**

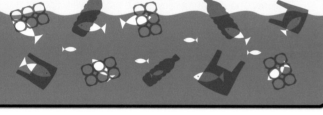

🏠 Home   @ Connect   # Discover   👤 Me      🔍 Search...   ✉ ⚙ ✍

Hi everyone. I'd like to thank you all for volunteering for Conmouth Beach clean-up tomorrow. Before we start, I'd like to give you some guidelines. First of all, do not pick up litter with your bare hands. There might be some broken glass in the sand. Wear gloves. Secondly, put all the rubbish in black plastic bags and leave the bags near the coffee shop. They'll be collected later. Next, don't waste any time. By 11 am, it's really hot on the beach, so we need to be done by then. Finally, enjoy yourselves, and thanks for volunteering. Let's go!

**1** *Danny told us not to pick up litter with our bare hands.*
**2** ...................................................................
...................................................................
**3** ...................................................................
...................................................................
**4** ...................................................................
...................................................................
**5** ...................................................................
...................................................................
**6** ...................................................................
...................................................................

**8** **Rewrite the dialogue in reported speech in your notebooks.**

**Amy:** Are you doing anything this weekend, Ben?
**Ben:** I was going to the football match, but it's been cancelled.
**Amy:** You could help me in my garden. I'm building a birdhouse.
**Ben:** That sounds like a good idea. What time should I be there?
**Amy:** You can come any time you want. You should call first, though.
**Ben:** Give me your number then. I don't think I have it.

## Special introductory verbs
**▶ pp. GR18-20**

**9** **Rewrite the sentences in reported speech. Use the verbs in the list.**

- invite • allow • admit • suggest • apologise
- remind • boast • complain • warn • promise

**1** "Sorry for throwing the rubbish in the wrong bin," said Rory to Amy.
...................................................................
...................................................................

**2** "Don't forget to take the recycling out," Sam told me.
...................................................................
...................................................................

**3** "Yes, you can plant a tree in the garden," Dan said to me.
...................................................................
...................................................................

**4** "Be careful you don't leave litter on the beach," Fiona said to us
...................................................................
...................................................................

**5** "Don't worry. I'll be at the animal shelter on time", said Polly to Tony.
...................................................................
...................................................................

**6** "No one does more to help the environment than me," said Oliver.
...................................................................
...................................................................

**7** "Do you fancy coming to the Save the Whales meeting tomorrow?" said Cal to me.
...................................................................
...................................................................

**8** "Why don't we create a garden on our rooftop?," said Max.
...................................................................
...................................................................

**9** "Yes, it was me who put the wrong rubbish in the recycling bin," said Steve.
...................................................................
...................................................................

**10** "You missed the tree planting on Sunday!" Beth said to me.
...................................................................
...................................................................

**10** 💬 **SPEAKING** **Imagine you are organising an event to plant trees in the local park. In pairs, act out a dialogue. Ask and answer questions. A third person takes notes, then reports the dialogue to another group.**

# Skills in Action

## Vocabulary
### Carbon footprints

**1** Fill in the gaps with words from the list.

• carpool • local • energy-efficient • economy
• paperless • electric • detergent • reusable
• organic • compost

## How **Big** is Your
# Carbon Footprint?

Your carbon footprint is the amount of carbon dioxide you create. This is important because carbon dioxide is mainly responsible for global warming. How big is your carbon footprint? Take this test by circling 'Yes' or 'No'.

| Do you … | |
|---|---|
| use a cold-water **1)** ........................? | **Yes / No** |
| grow **2)** ........................ food? | **Yes / No** |
| go **3)** ........................ with digital bills and statements? | **Yes / No** |
| drink from **4)** ........................ coffee cups? | **Yes / No** |
| **5)** .................... or use public transport to get to work? | **Yes / No** |
| buy **6)** ........................ products? | **Yes / No** |
| have **7)** ........................ appliances at home? | **Yes / No** |
| drive a(n) **8)** ........................ car? | **Yes / No** |
| go **9)** ........................ class when you fly? | **Yes / No** |
| **10)** ........................ your food waste? | **Yes / No** |

**So how many times did you answer 'Yes'?**

**1-3** You might need to make some changes to the way you live your life.

**4-7** You care about the environment and are doing quite well, but the planet always needs a little more help.

**8-10** You obviously care about the planet and want to leave it in a good condition for the next generation.

**2** Do the quiz. How environmentally friendly are you? What could you do to reduce your carbon footprint more? Tell your partner.

## Listening

**3** 🎧 You will hear four people talking about how they have become more eco-friendly. Listen and match the speakers (1-4) to the statements (A-E). One statement is extra.

**A** There are more advantages than I realised.
**B** I have suggested doing this to my friends.
**C** I did it because I wanted to save money.
**D** I can't get the exercise I used to nowadays.
**E** The main reason for doing it was to get fitter.

| | |
|---|---|
| Speaker 1 | |
| Speaker 2 | |
| Speaker 3 | |
| Speaker 4 | |

## Everyday English
### Making proposals – Agreeing/Disagreeing

**4** What proposals does Sam make for a green office?

🎧 Listen, read and check.

**S:** Sam        **J:** Mrs Jacobs

**S:** Hi, Mrs Jacobs. Yesterday, you asked the staff for ideas for making the office greener. I have a few suggestions for you.

**J:** Excellent. Let's hear the first one.

**S:** OK. Firstly, it's important to go paperless. For example, instead of printing reports and sending letters, it could be done digitally. That would help the environment and save the company money, too.

**J:** I like the sound of that. What else do you propose?

**S:** I think, it's worth considering green challenges for the staff. For instance, a month using no plastic knives and forks. Anyone who succeeds could get rewards. This would motivate staff and it's fun at the same time.

**J:** That sounds interesting, but I'm not sure it will work.

**S:** How about putting recycling bins on every floor? That would mean all our office waste going to the right places.

**J:** You're absolutely right. That would make a big difference. Anyway, put your proposals in writing and I'll make sure management see them.

**S:** I'll do that straightaway, Mrs Jacobs. Thank you.

**5** 👥👥 Use sentences/phrases from the language box to act out a dialogue about how to make your house greener.

| Making proposals |
|---|
| • Why don't you/we …? / How about …? • It's a good idea to … • It would be a good/great etc idea to … |
| **Agreeing/Disagreeing** |
| • I couldn't agree with you more. / You're absolutely right. • I'm not (so) sure about that. • I'm sorry, but I don't agree. |

## Intonation: prepositions

**6 a)** 🎧 Listen and underline the stressed prepositions.

1 Come on!
2 There's no one to go with.
3 I can't rely on her.
4 Who's he talking to?
5 Pick it up.

**b)** Read the sentences below. Mind the intonation.

• Don't throw that out! • Animals depend on us.
• Let's head off. • Who are you waiting for?

## Reading & Writing

**7** Read the proposal and fill in the gaps (1-6) with a word formed from the word in brackets.

**To:** Harriet Dawkins, Manager, 'The Healthy Appetite'
**From:** Joel Blakely, Head Waiter
**Subject:** Going green

**Introduction**
As **1)** ........................... **(request)** by the Manager, I am writing this proposal to set out ways for The Healthy Appetite restaurant to become more eco-friendly.

**A** ...............................
It would be a good idea to buy meat, milk and eggs from local farmers. This would mean food would not have to travel long distances, **2)** ........................... **(reduce)** its carbon footprint. Doing this could help both the environment and the local economy.

**B** ...............................
It is worth considering giving away or reusing food. At the end of an evening, there is always food left over. We could send this to the homeless shelter or we could reuse it in different dishes. By doing this, we could **3)** ........................... **(drastic)** cut down on food waste.

**C** ...............................
It is important to use green cleaning supplies. Most cleaning supplies use highly toxic chemicals. We should only buy cleaning supplies that **4)** ........................... **(clear)** state they do not harm the environment.

**Conclusion**
I believe that The Healthy Appetite should buy locally sourced products, give away or reuse leftover food and use eco-friendly cleaning products. With these **5)** ................................ **(recommend)**, we could be the **6)** ........................... **(green)** restaurant in the area.

### Writing Tip

**Proposals**

Proposals are formal pieces of writing to people in authority. They provide solutions to a problem or suggestions on how to achieve something in the future. The information is presented under sub-headings to make the proposal easy to read. Each suggestion/solution needs to be followed by examples/reasons. Proposals begin with an introduction saying why the proposal is being written and end with a summary of all the solutions/suggestions and the expected result.

**8** Fill in gaps A-C in the proposal with the sub-headings below. Two are extra.

• Clean and green • A new menu • Waste nothing
• Stay local • Online advertising

## Writing (a proposal)

**9** Read the task and answer the questions.

Your manager, Martin Oberman, has asked you to propose ways to make the office more eco-friendly. Write your proposal (120-180 words). Think about: office supplies, saving energy, going paperless.

**1** What are you going to write? Who for?
**2** What should you write about? How many words should your piece of writing be?

**10** **a)** Match the suggestions with the reasons/ examples. Which of the headings in the task does each match? Can you think of more suggestions?

**Suggestions**
**1** ☐ have digital files and put bills and statements online
**2** ☐ change to energy-efficient appliances to reduce energy consumption
**3** ☐ buy recycled paper and eco-friendly products

**Reasons/Examples**
**a** fewer trees cut down and less water pollution
**b** save paper and reduce the need for printouts
**c** buy LED light bulbs and use fans instead of air-conditioning

**b)** Use the ideas in Ex. 10a as well as your own to write your proposal for the task in Ex. 9. Follow the plan.

**Plan**
**To:** *Martin Oberman, Manager*
**From:** *(your name and position)*
**Subject:** *Going green*
**Para 1:** Introduction: the reason for the proposal
**Para 2:** first suggestion with reasons/examples
**Para 3:** second suggestion with reasons/examples
**Para 4:** third suggestion with reasons/examples
**Para 5:** Conclusion: summary of suggestions & expected results

**VALUES**

**Environmentalism**
*The Earth is what we all have in common.*
**Wendell Berry**

# 10 Culture

## Listening & Reading

**1** **Which of the following statements are true about Seaweek? Tick.**

🎧 **Listen, read and check.**

1 Seaweek is week-long festival. ........
2 Seaweek takes place every year. ........
3 People can volunteer to organise events. ........
4 More than 100,000 people take part. ........
5 There is an app to track divers underwater. ........
6 More information can be found online. ........

**2** **Read the leaflet again. For questions 1-3, choose the correct answer (A, B, C or D).**

1 What is the aim of Seaweek?
  A to raise money for an environmental organisation
  B to give information about sea life and its problems
  C to encourage young people to take up water sports
  D to persuade tourists to protect the seas and beaches

2 What do people like best about Seaweek?
  A guided water sport activities
  B the Marine Studies Centre app
  C the driftwood sculpture competition
  D free admission

3 What should readers who want to join in do?
  A spread the word online
  B write to other participants
  C get information from the organisers
  D research sea life worldwide

## Speaking & Writing

**3** 👥 (THINK) **What event would you organise to support Seaweek? Tell the class.**

**4** **ICT Is there a similar event in your country or another country? Collect information under the headings:** *what it is – who organises it – what happens.* **Use your notes to present the event to the class.**

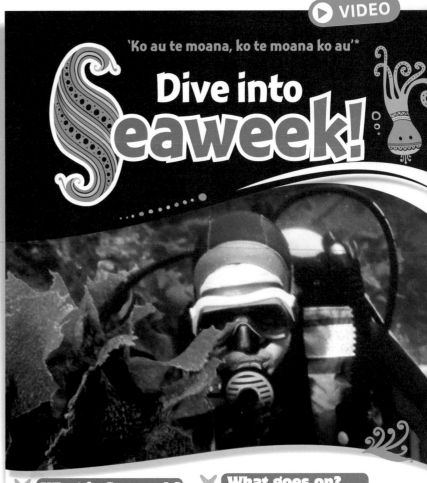

▶ VIDEO

'Ko au te moana, ko te moana ko au'*

# Dive into Seaweek!

### What is Seaweek?

Seaweek is an eight-day celebration of the beauty and wonders of life underwater. Held annually in New Zealand at the beginning of March, it's a fun eight days of events for all the family to educate them about the sea, its ecosystems and the challenges it faces.

### Who are we?

We are the New Zealand Association for Environmental Education (NZAEE). We raise awareness about the sea and the problems it's facing. The NZAEE has also been in schools across the country to promote environmental issues. Seaweek is run by members of the NZAEE, but also by volunteers who run their own events all over the country.

### What goes on?

Seaweek attracts over 120,000 participants every year and hosts over 250 events. The most popular activities are water sport days, when people of all ages go snorkelling, kayaking and exploring areas of the sea under the supervision of experienced guides. Why not download the Marine Studies Centre app? Look at a 1m² section of seashore and send info about the sea life it contains. There are also loads of competitions across New Zealand including a driftwood sculpture competition and lots more. All events are free to the public.

### How can you join in?

Take part in any of the events or sign up to run your own event. Seaweek will also be promoted on TV shows, radio channels and by local newspapers and magazines. Subscribe to our e-newsletter for more details and don't forget to check out social media sites for updates.

* 'I am the sea, the sea is me' in Maori, the native language of New Zealand

 **Check these words**

wonder, promote, run, supervision, driftwood

## Vocabulary

### 1 Choose the correct word.

1 All **cardboard/food/light** tins go in this bin.
2 Your stomach **acid/ecosystem/bacteria** helps you digest food.
3 Don't throw away vegetable **bags/grounds/peelings** – they can be recycled.
4 This restaurant is famous for its local **appliances/packaging/products**.
5 Global population **growth/change/production** is about 83 million people a year.
6 Companies are using too much **plastic/natural/global** packaging.
7 We all **take/go/play** a role in saving the Earth.
8 Birds' sleep can be interrupted by **noise/electric/endangered** pollution.

*(8 x 2 = 16)*

### 2 Fill in: *rotting, organic, electric, carbon, reusable, warming, carpool, compost, economy, rain.*

1 I drive a(n) ................................ car now.
2 Have you read the article about global ......................... ?
3 It's easier than you think to grow your own ...................... food.
4 The buildings have been damaged by acid .................... .
5 How can we make our ........................ footprint smaller?
6 The coffee shop encourages customers to bring in a(n) ................................ coffee cup.
7 I ................................ to work to reduce air pollution.
8 Tony only flies ................................ class on a plane.
9 A vulture's stomach kills bacteria from ......................... animals.
10 We ................................ our food waste.

*(10 x 2 = 20)*

### 3 Choose the correct item.

1 Kate is heading **up/off** the wildlife charity's local branch.
2 The coral reefs are **on/at** risk from scuba divers.
3 I felt seasick as we headed **out/over** on the rough sea.
4 The rainforest is **under/by** threat from deforestation.
5 How can we look after species **in/from** danger?

*(5 x 2 = 10)*

## Grammar

### 4 Rewrite the sentences in reported speech in your notebook.

1 "Switch off the lights before you leave," he told us.
2 "What is a sea cucumber like?" Amy asked.
3 "I had trouble getting to work today," said Mia.
4 "Have you taken out the recycling?" Nina asked Sam.
5 "Luke has to go before 5:00," said Kevin.
6 "The beach clean-up will be cancelled if it rains tomorrow," Rachel said to Steve.

*(6 x 4 = 24)*

### 5 Rewrite the sentences as reported speech in your notebook, using the verbs in brackets.

1 "You should cycle every day," Fran said to Sue. **(advise)**
2 "Don't forget to buy rechargeable batteries," Zoe told Henry. **(remind)**
3 "Sorry I'm late for the meeting," said Kim. **(apologise)**
4 "I cleaned up the beach all by myself," Harry said. **(boast)**
5 "Don't put used batteries in the recycling bin," Debbie told me. **(warn)**

*(5 x 2 = 10)*

## Everyday English

### 6 Match the exchanges.

1 ☐ I have a few recommendations.
2 ☐ To begin with, staff could carpool to work every day.
3 ☐ What else do you propose?
4 ☐ Let's hear your suggestions.
5 ☐ Put your proposals in writing, please.

a I'll do that straightaway. Thank you.
b That's a good idea.
c Let's hear the first one.
d It's also worth putting in fans.
e First of all, we could go paperless.

*(5 x 4 = 20)*

*Total 100*

## Competences

**GOOD** ✓
**VERY GOOD** ✓✓
**EXCELLENT** ✓✓✓

**Lexical Competence**
understand words/phrases related to:
• environmental problems
• waste
• carbon footprints

**Reading Competence**
• understand texts related to environmental problems (read for specific information – T/F/DS; multiple choice)

**Listening Competence**
• listen to and understand monologues related to carbon footprints (listen for key information – multiple matching)

**Speaking Competence**
• make proposals – agree/disagree

**Writing Competence**
• write a proposal

# 11

# Buying, buying, bought!

## THE POWER OF ADVERTISING

## Vocabulary

### Marketing & Advertising

**1** **Fill in:** *spot, slogan, jingle, commercial, audience, marketing, display, research, hoarding, time.* **Check in your dictionary.**

1 Market ............................. shows that 50% of our customers shop online.

2 An advertising ............................. is a short phrase that helps customers remember a product.

3 Our company is renting space to advertise on a huge roadside ............................. .

4 The average radio advertising ............................. is 30 to 60 seconds long.

5 Have you seen that funny TV ............................. for aftershave?

6 That toothpaste ............................. is so catchy that I can't get it out of my head!

7 The window ............................. was so attractive that it drew a huge crowd inside.

8 TV prime ............................. advertising slots cost more because more people are watching then.

9 With the rise of the Internet, digital ............................. has become the hot new advertising trend.

10 Advertising companies have to consider the target ............................. of the advertisements they are creating.

## Listening & Reading

**2** **Think of your favourite advertisement. Why do you like it?** 🎧 **Listen to and read the article. Are any of the advertising techniques mentioned used in your favourite advertisement?**

*Like it or not, advertisements have a mysterious power to grab our attention and stick in our mind. Rosin Pringle takes a look at the sneaky techniques advertisers use on customers.*

**1** There's a well-known saying in the retail world: "It pays to advertise." Sometimes, word-of-mouth is enough, when customers tell others about the **positive** experience they've had with a product or service, but for most companies it's necessary to spend money on advertising. And to make sure this is money well spent, it's best to ask the professionals. These days, advertising agencies know as much about the human mind as psychologists. They know about our hopes and fears, and are able to use this information to **create** ads that make ordinary products seem extraordinary.

**3** **Read the article again and match the headings (A-F) to the paragraphs (1-6). Then explain the words in bold.**

A **WE LIKE WHAT WE RECOGNISE**

B **LEAVE IT TO THE EXPERTS**

C **AN AMUSING DISTRACTION**

D **FREE FROM ITS CONTROL**

E **EVERYONE ELSE IS DOING IT**

F **NO TIME TO LOSE**

**4** **THINK** **Choose two types of advertising from the text and describe them in your own words.**

**2** One technique advertisers use is FOMO, or 'fear of missing out'. This often involves ads telling us that something is scarce. For example, they might put a time **limit** on an offer, using phrases like 'while stocks last' or 'for one day only'. These ads make us think that an offer will never appear again, and that someone else will benefit from it unless we act fast. And this often has us **rushing** to the shops!

**3** Another method is the bandwagon technique. To 'jump on the bandwagon' means to join or support something that has become popular, and in the same way, ads like this **encourage** us to buy products because most other people do, or at least that's how that make it seem. This technique plays on our **worry** of not being part of the group. So, these ads often show huge crowds of people with a product, or have phrases like 'Americans love …' or '9 out of 10 people choose …'.

**4** One of the most common and easy ways to **spot** advertising techniques is repetition. And although you might think it would be **annoying** to experience the same ad again and again, it actually works. Why? Well, we tend to feel more comfortable with things that we know something about. So, when we are faced with a choice of products at the supermarket, one known and one unknown, we will usually choose the one we have heard of before.

**5** Humour is another technique that advertisers use. Naturally, everyone enjoys a joke, but studies have also shown that humour in ads is very **effective** at making us think less about the qualities of a product. When we see a funny ad, we often stop thinking about whether it would be a good idea to buy the product – we just learn to associate it with a positive feeling. And that's exactly what advertisers want – for us to buy things without thinking **deeply** about whether we need them or not!

**6** These days, whether it is while walking down the street or looking at media, it is impossible to escape the power of ads. And even though we might be **aware** of some of the techniques advertisers use, they still have plenty of other tricks up their sleeves! So, how can we make better **decisions** as customers? Well, this calls for some common sense. The next time you find yourself putting items you hadn't planned to buy in your shopping trolley, ask yourself why. Do you really need the product, or is it actually the power of advertising?

 **Check these words**

grab sb's attention, sneaky, retail, scarce, support, experience

**5** COLLOCATIONS **Find the words in the text that describe the following. Complete the phrases and use them to make sentences based on the text.**

1 ................... world
2 ................... experience
3 ................... agencies
4 ................... mind
5 ................... limit
6 ................... feeling
7 ................... sense
8 ................... trolley

**6** PREPOSITIONS **Fill in: out, with, from, of, on.**

1 It's a known fact that adverts play ............ our feelings.
2 The ad claimed that nine ............ of ten cats preferred their pet food.
3 Steve wasn't aware ............ the deals available from online shops.
4 The bookshop benefited a lot ............ the ad they placed in the local paper.
5 People associate this brand of chocolate ............ quality.

**7** WORDS EASILY CONFUSED **Choose the correct word. Check in your dictionary.**

1 This greengrocer's always has a wonderful display of farm fresh **produce/products**.
2 I'm afraid you cannot exchange it without a **recipe/receipt**.
3 Everyone in the supermarket was given free chocolate **samples/examples**.
4 Our agency creates ads for a number of world-famous **clients/customers**.

**8** PHRASAL VERBS **Fill in the correct particle. Then try to make up a story using the phrasal verbs in the box.**

> **call after:** to name sb/sth after sb/sth else
> **call back:** to return a phone call
> **call for: 1)** to demand; **2)** to pick up sb
> **call in:** to make a short visit
> **call off:** to cancel

1 Someone is on the other line – I'll call you ............ in five minutes.
2 The campaign was called ............ because of the high cost.
3 Bob called his dog .......... a character in his favourite ad.
4 I'll call ............ you at 10.00 so we can go shopping together.
5 The success of our campaign calls ............ a celebration!
6 Mr Smith called ............ to see you this morning.

## Speaking & Writing

**9** THINK **Which advertising method is the most effective in your opinion?**

**10** ICT **You have been asked to create a video ad for the media for a new piece of technology. Which of the techniques in the text would you use? Write an outline for the ad and present it to the class. The class votes for the best advert.**

91

# Grammar in Use

| BLOG | WHAT'S NEW? | SUPPORT | MEMBERS | 🔍 |

## GEMMA'S
## shopping blog

*America's famous Cyber Monday sales are now yet **another** event in **all** online stores the world over. **Each** year in November, on the Monday after Thanksgiving, online retailers offer reduced prices to attract customers with fantastic bargains. Here are a few hot tips that **every** serious shopper will find useful!*

**Start early**

**Either** a few days ahead of time **or** even the day before is when offers are advertised. The earlier you find out about them the better.

**Be quick**

When the offer goes live (usually at midnight on Sunday) be first in the queue, even if that means staying up late! Clever shoppers don't wait until the morning, and **neither** should you!

**Buy wisely**

Don't buy something just because the price seems low. Plenty of items like TVs and jewellery are often cheaper at other times of the year.

**Do your homework**

**Both** ads and emails give some information on sales and offers. But don't just rely on them. Check out other important details on social media.

**Compare prices**

How much money do you have to pay for the same product at different retailers? **Several** phone apps let you check out the differences and get the best deal to be had anywhere.

*If you've got **another** useful tip, please post a comment!*

## Determiners ▶ pp. GR20-21

**1** **Read the blog entry. Look at the determiners in bold. Which:** *has a positive meaning? has a negative meaning? takes a plural verb? is used with singular countable nouns? takes either a verb in the singular or plural depending on the subject which follows it? refers to an additional part of something already mentioned?*

**2** **Choose the correct item. Give reasons.**

1  **Neither/Either** Pam nor Faye went to the mall.
2  **The whole/All** the shops are closed today.
3  You can buy the product **either/neither** online or at our store.
4  **None/Every** of the shoes I liked were in the sale.
5  **All/None** of our electrical goods are guaranteed for two years, so you don't have to worry!
6  We are proud to say that **each/every** one of our ads this year has been successful.
7  Lucy spent **her whole/all her** money on a new outfit.
8  **Both/Either** Colin and Roger work in marketing.

**3** **Read the sentences and correct the mistakes.**

1  Both Liam and his brother goes to the mall on Saturdays.
2  Either Tracy's nor Lacy's will have the bag you're looking for.
3  The two girls were comparing their new clothes with each one.
4  Mary came out of the shop with lots of shopping bags in every hand.
5  Neither advert are very funny, if you ask me.
6  Sally never shops online, and Matt doesn't neither.
7  All the items in the display is reduced in price.
8  Neither the restaurant nor the café are open on Sundays.

**4** **Rewrite the sentences using the words in brackets.**

1  James doesn't like TV commercials. Susan doesn't either. **(neither)**
.......................................................................
2  Not a single customer was satisfied with the product. **(none)**
.......................................................................
3  Channel X will broadcast the ad or else Channel Y will. **(either)** .......................................................................
4  Using social media is a good way of advertising. Sending emails is too. **(both)**
.......................................................................
5  Marge spent all morning shopping. **(whole)**
.......................................................................
6  We're giving each of our customers a five-pound voucher today. **(every one)**
.......................................................................

**5** 👥👥 **SPEAKING** **Think of shops in your area. Compare them using determiners.**

*Both Allen's and Crystal sell clothes.*
*Neither Allen's nor Crystal is near my house.*

## Countable/Uncountable nouns – Quantifiers & Partitives
▶ pp. GR21-22

**6** a) **List all the nouns in the blog entry in Ex. 1. Which are** *countable*? *uncountable*?

b) **Look at the highlighted words in the blog entry in Ex. 1. Which do we use with countable nouns? uncountable nouns?**

**7 Choose the correct item. Give reasons.**

1 A: I'm making **some/a** tea. Would you like a cup?
   B: Yes please, and **a few/a little** biscuits would be nice!

2 A: I haven't got **many/enough** time to go to the supermarket today.
   B: Don't worry. We've got **plenty/several** of food until tomorrow.

3 A: They show **too much/too many** ads on TV.
   B: I agree. I'm sure **few/little** people bother to watch them.

4 A: There aren't **any/some** more sales in the shops until the summer.
   B: I know. We've got **a couple of/a bit of** months to wait until then.

5 A: They've sold **both/all** the loaves in the baker's.
   B: Really? There was **dozens of/plenty of** bread when I passed by this morning.

6 A: Have you got **many/any** fresh goat's milk today?
   B: Yes, we've got **lots of/lots**.

**8 Fill in:** *both, plenty, a few, much, a lot of, all, a little, a bit, several, many, little, enough*. **Two items are extra.**

1 I can't come shopping with you. I've got ................ work.
2 How .................... butter do you need for the recipe?
3 Don't buy too .................... oranges.
4 .................... milk and cheese are dairy products.
5 Who ate .................... the chocolates in the box?
6 There are ............ of biscuits. Don't buy any.
7 We've got .................... apples. There are enough for an apple pie.
8 There's very .................... time. We'd better hurry.
9 We've got .................... food to feed everyone.
10 Add .................... salt to the soup.

**9 Fill in:** *bag, carton, tin, packet, jar, tube, bowl, box, bottle, pot.*

1) a *tin* of tuna/beans/corn; 2) a .............. of toothpaste/glue/fish paste; 3) a .............. of milk/water/lemonade; 4) a .............. of honey/jam/mayonnaise; 5) a ................ of flour/sugar; 6) a ............... of yogurt/tea/coffee; 7) a ............... of apple juice/milk/buttermilk; 8) a .............. of soup/cereal/ice cream; 9) a .............. of biscuits/crisps/spaghetti; 10) a ............... of cereal/chocolates/washing powder

**10** 👥 **SPEAKING** **You are having a dinner party this Saturday. Decide on what to buy.**

**some/any/no/every & compounds**
▶ p. GR22

**11 Choose the correct item.**

1 In the town centre, there are outdoor advertisements **anywhere/somewhere/everywhere** you look.
2 Does **anyone/nobody/someone** remember a favourite ad from their childhood?
3 There's **anything/nothing/not anything** I'd like better than to go shopping in town and then go **anywhere/nowhere/somewhere** for lunch.
4 What a strange ad! Can **anybody/everybody/nobody** understand it?
5 Would you like **any/some/every** help carrying your shopping bags?
6 **Anyone/Everyone/Someone** in the office clapped when Barry explained his marketing plan.

**12 Fill in** *some/any/no/every* **or one of their compounds.**

1 A: Would you like .................... assistance?
   B: Yes, thank you. Is there .................... I could try these jeans on?
2 A: Has .................... got change for this £20 note?
   B: Hold on. I've got .................... coins in my purse.
3 A: We need to start the meeting. Is .................... here?
   B: Greg said .................... about meeting a client.
4 A: .................... pays in cash anymore. They prefer paying with their cards.
   B: Yes, you see people using them ...................., even in coffee shops.
5 A: How about going .................... in the country this Saturday? I'm fed up going shopping .................... weekend.
   B: OK. There's .................... very interesting in the shops lately anyway.
6 A: Can .................... exchange this jumper for me, please? I've been waiting for five minutes.
   B: I'm sorry, madam. .................... will be with you in just a second.

**13** 👥 **SPEAKING**
**Look at the picture. Act out a dialogue around it. Use** *some/any/no/every* **& their compounds.**

A: *I could do with some new trainers. I haven't got anything to wear at the gym.*
B: *And I want to get something for my brother. Shall we go inside and see if they've got any of those T-shirts he likes?*

# Skills in Action

## Vocabulary

### Online shopping – Customer complaints

**1** **Fill in:** *damaged, cracked, missing, scratched, torn, weak, broken, dead.*

**A** The screen was so badly **1)** ....................... that I couldn't see anything clearly.

**B** Three of the buttons down the front were **2)** ...................., so I couldn't even do it up!

**C** The first time I started to play with it, I found that the battery was completely **3)** ....................... . I had to plug it into the main electricity supply.

**D** When I unpacked it I saw that the glass door was **4)** ....................... right across the front from side to side. I can't cook with it.

**E** The signal is so **5)** ....................... that I can't stay connected to the Internet.

**F** I was looking forward to a good read but no such luck. Several pages in the front and back were badly **6)** ................... .

**G** I bought it specially for my trip, but the handle on top was completely **7)** ....................... . It came off in my hand in two pieces.

**H** The problem is it's got a **8)** ....................... button. Every time I try to take a picture, it sticks.

**2** **THINK** Match the complaints (A-H) in Ex. 1 to the products in the list. Two products do not match. Think of a further problem for each product.

- microwave • printer • washing machine • book
- wireless video game controller • Wi-Fi booster
- shirt • digital camera • suitcase • e-reader

## Listening

**3** You will hear Amanda Brown, the manager of a chain store, explaining to a radio presenter how to return things bought online. For questions 1-6, write one or two words or a number or a date or a time in the gap.

**1** Amanda says that online customers may have ............. ................................... returning products.

**2** You can return a product to Home For You ..................... after delivery.

**3** Home For You stores close at ............. pm on weekdays.

**4** Home For You can collect returned items from ............. .................... different pick-up points.

**5** Items can also be collected from a customer's ............. ....................... .

**6** To return an item, you must show which ....................... .................... you used to pay for it.

## Everyday English

### Complaining about a product

**4** Read the first exchange. How was the customer's problem solved?

Listen and read to find out.

> **E:** Employee          **C:** Customer
>
> **E:** Good afternoon. Customer Service. Trisha speaking. How can I help?
>
> **C:** Hello. I'm calling about a digital camera I ordered from you last week. They delivered it this morning but it was damaged when I unboxed it.
>
> **E:** Oh dear! What's wrong with it exactly?
>
> **C:** The case is cracked.
>
> **E:** Can I have your name and order number?
>
> **C:** Yes, it's Brian Jones. The order number is 773326.
>
> **E:** Could I have your email address as well?
>
> **C:** Sure, it's bjones100@netfix.com.
>
> **E:** Let me email you a return slip, sir. Print it out, fill in the details and return it to us with the camera.
>
> **C:** OK. Then what?
>
> **E:** We can either exchange it for another one or give you a full refund. It's up to you.
>
> **C:** I'd prefer a refund, please.
>
> **E:** Certainly, sir. The email has been sent. Let us know if there is anything else we can do for you.
>
> **C:** No that's OK ... Thank you for your help.
>
> **E:** You're most welcome.

**5** You ordered a pair of jeans online but when they arrived the zip was broken. Use sentences/phrases from the language box to act out a dialogue similar to the one in Ex. 4.

| Complaining about a product | Responding |
|---|---|
| • It was (damaged/broken, etc) when it arrived. <br> • What can be done about it? | • I'm so sorry. <br> • We can sort it out. <br> • What I suggest is (to) ... |

### Intonation: exclamations

**6** **a)** **Fill in:** *what (a/an), how, so* or *such (a/an).*

Listen and check, then repeat.

**1** .................... expensive!

**2** That's ..................... kind of you!

**3** Filming the advert was ................... exciting experience!

**4** .................... busy day!

**b)** Form similar sentences. Mind the intonation.

## Reading & Writing

**7** **a) Read the complaint form and fill in gaps 1-6 with the words in the list.**

• any  • some  • nothing  • someone  • every  • no

| Customer Complaint Form | |
|---|---|
| **Name:** Eliza Harris | **Contact details (phone/email):** 095 035 896 |
| **Product description:** robot vacuum cleaner, model S200 | **Order number:** 5905911 |
| **Location of purchase:** company website | **Date of purchase:** 17/12/.... |
| | **Date of complaint:** 24/12/.... |

**Complaint details:**

I am writing to complain about a robot vacuum cleaner, model S200 that I ordered from your website a week ago.

When it arrived, **1)** .................. of the accessories were missing; there was **2)** .................. spare filter or brush as advertised.

I spoke to **3)** .................. in customer service who assured me they would send the missing accessories immediately. However, I have since become aware of another issue, **4)** .................. time I tried to use it, it started sticking in one spot and wouldn't move around the floor properly. I have tried turning it off and on, and checking the battery, but **5)** .................. seems to work. As a result, I am unable to get **6)** .................. cleaning done unless I do it myself.

I would therefore like to return the vacuum cleaner and exchange it for a new one or a full refund. Thanking you in advance.

**Signature:**

*E. Harris*

**b) What information is included in the details of the complaint and in what order? Choose three of the following:**

• action requested  • writer's opinion of the website
• what was wrong with the product
• action writer plans to take
• when and where the product was purchased/ordered

**8** **Read the sentences.** Which use: *mild, polite language*? *strong, insulting language*? **What language tone does the person use on the form in Ex. 7?**

1 Your prompt attention to this matter would be appreciated.
2 Could you please send me a replacement as soon as possible?
3 I am quite disgusted with the smart TV I bought from you recently.
4 I demand you send me a full refund or I shall take you to court.
5 I am writing to complain about a faulty fitness tracker which I purchased from you.
6 I shall warn people I know not to buy from your website.

## Writing (a complaint form)

**9** **Read the task and answer the questions.**

> You bought an electronic device from an online store. When it was delivered to you, you found it was faulty. Complete a complaint form (120-180 words) to be sent to the store.

1 What are you going to write?
2 Who is going to read it?
3 What should you write about?
4 How many words should you write?

**10** **a)** **BRAINSTORMING** **Make notes under the headings:** *product – when/where purchased – problem – action requested*.

**b)** **Use your notes in Ex. 10a to write your complaint. Follow the plan.**

**Plan**

**Complaint details**
**Para 1:** reason for writing (state complaint, product, when/where purchased)
**Para 2:** complaint in detail
**Para 3:** action requested, closing remarks

**VALUES**

**Politeness**
*Politeness is to human nature what warmth is to wax.*

**Arthur Schopenhauer**

# How did BLACK FRIDAY get its name?

*Ruby Smythe, Sales Editor, reports.*

Thanksgiving in the USA falls on the fourth Thursday in November and the very next day is the Black Friday sales! Although essentially an American invention, it's a date that shoppers **worldwide** look forward to. But why is this particular Friday called black?

Actually, the name originates from a financial crisis, not a shopping day! On Friday 24th September, 1869, two Wall Street financiers, Jay Gould and Jim Fisk, bought up all the nation's gold stocks, hoping to sell them for high prices. Unfortunately, there was a stock market crash and lots of unlucky investors went bankrupt that day.

There is another story about the name Black Friday that links it to retailers. Traditionally, **accounts** were kept using black and red ink. If shops were losing money all year, they would be 'in the red' and the accounts written in red ink. On the day after Thanksgiving, which marks the beginning of the festive shopping period, people would start spending more money and the shops started to 'go into the black'. Retailers **recorded** these **profits** in black ink.

The real story behind Black Friday, however, lies with the Philadelphia police. Historically, the city of Philadelphia is the home of the Army-Navy football game on the Saturday after Thanksgiving. In the 1950s, shoppers would flood the city stores on Friday before staying over for the match the next day. Instead of taking the day off and enjoying a long four-day weekend, the police had a very black Friday indeed. They had to deal with huge **traffic jams, shoplifting** and even violent shoppers.

By the late 1980s, Black Friday sales had **spread** across all America. Today, stores are opening earlier and earlier. In fact, you can go straight out shopping after your Thanksgiving meal. Black Friday is now a four-day event **including** Small Business Saturday/Sunday and **Cyber Monday**. An estimated 60% of Americans visit stores that weekend and even more – around 80% – hunt for **bargains** online.

✓ **Check these words**

originate, financial crisis, stock, crash, investor, bankrupt, retailer, estimated

## Listening & Reading

**1** Look at the picture and read the title. Do you know the answer to the question?

🎧 Listen and read to see if you were right.

**2** Read the text again and complete the summary. Use ONE word in each gap. Then explain the words in bold.

The Black Friday sales are on the day after **1)** .................. celebrations every year in November. The name was first used in Wall Street, where there was a major stock market **2)** .................. one Friday in 1869. When retailers make a **3)** .................. , they 'go into the black', which may explain the name. However, the common explanation is that the **4)** .................. force used to have a 'black' day once a year, controlling shopping crowds and traffic. Since the 1980s, Black Friday has become a national event, taking place over **5)** .................. days.

## Speaking & Writing

**3**  🗨 **THINK** Why do businesses participate in Black Friday? Make a list of reasons and compare with your partner.

**4** **ICT** Collect information about another popular sales period in your country or another country. Make notes under the headings: *Name/Time of year – When first popular – How big today – Other interesting information*. **Write a short magazine article about it.**

## Vocabulary

**1 Choose the correct word.**

1 You can see lots of **hoardings/displays/commercials** on motorways.
2 Look at that amazing **shop/window/product** display!
3 Advertisers use clever **demonstration/marketing/research** strategies.
4 We advertise our product in a 30-second radio **time/spot/audience**.
5 They put a time **mind/sense/limit** on the offer to attract customers.
6 Advertising **jingles/slogans/storylines** should be just a few words long.
7 Advertising companies do their best to **rush/grab/support** our attention when it comes to advertising a product.
8 Can you **spot/encourage/rush** the difference between the two ads?

*(8 x 2 = 16)*

**2 Fill in:** *cracked, weak, scratched, torn, broken*.

1 The door handle was ..................... so the oven wouldn't close.
2 The leather sofa was badly ..................... in the house move.
3 This shirt is ...................; there's a big hole in the sleeve.
4 When the phone arrived, it was ..................... right across the screen.
5 Our smart TV signal is so ..................... that it can't connect to the Internet

*(5 x 2 = 10)*

**3 Choose the correct item.**

1 Customers can call **in/off** to our after-sales service office anytime.
2 Ads often play **on/off** people's feelings in order to sell.
3 He informed us **about/for** this week's special deals.
4 Lots of products are called **for/after** the people who invented them.
5 Shopping online can mean buying **with/at** a cheaper price.

*(5 x 2 = 10)*

## Grammar

**4 Rewrite the sentences using the words in brackets in your notebook.**

1 January is a busy sales month and so is June. **(both)**
2 John or May is giving the presentation. **(either)**
3 We've spent all our budget on advertising. **(whole)**
4 Sheila didn't like any of the jeans in the shop. **(none)**
5 Lynn and her sisters don't shop online. **(neither)**
6 There aren't any ads on this TV channel. **(no)**

*(6 x 4 = 24)*

**5 Choose the correct item.**

1 The stores are **enough/much/too** crowded today.
2 We'll be back in a **few/a little/few** minutes.
3 Would you like **much/some/a bit** help?
4 How **many/much/few** will the repair cost?
5 We've got **several of/any/plenty of** bargains in the store today!

*(5 x 2 = 10)*

**6 Fill in:** *someone, anything, nowhere, everything, some*.

1 I can't find any brown rice; ................... seems to sell it!
2 Would you like ................... help with those parcels?
3 Is there ................... we can do to improve sales?
4 Wait for the sales to buy, when ................... is cheaper.
5 I can't exchange this, sir; ................... has used it!

*(5 x 3 = 15)*

## Everyday English

**7 Match the exchanges.**

1 ☐ Can I be of assistance?
2 ☐ What's the problem?
3 ☐ I'd like a refund, please.
4 ☐ The lid is cracked.
5 ☐ You've been most helpful.

a Glad to be of help.
b I'm so sorry.
c I'd like to return a faulty product.
d All the buttons are missing.
e Certainly, madam.

*(5 x 3 = 15)*

*Total 100*

## Competences

GOOD ✓

VERY GOOD ✓✓

EXCELLENT ✓✓✓

**Lexical Competence**
understand words/phrases related to:
• marketing & advertising
• online shopping – customer complaints

**Reading Competence**
• understand texts related to advertising and shopping (read for key information – match headings to paragraphs; text completion)

**Listening Competence**
• listen to & understand texts related to shopping (listen for specific information – sentence completion)

**Speaking Competence**
• complain about a product

**Writing Competence**
• complete an online complaint form
• write an article about a sales period

| Vocabulary: food; healthy living | Everyday English: Asking for/Giving advice |
|---|---|
| Grammar: clauses of concession; clauses of result/purpose/reason; intensifiers | Writing: a forum post giving advice |

# Health is wealth

CULTURED MEAT

These days, people are becoming more and more **concerned** about what they eat. For one, people are more aware of the importance of having a healthy diet. As a result, many people try to cut down on processed foods, and salt and sugar. But another issue on people's minds these days is the environment, particularly global warming. This means that a lot of people want to eat foods that are produced in an eco-friendly way, and this is where cultured meat comes in.

Cultured meat, also known as cell-based meat, is meat that is produced from animal cells. Basically, a cell is taken from a living animal and then placed in a laboratory under special conditions until a 'culture' appears. When this happens, the cell starts making new cells, and these new cells do the same, until some meat is grown. This meat doesn't look like a chicken breast or beef steak, though. Instead, cultured meat is more **'mushy'** – but this mushy meat can be made into burgers, sausages, chicken nuggets and more. Scientists can choose which types of cells they want to grow, such as muscle cells or fat cells, in order to make different types of meat.

Research into cultured meat started in the early 2000s, and a major breakthrough came in 2013 when the first cell-based burger, made by a group of Dutch scientists, was cooked and eaten in front of an **audience** in London. Since then, a lot of cultured meat companies have been set up, each trying to make the first tasty, cultured meat product that they can sell to the public. It hasn't been easy, though, especially when it comes to cost. One American company says it costs them $50 to make a single chicken nugget! So, it will be some time before cultured meat is **affordable** for customers.

## Vocabulary

### Food

**1** How do carbohydrates, protein, fibre and fat help our body? Use the ideas in the list to discuss with your partner.

- build and repair muscle tissue • give the body energy
- protect the organs • keep the digestive system healthy
- help the body absorb vitamins

**2 a)** Which of the foods in the lists (1-4) are rich in: *carbohydrates*, *protein*, *fibre*, *fat*?

**1** wholegrain bread and cereals, beans, peas, nuts, seeds, lentils, fruit, vegetables ..........................

**2** dairy products, dark chocolate, olives, eggs, avocados, coconuts, oily fish ..........................

**3** seafood, lean meat and poultry, eggs, beans, peas, soy products ..........................

**4** soya, pasta, rice, sugar, honey, soft drinks, bread, potatoes ..........................

**b)** Add one more food to each of the categories in Ex. 2a. Compare with your partner.

## Reading & Listening

**3** What do you think cultured meat is? Do you think it has a positive impact on the environment?
Listen and read to find out.

**4 a)** Read the article and for questions 1-4 choose the best answer (A,B C or D).

**1** What is the writer's main purpose?
- **A** to encourage people to eat cultured meat
- **B** to list the health benefits of cultured meat
- **C** to describe how cultured meat was invented
- **D** to explain why cultured meat could change the world

**2** What does writer say about cultured meat after it has grown?
- **A** It always has a lot of fat.
- **B** It doesn't have a solid form.
- **C** It is ready for customers to eat.
- **D** It looks like a real piece of meat.

But even if it becomes affordable, is there any real **point** in giving people cultured meat instead of real meat? For one, there is the moral reason. Whereas around 70 billion animals are killed each year for meat, cultured meat wouldn't harm a single **creature**. The main reason these companies have started, though, is to save the environment. Right now, animal farming is the cause of 18% of greenhouse gas emissions – more than all cars, trucks, planes and trains put together! This makes it one of the major causes of global warming. But a cultured meat industry would produce 96% fewer greenhouse gas emissions. Also, keeping animals on farms uses up a huge amount of water. For example, around 15,000 litres of water is used to produce just one kilogram of beef! And farming also causes a lot of water and soil pollution from pesticides and fertilisers.

Taking all this into account, cultured meat could play a huge role in saving our planet. It's clear that becoming a **vegan** or vegetarian is better for the environment than being a meat eater – but people have been eating meat for centuries, and this is unlikely to change. But, with cultured meat, we could give people a kinder and more environmentally friendly way to eat the food they enjoy. So, if scientists can make it as tasty and as affordable as real meat, maybe cultured meat will find its way onto our restaurant menus and supermarket shelves in the near future.

> ✓ **Check these words**
>
> culture, breakthrough, set up, moral, pesticide, fertiliser

**3** What is the biggest challenge for cultured meat companies?
  **A** lowering their production costs
  **B** making their products taste nice
  **C** getting permission to sell their products
  **D** persuading people to buy their products

**4** According to the writer, animal farming
  **A** doesn't require a lot of water.
  **B** hasn't had a big impact on global warming.
  **C** is more harmful to the environment than transport.
  **D** causes more than half of all greenhouse gas emissions.

**b)** Explain the words in bold.

**5** PREPOSITIONS  Fill in: *about, in, on, of (x2)*.

**1** Tim should be more concerned .............. the amount of sugar in his diet.

**2** Most people these days are aware .............. the dangers of a high-salt diet.

**3** There's no point .............. going to the supermarket – we can order what we need online .

**4** An unhealthy diet is the leading cause .............. heart disease worldwide.

**5** The importance of eating healthily is .............. most people's minds these days.

**6** COLLOCATIONS  Find and complete the words in the text that describe the following. Then use the phrases to make sentences.

**1** ....................... diet        **5** ....................... breast
**2** ....................... foods       **6** ....................... reason
**3** ....................... warming     **7** ....................... farming
**4** ....................... cells       **8** ....................... pollution

**7** WORDS EASILY CONFUSED  Choose the correct word. Check in your dictionary.

**1** The restaurant **raises/rises** its prices every few years.

**2** It was difficult to make a **choice/option** between the ice cream and the cheesecake.

**3** A lack of vitamin D in your diet can greatly **affect/effect** your mood.

**4** Peter has a large garden where he **produces/develops** his own vegetables.

**8** PHRASAL VERBS  Fill in the correct particle(s).

> **cut down (on sth):** to eat, drink or use less of sth
> **cut in:** to interrupt sb/sth
> **cut off: 1)** to isolate sb/sth; **2)** to stop providing sth; **3)** to disconnect sb (while on the phone)
> **(be) cut out (for sth):** to have the qualities to do sth

**1** When Bob lived in the countryside, he felt really cut ................... from society.

**2** We seem to have been cut ............... during our last call.

**3** Frank was warned to cut ................... the amount of sugar in his diet.

**4** Jack didn't pay the bill, so they cut ................... his electricity.

**5** I don't think Laura is cut ................... to be a chef.

**6** I'm sorry to cut ..................., but did either of your order the duck?

## Speaking & Writing

**9** 💬 THINK 🎧 Listen to a monologue and note down the negatives of cultured meat. Then, read the fourth paragraph of the text again and note down the positives of cultured meat. Use your notes from both sources, as well as your own ideas, to have a class debate based on the following statement: *"Cultured meat is the food of the future."* Record your debate.

**10** ICT  Collect information about other possible foods of the future, e.g. insects, seaweed. Make notes. Prepare and give a presentation.

# Grammar in Use

## Goji Berry
### A True Superfood

Due to the fact that they are so nutritious, goji berries are fast becoming the most popular superfood on the market. While most fruits don't contain much protein, these small red berries are packed with it. In fact, goji berries have so much protein that you can get 14% of your daily recommended intake from a 100-gram serving. But that's not all! Goji berries also contain absolutely huge amounts of vitamins A, C, calcium and iron. Originally, goji berries were only grown in the Himalaya region in Asia, but now many countries around the world grow them so that they can be sold fresher and for a cheaper price to local consumers.

## Clauses of concession

**1** Read the theory. Find two examples in the text.

### Clauses of concession ▷ p. GR22

Clauses of concession are used to express contrast. They are introduced with: *but*, *although*, *even though*, *though*, *in spite of*, *despite*, *while/whereas*, *yet/still*.
*Despite its bitter taste, Peter drank all of the tea.*

**2** Choose the correct item.

**1** My sister is a vegetarian **whereas/however** I eat meat regularly.

**2** I've been exercising a lot recently, **yet/while** I haven't lost much weight.

**3** Mary made fish soup **but/in spite of** her children didn't like it.

**4** **Still/Despite** being slightly overweight, Steve is a great footballer.

**5** I eat a lot of dairy products like cheese and yoghurt. I never drink milk, **though/although**.

**6** **Although/Whereas** John had been taking the medicine for a week, he still didn't feel any better.

**3** Complete the sentences.

**1** Jason went to bed early but he feels tired today.
Although ......................................................... .

**2** Sue is really fit but her husband doesn't do any exercise at all.
Whereas ......................................................... .

**3** Jessica has taken up yoga but she still feels stressed.
In spite ......................................................... .

**4** George doesn't like vegetables but he tries to eat at least one portion a day.
Despite ......................................................... .

**5** Greta is a talented cook but she rarely makes dinner for her family. Though ......................................................... .

**4** 🗣 **SPEAKING** Think of a person you both know. Talk about them using clauses of concession.

A: *Although Bob works long hours, he still finds time to exercise.*

B: *Despite the long hours, Laura loves working as a chef.*

**5** Read the theory. Identify the types of clauses in the highlighted sections in the text in Ex. 1.

### Clauses of result/purpose/reason
▷ pp. GR23-24

**Clauses of result** are used to express result. They are introduced with: *such/so … that*, *as a result*, *therefore*, *consequently*. *Dr Hanson is so popular that it's sometimes difficult to get an appointment with him.*
**Clauses of purpose** are used to explain why somebody does something. They are introduced with: *to-infinitive*, *in order (not) to*, *so as (not) to*, *so that*, *in order that*, *in case*. *Keith has started cycling to work so that he can lose some weight.*
**Clauses of reason** explain why something happens. They are introduced with: *because*, *since/as*, *the/a reason for/why*, *now (that)*, *for*. *The reason why he avoids eating pizza is that he's allergic to dairy products.*

**6** Choose the correct item, A, B or C.

**1** Jack went to the market ........... buy some fresh fruit and vegetables.
**A** in order to    **B** so that    **C** since

**2** James tries to exercise daily ........... he can stay in good shape.
**A** therefore    **B** in case    **C** so that

**3** Ann's job as a supermarket manager is ........... stressful that she's considering changing careers.
**A** as    **B** so    **C** such

**4** Paul broke his ankle. ..........., he couldn't play football for six months.
**A** The reason for    **B** Such    **C** As a result

**5** ........... Lucy got promoted is because she is hard working.
**A** Consequently    **B** Now that
**C** The reason why

**6** .......... you're better, you can come with us on the skiing trip.
**A** Now that    **B** In order that    **C** For

**7** Fill in: *in order not to*, *the reason for*, *such*, *in case*, *now that*, *therefore*, *as*, *so that*.

1 Peter stayed home from work ................................... spread his cold around the office.
2 Lisa is a strict vegetarian. ..................................., she won't eat this meal you've prepared.
3 Paul was in .................................. terrible pain that he couldn't stop screaming.
4 Greg's nervous .................................. he has just received the results of his blood tests.
5 Take a book with you .................................. you have to wait to see the dentist.
6 .................................. Jane is a qualified nurse, she plans to look for work abroad.
7 .................................. Kevin's bad mood is that he has to work a double shift at the hospital.
8 Eat plenty of fruit and vegetables .................................. you have enough nutrients in your diet.

**8** Rewrite the sentences as one sentence using the word(s) in brackets.

1 He went to bed early. He didn't want to feel tired at work. **(so as not to)**
....................................................................
....................................................................
2 Lisa's not joining us at the cinema. She's got an upset stomach. **(the reason why)**
....................................................................
....................................................................
3 Take some aspirin with you on the trip. You might get a headache. **(in case)**
....................................................................
....................................................................
4 Brian had terrible backache. He had to take the day off work. **(such)**
....................................................................
....................................................................
5 The runners drank lots of water. They didn't want to get dehydrated. **(so that)**
....................................................................
....................................................................

**9** 👥 SPEAKING Start a sentence. Your partner completes it using words/phrases that express result, purpose or reason.

A: *We ate out at an Italian restaurant yesterday …*
B: *… since we wanted to celebrate my brother's promotion at work. We arrived at the restaurant early …*
A: *… so that we could get a table. etc*

**10** Read the theory. Find an example in the text in Ex. 1.

## Intensifiers ▶p. GR24

We use words like *very*, *really*, *extremely*, etc. to make adjectives stronger. *He is **very careful** with what he eats.*
We do not normally use *very* with strong adjectives e.g. *awful*, *brilliant*, *amazing*, *delicious*, *disgusting*, *excellent*, *huge*, *enormous*, *ideal*, *wonderful*, etc.
Instead, we can use intensifiers such as *absolutely*, *completely*, *exceptionally*, *utterly*, *really*, *quite*, *totally*. *This dish is **absolutely delicious**.*
We can use *a lot*, *a great deal*, *a good deal*, *much*, *far*, etc with comparative adjectives. *Tom is **a lot healthier** than me.*

**11** Choose the word in bold that does not fit in each sentence.

1 The city's main hospital is **really/absolutely/extremely** huge.
2 The meal was **totally/utterly/very** awful.
3 A piece of fruit is a **really/far/much** better snack than a bar of chocolate.
4 Laura is **a lot/extremely/a great deal** fitter than me.
5 Tony is a(n) **lot/really/exceptionally** brilliant chef.
6 This restaurant serves **completely/really/very** nice vegetarian food.

**12** Use one of the words in brackets to make the sentences stronger.

1 The cakes Sarah makes are amazing. **(quite/ a great deal)**
*The cakes Sarah makes are **quite** amazing.*
2 George felt awful when he had the flu. **(very/absolutely)**
3 The care John received at the hospital was excellent. **(really/extremely)**
4 The rooms here are more spacious than in most hospitals. **(far/completely)**
5 Getting enough sleep each night is important for your health. **(extremely/a lot)**
6 We've got some brilliant news – Kate is pregnant! **(very/totally)**

**13** 👥 SPEAKING Say a sentence. Your partner makes it stronger.

A: *John works hard at the gym.*
B: *That's true. He works **extremely** hard.*

# Skills in Action

## Vocabulary

### Healthy living

**1** **a)** **Fill in:** *floss, limit, eliminate, consume, maintain, exercise, remove, apply.* **Check in your dictionary.**

1) ........................ a healthy weight by being active and following a balanced diet.
2) ........................ sunscreen in sunny weather, especially if you have fair skin.
3) ........................ for at least 30 minutes a day, including both cardio and strength training.
4) ........................ at least five servings of fruit and vegetables per day.
5) ........................ and brush your teeth twice a day for at least two minutes.
6) ........................ your use of devices before bedtime and get eight hours of sleep a night.
7) ........................ sugary fizzy drinks from your diet completely.
8) ........................ yourself from stressful situations as much as possible and take care of your mental health.

**b)** **THINK** **Think of two more healthy living tips for teens.**

## Listening

**2** **You will hear four people talking about teen health. Listen and match the statements (A-E) to the speakers (1-4). One statement does not fit.**

A  I continue doing something that I know is unhealthy.
B  I didn't act fast enough to change my unhealthy lifestyle.
C  I recently gave up a bad habit.
D  At first, I didn't think I needed medical help.
E  I thought I was healthier than I actually am.

| | |
|---|---|
| Speaker 1 | |
| Speaker 2 | |
| Speaker 3 | |
| Speaker 4 | |

## Everyday English

### Asking for/Giving advice

**3** **Read the first exchange in the dialogue. What advice do you think Jane will get?**
**Listen and read to find out.**

| | |
|---|---|
| **Sam:** | Are you looking forward to going backpacking in Southeast Asia next month, Jane? |
| **Jane:** | Yes, I guess so. I'm just a bit worried about things going wrong while I'm there. I mean, what if I have a health problem or something? |
| **Sam:** | Hmm, well, if I were in your shoes, I'd definitely look into getting some vaccines before your trip. This way, you would protect yourself from catching certain diseases. I think it's what most people do when they travel there. |
| **Jane:** | I hadn't thought of that. And what is your advice about travel insurance? To be honest I'm not sure it's worth the money. |
| **Sam:** | If you ask me, you should definitely get it! It would mean your health expenses would be covered in case of an emergency. |
| **Jane:** | Thanks for your advice, Sam. |
| **Sam:** | No problem. I hope you enjoy your trip. |

**4** **Imagine you want to get fitter. Use the prompts, or your own ideas, and the phrases in the language box to act out a dialogue similar to the one in Ex. 3.**

• limit sugary foods and drinks ➡ consume nutritious meals
• start an exercise routine ➡ build strength

| Asking for advice | Giving advice |
|---|---|
| • What is your advice about ...? | • If you ask me, ... |
| • Would it be a good idea to ...? | • A good idea would/ might be to ... |

### Intonation: direct/indirect questions

**5** **a)** **Listen to the examples and repeat. Note the difference in intonation.**

**Direct question:** *"Where is James?"*
**Indirect question:** *"Could you tell me where James is?"*

**b)** **Rewrite the questions (1-4) as indirect questions. Use the words/phrases in brackets. Then say the indirect questions to your partner.**

1  Where is the nearest hospital? **(Would you mind)**
2  When is Frank having his operation? **(Do you know)**
3  Who is that man over there? **(Could)**
4  How can I reach Bob? **(Do you have any idea)**

## Reading & Writing

**6** **a)** Read the forum entry and fill in the gaps with the words derived from the words in brackets.

Staying
SAFE
in the Kitchen

Hi everyone! In this forum, I've read a lot of posts with
1) ........................... (impress) recipes, but I've never come
across a post about health and 2) ........................... (safe) in
the kitchen. So, here are some tips about how you can stay
safe while cooking.
**First**, wash your hands before you start cooking. They might
be covered in germs, so it's important to clean them before
you 3) ........................... (hand) food. Also, while you're
cooking, wash your hands 4) ........................... (immediate)
after you touch raw meat.
**Secondly**, there are some steps you can take to avoid
accidents in the kitchen. For example, you should turn pot
handles away from the front of the cooker, so that you don't
bump into them 5) ........................... (accident). And make
sure to keep the floor dry – you don't want to slip while
you're carrying a pot of boiling water.
**Lastly**, you need to be prepared if something goes wrong
in the kitchen. For example, it's common to get minor
burns, so always have some cream close by. And most
6) ........................... (important), get a fire extinguisher and
learn how to use it.
So, that's it. These tips might not help you make a
7) ........................... (taste) cheesecake, but they *will* keep
you safe in the kitchen.

Leave a comment if you can think of anything else!

**b)** What is each paragraph about?

 **Writing Tip**

**Forum posts**
Forum posts are public messages on the Internet. They
include a title that lets readers know what the post is
about. Forum posts often include an invitation for readers
to reply to the post with their comments. They are usually
informal in style. We can put a word or phrase in **bold** or
*italics* to emphasise it.

**7** Has the writer in the forum post in Ex. 6
used bold text and italics? What do they
want to emphasise? Do you think the title is
appropriate?

## Writing (a forum post)

**8** Read the task and answer the questions.

You are a member of an online forum about
world travel. Write a forum post giving health
advice for people who plan to travel abroad. Write
your forum post in 120-180 words.

1 What are you going to write? Who for?
2 What should you write about? How many paragraphs
should you include?
3 How many words should your piece of writing be?

**9** **a)** **BRAINSTORMING** Match the pieces of
advice (1-3) to the reasons/expected results
(a-c).

1 ☐ don't eat in dirty restaurants
2 ☐ get vaccines before your trip
3 ☐ take out travel insurance

a health expenses covered in case of emergency
b protect yourself from catching certain diseases
c help avoid getting food poisoning and certain illnesses

**b)** Use your answers to write your forum
post. Follow the plan. Give your post an
appropriate title.

**Plan**

Title
**Para 1:** introduce the topic
**Para 2:** first piece of advice with reasons/expected
results
**Para 3:** second piece of advice with reasons/expected
results
**Para 4:** third piece of advice with reasons/expected
results
**Para 5:** conclusion; invite reader to post comments

**VALUES**

**Health**
*A life without health is like a river
without water.*
**Maxime Lagacé**

▶ **VIDEO**

# The NHS

1. ☐ Ask a British person what they are most proud of about their country, and you will get a variety of answers: some might say the structure of their government, their famous writers and artists, or maybe even their sports teams. But something else that would definitely be **mentioned** is the NHS.

2. ☐ The NHS (National Health Service) is the healthcare system of the UK. It was **launched** on 5th July, 1948 by the Health Secretary Aneurin Bevan, who believed that **quality** healthcare should be available to everyone, both rich and poor, in the country. Consequently, healthcare became free in the UK, and all hospitals, doctors and nurses became part of the NHS.

3. ☐ Today, apart from dental and optical care, most healthcare remains free for all UK **residents**. Funds for the NHS come from government taxes and National Insurance contributions, which most workers have to pay. On average, this means each British person pays around £2,000 per year to the NHS.

4. ☐ Since its beginnings, the NHS has done a lot to improve the health of the British public. Diseases such as polio and tuberculosis have been wiped out, while life expectancy has risen to 81 years old. Also, many new treatments have been developed by the NHS, such as in vitro fertilisation (IVF), a fertility treatment, which brought the world's 'first test-tube baby' in 1978. And in 1994, the NHS Organ Donor Register was **set up**, which has so far saved around 50,000 lives.

5. ☐ Despite its many successes, the NHS has still received some criticism. Since it is a public service, and governments usually try to keep taxes low, the NHS has to work on a **limited** budget. As a result, there is sometimes a lack of staff and equipment in hospitals, and some treatments are not available in some areas of the country. Some people even have to pay for private healthcare instead.

6. ☐ Nevertheless, most British people say the positives of the NHS outweigh its negatives. British people know that they will always receive healthcare from the best doctors and nurses. For this reason, the NHS holds a **unique** place in the hearts of the British public.

**DID YOU KNOW?**
- The NHS helps over 1 million patients every 36 hours!
- The NHS employs around 1.7 million people in the UK!
- During the opening ceremony of the London 2012 Olympics, one part celebrated the NHS!

✓ **Check these words**

structure, healthcare, National Insurance contributions, wipe out, life expectancy, in vitro fertilisation (IVF), budget

## Listening & Reading

1 **What is the NHS? How are these names related to it:** *Aneurin Bevan, in vitro fertilisation, Organ Donor Register*?

🎧 Listen and read to find out. Then explain the words in bold.

2 **Choose the most suitable heading from the list (A-H) for each paragraph (1-6). Two headings are extra.**

| | |
|---|---|
| **A** Working in the System | **F** One Man's Vision |
| **B** Giving Peace of Mind | **G** Admired by the Nation |
| **C** An Unknown Future | **H** Problems with the System |
| **D** A List of Achievements | |
| **E** How It's Paid For | |

## Speaking & Writing

3 💬 THINK Which do you think is better for a country to have, a public healthcare system like the NHS, or a private healthcare system, in which people must pay doctors, hospitals, etc when they need treatment? Have a class debate.

4 **ICT** Collect information about the healthcare system in your country. Make notes under the headings: *how it started – services it provides – achievements – problems – what citizens think of it.* Write a short article about it. Use subheadings. Tell the class.

## Vocabulary

### 1 Choose the correct item.

1 To protect your skin, **absorb/apply/consume** sunscreen in sunny weather.

2 I think you should **limit/maintain/eliminate** dairy products from your diet.

3 Many people become vegan for **affordable/moral/limited** reasons.

4 Under **processed/certain/concerned** conditions, the cells start growing.

5 The scientists celebrated making a(n) **active/quality/major** breakthrough.

6 Ann **builds/develops/produces** jam from the fruit she grows in her garden.

7 Fat helps the body by protecting our **organs/tissues/systems**.

*(7 x 2 = 14)*

### 2 Match the words to form collocations.

1 ☐ muscle       a bread
2 ☐ oily         b system
3 ☐ dark         c drinks
4 ☐ wholegrain   d tissue
5 ☐ digestive    e meat
6 ☐ dairy        f chocolate
7 ☐ lean         g fish
8 ☐ soft         h products

*(8 X 2 = 16)*

### 3 Choose the correct item.

1 Are you aware **of/in** the benefits of a vegan diet?

2 There's no point **in/on** cooking if the children aren't hungry.

3 Most people are concerned **with/about** eating too much processed food.

4 Bill doesn't enjoy working outdoors, so I don't think he is cut **out/down** to be a farmer.

5 You should try to cut **down/out** on the amount of fried food you eat.

*(5 X 3 = 15)*

## Grammar

### 4 Join the sentences using the words in brackets.

1 She went on a diet. She didn't lose any weight. **(although)**

2 She eats so much protein. She's a bodybuilder. **(reason)**

3 Lisa's a vegetarian. Her brother eats a lot of meat. **(whereas)**

4 Tim is a fitness trainer. He eats a lot of fast food. **(spite)**

5 Take a bottle of water with you. You feel thirsty. **(case)**

*(5 X 4 = 20)*

### 5 Choose the correct item.

1 The trainer created a(n) **totally/extremely** ideal training programme for me.

2 The doctor who treated me was **really/a good deal** friendly.

3 Greg's classmates gave him a(n) **very/absolutely** enormous get-well card.

4 This medicine is **totally/far** more useful for your problem.

5 The food in the restaurant was **very/absolutely** disgusting.

*(5 X 3 = 15)*

## Everyday English

### 6 Match the exchanges.

1 ☐ What steps should I take to get fit?

2 ☐ If you ask me, you should get more sleep.

3 ☐ What is your advice about giving up sugar?

4 ☐ I'm not sure getting a gym membership is worth the money.

a If I were in your shoes, I'd try to cut down rather than eliminating it completely.

b A good idea might be to exercise more.

c If you ask me, it's probably not.

d I hadn't thought of that.

*(4 X 5 = 20)*

*Total 100*

## Competences

GOOD ✓

VERY GOOD ✓✓

EXCELLENT ✓✓✓

**Lexical Competence**
understand words/phrases related to:
• food
• healthy living

**Reading Competence**
• understand texts related to food and health (read for specific information – multiple choice; read for key information – match headings to paragraphs)

**Listening Competence**
• listen to and understand monologues related to healthy living (listen for specific information – multiple matching)

**Speaking Competence**
• ask for/give advice

**Writing Competence**
• write a forum post giving health advice for travelling abroad
• write an article about a healthcare system

# Values: Commitment

## lifestyle lessons

*Lifestyle coach Wendy answers your questions …*

Home▾ **Ask Question**▾ Questions▾ User▾ Contact us   **About Us** | **Join Now**

**Q: How can I stay committed to a healthy lifestyle?**

I've lost count of the number of times I've tried to change my lifestyle for the better. I've read lots of books on how to lead a healthy lifestyle, so I know all about eating healthily, exercising regularly and getting enough sleep … the problem is, after a few weeks of following a new lifestyle, I always return to my old bad **habits**.

*Tim Mack, office worker*

**A:** First of all, Tim, I'm delighted to hear that you want to change your habits and improve your life. Staying committed to a healthy lifestyle, though, can be difficult. Here are some tips to help you **keep on track**!

### Be realistic

The first step to a healthier lifestyle is to make a **realistic** lifestyle plan. This should be an **uncomplicated** plan that you can stick to easily for a long time. So, instead of planning to do **intensive** exercise every day, plan to do some light exercise four times a week – something that you look forward to doing rather than **dread**! The same goes for diet. For example, don't try to avoid desserts completely – allow yourself some 'cheat days'. If you start with unrealistic goals, you'll be far more likely to give up quickly.

### Record your progress

To stay committed to a lifestyle plan, it's important for you to be able to see your **progress**. If losing weight is your goal, weigh yourself at the start of your plan and then every week or so, and write down the number in a journal. You can do the same for exercise – with the number of push-ups you can do, or the number of miles you can run, for example. When you see that your lifestyle changes are making a difference, you'll feel **motivated** to continue.

### Accept mistakes

Nobody's perfect, so don't expect yourself to stick to your lifestyle plan perfectly, either. I've seen it many times with my clients – people **abandoning** their lifestyle plans just because they've made mistakes. But even if you eat unhealthily at a party or forget to go for a run one day, don't throw out your lifestyle plan completely. In fact, even if you have a bad week or month, you can still **turn it around**. Basically, don't have an 'all or nothing' mindset. Accept you will make mistakes and give yourself a fresh start each morning.

**Read more**

**1** Read the question (Q) at the beginning of the advice column. What advice do you think might be given?

🎧 Listen and read to find out.

**2** Read the text again and decide if the sentences are *T* (True), *F* (False) or *DS* (Doesn't Say). Then explain the words/phrases in bold.

1 Tim has done some research on how to live healthily.    .........
2 Wendy advises Tim to have a very challenging exercise routine.    .........
3 Wendy says Tim should write about his feelings in a journal.    .........
4 Some of Wendy's clients have failed to follow their lifestyle plans.    .........
5 Most people will break their diet at some point.    .........

**3** THINK Think of two other situations where it is important to show commitment.

**4** Create a lifestyle plan for yourself. Write a short text under the following headings: *diet – exercise – sleep – how you will stick to your plan*. **Present your plan to the class.**

# Public Speaking Skills

**1** Read the task. What type of speech does it ask for: *informative*, *persuasive* or *ceremonial*?

You are a lifestyle coach. Give a talk to a group of college students on healthy habits.

**2** Listen to and read the model. Then, with a partner, decide what non-verbal communication you could use at the underlined parts of the speech. Then present your speech to the class. One partner reads the model while the other makes the gestures.

**3** **ICT** Do some research about the best way to prepare for an exam. Prepare and then give a presentation to the rest of the class on how they should be in the best possible shape for their next exam. Use appropriate non-verbal communication.

Hello, everyone. My name's Kim Lo. Today, I'm going to talk about some healthy habits you can add to your daily routine – <u>little</u> things that can give you <u>big</u> rewards. So, let's get started.

First, a survey. How many of you got at least seven hours' sleep last night? <u>Hands up</u>. Today, around 20% of teens and young adults get less than 5 hours of sleep a night, while the average is around 6.5 hours. And there are negative consequences to this. For one, a lack of sleep weakens your immune system, so you're more likely to get sick. It has also been linked to weight gain and can even cause memory loss. We should all try to get at least seven hours of sleep a night, because it's so important to your health.

Now, <u>let's move on</u> to nutrition. We all know about the importance of a balanced diet, but something we often forget about is water. It's very important to drink enough liquids. When we are thirsty, we often confuse this feeling with being hungry, so we tend to overeat. Also, dehydration can cause low blood pressure and skin problems. But there's a huge difference between drinking water and drinking other liquids like fizzy drinks and energy drinks. These are usually full of sugar, so they're very <u>bad</u> for your health. My advice is to make water your number one drink – and try to get around eight glasses a day. That's not so hard, is it?

Lastly, I want to give you an exercise tip. Most experts advise us to exercise at least four times a week for around thirty minutes. So, a lot of people jog or cycle, and this is great, but we shouldn't forget about strength training. That's right, <u>it isn't just for bodybuilders</u> – it should be part of <u>everyone's</u> exercise routine! It keeps your bones and muscles healthy, it's good for your heart, and it helps you control your weight. And you don't need to lift weights. Exercises that use your own body's weight, like push-ups and squats, are very effective.

So, today I've presented you with three healthy habits that a lot of us don't always think about. I think that if you can get enough sleep, drink enough water, and do some strength training, you can really improve your <u>whole life</u>.

# CLIL: PSHE

## Reading & Listening

**1** **a)** **How much do you know about road safety? Do the quiz.**

**1** When is it OK to use a **handheld** mobile device while driving?

A when you are stopped at a traffic light
B when you are waiting in traffic
C when you are safely parked somewhere

**2** Which statement is TRUE about speed limits?

A It's always safe to travel at the speed limit.
B You should travel as close as possible to the speed limit.
C Travelling at the speed limit isn't safe under some conditions.

**3** Which age group has the highest rate of car accidents around the world?

A 16-29    B 30-59    C 60+

**4** Where do most road accidents happen?

A on country roads
B in city centres
C on motorways

**5** If you ride a motorbike, the law **requires** you to wear

A leather motorcycle boots.
B an **approved** helmet.
C illuminated clothing at all times.

**6** What should cyclists do at a junction with a stop sign?

A stop cycling
B slow down
C continue if the road is empty

**7** It is illegal to drive through a zebra crossing when a pedestrian

A is waiting at the side of the road to cross.
B has already started crossing the road.
C has held up their hand to cross the road.

**8** Which of the following activities done by pedestrians is the most dangerous?

A texting
B talking on the phone
C listening to music with earphones

**b)** 🎧 **Listen and check your answers. Then explain the words in bold.**

---

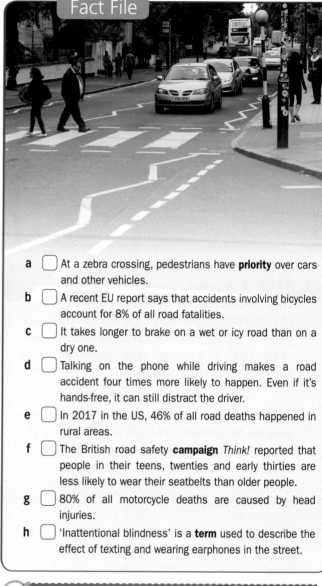

**Fact File**

**a** ☐ At a zebra crossing, pedestrians have **priority** over cars and other vehicles.

**b** ☐ A recent EU report says that accidents involving bicycles account for 8% of all road fatalities.

**c** ☐ It takes longer to brake on a wet or icy road than on a dry one.

**d** ☐ Talking on the phone while driving makes a road accident four times more likely to happen. Even if it's hands-free, it can still distract the driver.

**e** ☐ In 2017 in the US, 46% of all road deaths happened in rural areas.

**f** ☐ The British road safety **campaign** *Think!* reported that people in their teens, twenties and early thirties are less likely to wear their seatbelts than older people.

**g** ☐ 80% of all motorcycle deaths are caused by head injuries.

**h** ☐ 'Inattentional blindness' is a **term** used to describe the effect of texting and wearing earphones in the street.

✓ **Check these words**

speed limit, motorway, account for, fatality, brake, distract, rural

**2** **Read the fact file and label each fact (a-h) according to the questions (1-8) in Ex. 1a they refer to.**

## Speaking & Writing

**3** 👥 THINK **Which of the rules/laws mentioned in the quiz is most important to you? Why?**

**4** 💬 **ICT** **Collect more information about road safety and write your own quiz. Think about:** *motorists, motorcyclists, cyclists, pedestrians.* **Swap your quiz with another group and do it. How many answers did you get right?**

# CLIL: Biology

## Reading & Listening

**1** How does our voice work?
🎧 Listen and read to find out.

**2** Read the text and label the diagram. Use the highlighted words/phrases.

In today's world, we communicate a lot through email and social media, but let's not forget about our most basic **communication tool** – our voice. It's a tool we use every day, but how does it actually work? Basically, when we produce speech, three things are working together in our bodies: the power source, the vibrator and the resonator.

### The power source

The air that we breathe is the power source behind our voice. When we breathe in, our lungs fill up with air. As we breathe out, with the help of the diaphragm below, this air **rushes** up through the trachea, or windpipe. Here, it provides the energy for the vocal folds, or cords, to work. The stronger the **stream** of air, the more **powerful** the sound we make.

### The vibrator

Our larynx, commonly called the voice box, sits on top of the windpipe. It is here that our two vocal folds are **situated**. There is one on either side of the larynx, opening and closing much like a pair of curtains. They open when we breathe in, and close when we **swallow** food or speak. When the air from our lungs travels up and reaches the folds, they close and then vibrate. There can be between 100 and 1,000 vibrations per second, depending on the pitch of our voice. The loudness or softness of the sound is controlled by muscles in the larynx, which create just the right amount of tension in the vocal folds.

✔ **Check these words**

power source, vibrator, resonator, vibration, pitch, tension, resonance tract, throat, sinuses

### The resonator

When the vocal folds vibrate, they produce a simple buzzing sound, a bit like the sound of a bee. So how does this buzzing get **transformed** into the actual words we use to communicate? The answer is through the resonance tract, which includes the nasal cavity (nose), oral cavity (mouth), throat and sinuses. When the buzzing sound occurs in our vocal folds, muscles in our throat and tongue come into play to help form that buzzing into recognisable sounds. These are **released** through our mouth as speech. We can compare it to someone blowing into the mouthpiece of a trumpet and producing clear musical notes that come out at the other end.

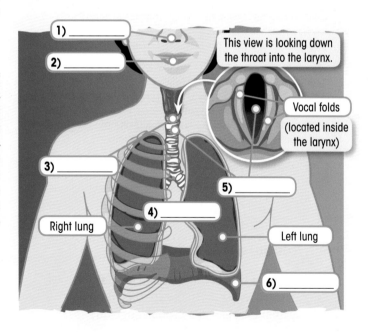

1) _____
2) _____

This view is looking down the throat into the larynx.

Vocal folds (located inside the larynx)

3) _____

5) _____

4) _____

Right lung

Left lung

6) _____

**3** Read the text again and answer the questions. Then explain the words/phrases in bold.

1 How do the vocal folds get the energy to work?
2 How does air travel up from our lungs?
3 Where is the voice box?
4 Where are the vocal folds?
5 What can we do when the vocal folds are closed?
6 What sound do the vocal folds make?
7 How does the resonance tract help us to form words?

## Speaking & Writing

**4** Use the diagram to explain how our voice works.

**5** 💬 ICT Collect information about how our ears work. Use a diagram. Present your findings to the class.

# CLIL: History

# Education in Victorian England

**1** Up until the 19th century, most people in England did not have access to a formal education. A large number of people could not read or write. This was before the Industrial Revolution and many people made their living as agricultural workers and had no need to read. Children in these days helped to **support** their families as early as they could. Boys went to work in the fields or learnt a trade from a young age and girls helped with cooking, cleaning and childcare in the home. Only wealthy families could afford the **luxury** of an education and they hired a tutor or a governess to come to their home or paid to attend a private school.

**2** However, during Queen Victoria's reign, free schools for poor children, both boys and girls, started to appear. Many of these children continued working, but got **time off** to attend school for a few hours each day. Classes had up to 70 or 80 pupils. Boys and girls sat separately and often used separate entrances.

**3** School subjects were mainly the '3 Rs', that is, reading, writing and arithmetic. There was also a lesson called 'drill', which was an early form of PE. Later, there were woodwork lessons for boys and sewing lessons for girls. Teachers were usually unmarried women and very few had **academic qualifications**. The pay wasn't very good, so men preferred to work in other jobs.

**4** Even though children got a basic education in Victorian England, very few went to secondary school or university. Universities had been established in the UK since medieval times but only men could attend. They studied arithmetic, geometry, astronomy, music theory, grammar, **logic**, and rhetoric and all the lessons were taught in Latin. In the 18th century a number of medical schools were established at universities and hospitals in Edinburgh, Glasgow and London.

**5** However, it wasn't until the mid 1800s that the higher education revolution took place. Many cities founded Mechanics Institutes that offered practical knowledge of the arts and sciences connected with **manufacturing**, mining and agriculture. The first women's college opened in 1849 and taught subjects including astronomy, geography, geology and fine art. In 1878 the University of London offered degrees in all the usual subjects – previously only offered to men – to women for the first time. It wasn't until the First World War, though, that women were allowed to attend a medical college in London.

**6**

| | |
|---|---|
| **1833** | The government awards grants to build schools for the poor across England and Wales. |
| **1844** | Children working in factories are allowed six half-days a week to go to school. |
| **1878** | The University of London accepts female students. |
| **1880** | School is made compulsory for children aged 5-10. |

✓ **Check these words**

agricultural, governess, rhetoric, grant, compulsory

## Reading & Listening

**1** Read the title of the text and look at the pictures. What do you think the education system was like in Victorian England?
🎧 Listen and read to find out.

**2** Read the text again and match the headings (A-I) to the paragraphs (1-6). Three headings are extra. Then explain the words/phrases in bold.

| | | | |
|---|---|---|---|
| **A** | What was taught | **F** | The teaching staff |
| **B** | No women allowed | **G** | Classroom rules |
| **C** | Important dates | **H** | Education opens up |
| **D** | University life | **I** | Basic schooling for all |
| **E** | Education for the few | | |

## Speaking & Writing

**3**  THINK In what ways was the education system of Victorian England different from the education system of most countries today? Make a list and compare with your partner. Then present your ideas to the class.

**4** ICT Collect information about the education system in the 19th century in your country or another country. Make notes under the headings: *Education before the 19th century – Private education – Basic education for all – What was taught – Higher level education.*

# CLIL: Environmental Studies

# Recycling symbols

We all know it's important to recycle, but with so many recycling symbols out there it's easy to end up getting it wrong. Here are a few of the most common symbols.

**1** Mobius loop
A triangle with three arrows chasing each other means that the object can be recycled. However, it does not always mean that it's made from recycled materials.

**2** Plastics code
A Mobius loop with a number in the middle means that the object is made of plastic. The numbers are from 1 to 7. This shows which type of plastic has been used.

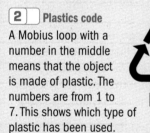

**3** Glass
This symbol **reminds** us to recycle a glass item in the correct recycling bin or at a **bottle bank**. Do not recycle glass that is broken!

**4** Aluminium
Recyclable aluminium does not just include drinks cans but also tin foil, foil lids and **wrappers**. They can be scrunched up into a ball to make them easier to recycle.

**5** Steel
This symbol of a magnet attracting a piece of steel is for steel objects. Things like pet food tins should go in the correct recycling bin. Bigger objects, like old cookers, can often be collected from your home by a recycling centre.

**6** Paper & Wood
FSC (the Forest Stewardship Council) is an organisation that protects the world's forests. This symbol means that a wood-based item has been produced from forests that are **managed** in an environmentally-friendly way.

**7** Electricals
Old electrical items with the crossed-out wheelie bin symbol should not be thrown into the normal rubbish.

Recycling centres accept them or, alternatively, smaller items can be taken to special collection points in big shops.

**8** Compostables
An item with the seedling symbol can be turned into fertiliser. Sometimes, your local **council** can collect it along with other garden waste. Do not place items with this symbol on your own compost heap unless the symbol includes the word 'HOME'.

**9** Tidy man
The tidy man symbol appears on many products. It is not actually a recycling symbol but instead it reminds **citizens** not to litter.

**10** The green dot
Two arrows wrapped around each other in a circle means that the makers of the product pay towards the cost of recycling. The product itself, though, is not necessarily recyclable.

## Reading & Listening

**1** Look at the recycling symbols in the text. Do you know what they all mean? 🎧 Listen, read and check.

**2** Read the text again and match statements A-J to paragraphs 1-10. Then explain the words/phrases in bold.

This symbol ...
**A** shows that an item can be used to help plants grow.
**B** encourages tidy habits.
**C** shows that the company that made an item supports recycling.
**D** means that an item is recyclable.
**E** has a numbering system.
**F** is only for items that are not in pieces.
**G** shows that you should change an item's shape before recycling it.
**H** might mean you can recycle an item in a shop.
**I** shows that an item has been made without harming the environment.
**J** might mean that a recyclable item can be collected from your home.

> ✓ **Check these words**
>
> chase, tin foil, scrunch, steel, seedling, fertiliser, compost heap

## Speaking & Writing

**3** THINK Where could you see these symbols, apart from on items mentioned in the text?

**4** ICT Do some research on the different codes used in the plastics code symbol. Think about: *types of plastic, products they're used for, whether they're recyclable or not.* **Make a poster and present it to the class.**

111

# Grammar Reference

## Unit 1

### Present simple

**Form:** main verb (+ -*s* in the third person singular)

| Affirmative | I/You/We/They **run**.<br>He/She/It **runs**. |
|---|---|
| **Negative** | I/You/We/They **do not/don't run**.<br>He/She/It **does not/doesn't run**. |
| **Interrogative** | **Do** I/you/we/they **run**?<br>**Does** he/she/it **run**? |
| **Short answers** | **Yes**, I/you/we/they **do**.<br>**Yes**, he/she/it **does**. |
| | **No**, I/you/we/they **don't**.<br>**No**, he/she/it **doesn't**. |

**Spelling 3rd-person singular affirmative**
- Most verbs take -*s* in the third-person singular.
  *I walk – he walks*
- Verbs ending in -*ss*, -*sh*, -*ch*, -*x* or -*o* take -*es*.
  *I miss – he misses, I wish – he wishes, I catch – he catches, I relax – he relaxes, I go – he goes*
- Verbs ending in consonant + *y* drop the -*y* and take -*ies*. *I try – he tries*
- Verbs ending in vowel + *y* take -*s*. *I pay – he pays*

**Use**
We use the **present simple** for:
- **daily routines/repeated actions** (especially with adverbs of frequency: *often*, *usually*, *always*, etc).
  *She usually **drives** to work in the morning.*
- **habits.** *Sue **walks** her dog twice a day.*
- **permanent states.** *John **works** as a travel agent.*
- **timetables/schedules** (future meaning).
  *The guided tour **starts** at 8:00 am.*
- **general truths and laws of nature.**
  *Temperatures **drop** in autumn.*
- **reviews/sports commentaries/narrations.**
  *Samuels **scores** the winning goal and **ends** the game.*

> **Time words/phrases used with the *present simple*:** every day/month/hour/summer/morning/evening, etc, usually, often, sometimes, always, etc, on Mondays/ Fridays, etc

### Adverbs of frequency

- **Adverbs of frequency** tell us how often sth happens. These are: always (100%), usually (90%), often (70%), sometimes (50%), occasionally (30%), rarely/seldom (10%), never (0%).
- **Adverbs of frequency** go **before** the **main verb** but **after** the main verb *be* and auxiliary verbs *be*, *have*, *do* and modals such as *will*, *can*, etc.
  *We **rarely** travel abroad. You must **never** throw litter on the ground.*

### Present continuous

**Form:** subject + verb *to be* (*am/is/are*) + main verb -*ing*

| Affirmative | Negative |
|---|---|
| I'm **walking**.<br>You're **walking**.<br>He/She/It's **walking**.<br>We/You/They're **walking**. | I'm not **walking**.<br>You **aren't walking**.<br>He/She/It **isn't walking**.<br>We/You/They **aren't walking**. |
| **Interrogative** | **Short answers** |
| **Am** I **walking**?<br>**Are** you **walking**?<br>**Is** he/she/it **walking**? | **Yes**, I am./**No**, I'm **not**.<br>**Yes**, you are./**No**, you **aren't**.<br>**Yes**, he/she/it **is**./<br>**No**, he/she/it **isn't**. |
| **Are** we/you/they **walking**? | **Yes**, we/you/they **are**./<br>**No**, we/you/they **aren't**. |

**Spelling of the present participle**
- Most verbs take -*ing* after the base form of the main verb. *cook – cooking, read – reading*
- Verbs ending in -*e* drop the -*e* and take -*ing*.
  *stare – staring, take – taking*
- Verbs ending in **one vowel** + **consonant** and which are stressed on the last syllable, **double the consonant** and take -*ing*. *drop – dropping, begin – beginning* **BUT** *enter – entering* (stress on 1st syllable)
- Verbs ending in -*ie* change the -*ie* to -*y* and add -*ing*.
  *lie – lying*

**Use**
We use the **present continuous** for:
- actions happening **now**, at the moment of speaking.
  *They **are packing** their suitcases at the moment. .*
- actions happening **around the time of speaking**.
  *Stella **is watering** our plants while we are away on holiday.*
- **fixed arrangements** in the **near future**, especially when we know the time and the place.
  *He's **leaving** for Ireland tomorrow morning.*
- **temporary situations**.
  *Harry **is spending** this weekend at his friend's in Dover.*
- **changing or developing situations**.
  *Plane tickets to London **are becoming** more and more expensive.*
- **frequently repeated actions**, with *always*, *constantly* and *continually*, to express annoyance or criticism.
  *You're **always driving** too fast.*

**Note: The following verbs do not usually have a continuous form:** *have* (= possess), *like*, *love*, *hate*, *want*, *know*, *remember*, *forget*, *understand*, *think*, *believe*, *cost*, etc. *I don't **remember** the name of our hotel.*

> **Time words/phrases used with the *present continuous*:** now, at the moment, at present, nowadays, these days, today, tomorrow, next week, etc

## Present simple vs Present continuous

| Present simple | Present continuous |
|---|---|
| **permanent states & facts** *He sells cars for a living.* | **temporary situations** *I am working from home this week.* |
| **habits/routines** *Amy usually eats lunch at school.* | **actions happening now/ around the time of speaking** *He's riding his bike now.* |
| **timetables (future)** *The bus leaves in 30 minutes.* | **future arrangements** *We're going to the theatre tonight.* |

## Stative verbs

**Stative verbs** are verbs which describe a state rather than an action, and do not usually have a continuous form. These are:

- verbs of the **senses** (*appear*, *feel*, *hear*, *look*, *see*, *smell*, *sound*, *taste*, etc). *You seem tired.*
- verbs of **perception** (*believe*, *forget*, *know*, *understand*, etc). *I don't know this song.*
- verbs which express **feelings** and **emotions** (*desire*, *enjoy*, *hate*, *like*, *love*, *prefer*, *want*, etc). *The children love playing in the snow.*
- other verbs: *agree*, *be*, *belong*, *contain*, *cost*, *fit*, *have*, *include*, *keep*, *need*, *owe*, *own*, etc. *They own a five-star hotel.*

Some of these verbs can be used in continuous tenses, but with a difference in meaning.

| Present simple | Present continuous |
|---|---|
| *I think we should turn left here.* (= believe) | *We are thinking of going for a hike.* (= are considering) |
| *He has a map of the area.* (= owns, possesses) | *Peter is having coffee.* (= is drinking) *She is having a dinner party tonight.* (= is hosting) *We are having fun.* (= are experiencing) |
| *I see the ocean from my window.* (= the ocean is visible) *I see why you're upset.* (= understand) | *He is seeing his old school friends tomorrow.* (= is meeting) |
| *My tea tastes sweet.* (= the flavour of the tea is) | *Kim is tasting the soup to check if it needs more pepper.* (= is trying) |
| *Her perfume smells like jasmine.* (= has the smell of) | *The dog is smelling its food.* (= is sniffing) |

| *The locals appear to be very friendly.* (= seem) | *Karen is appearing in the school play.* (= is performing) |
|---|---|
| *My hands feel rough.* (= have a rough texture) | *Ann is feeling the clothes to see if they're still wet.* (= is touching) |
| *David is quite funny* (character – permanent state) | *You are being very unreasonable.* (behaviour – temporary state) |
| *These jeans fit you well.* (= are the right size) | *They are fitting an air conditioner in their bedroom.* (= are putting) |
| *Eve looks confused.* (= appears/seems) | *He is looking at the map to see where the station is.* (= is taking a look at/reviewing) |

**Note:** The verb *enjoy* can be used in continuous tenses to express a **specific preference**. *Frank enjoys camping in the forest.* (general preference) **BUT** *We are enjoying a day at the beach.* (specific preference)
The verbs *look* (when we refer to somebody's appearance), *feel* (when we experience a particular emotion), *hurt* and *ache* can be used in simple or continuous tenses with no difference in meaning. *You look nice today.* = *You are looking nice today.*

## Present perfect

**Form:** subject + *have/has* + past participle of the main verb

| Affirmative | Negative |
|---|---|
| I/You/We/They **have/'ve worked.** He/She/It **has/'s worked.** | I/You/We/They **have not/ haven't worked.** He/She/It **has not/hasn't worked.** |
| **Interrogative** | **Short answers** |
| **Have** I/you/we/they **worked?** **Has** he/she/it **worked?** | **Yes,** I/you/we/they **have.**/ **No,** I/you/we/they **haven't.** **Yes,** he/she/it **has.**/ **No,** he/she/it **hasn't.** |

### Use

We use the **present perfect**:

- for actions which **started in the past** and **continue** up to the **present**, and also especially with stative verbs such as *be*, *have*, *like*, *know*, etc. *He has had the same car for fifteen years.* (= He got the car fifteen years ago and he still has it.)
- to talk about **a past action** which has a **visible** result in the **present**. *Brenda has heard some good news and she is very happy.*
- for actions which happened at an **unstated time** in the **past**. The action is more important than the time it happened. *She has moved into a new house.* (When? We don't know; it's not important.)

# Grammar Reference

- with *today*, *this morning/afternoon/week*, *so far*, etc when these periods of time are not finished at the time of speaking.
  *Adam **has cancelled** our dinner plans twice this week.* (The time period – this week – is not over yet. He may cancel our plans again.)
- for **recently completed actions**.
  *They **have** just **returned** from their trip.* (The action is complete. They are here now.)
- for **personal experiences/changes** which have happened.
  *It's the first time we **have visited** the USA.*

---

**Time words/phrases used with the *present perfect*:**
- *already* (normally in affirmative sentences)
  *I've **already** confirmed our hotel reservations.*
- *yet* (normally in interrogative or negative sentences)
  *Have you been on the London Eye **yet**?*
  *Marlon hasn't returned from Spain **yet**.*
- *just* (normally in affirmative sentences to show that an action finished a few minutes earlier)
  *Their plane has **just** landed.*
- *ever* (normally in affirmative and interrogative sentences)
  *This hotel is the best we've **ever** stayed at. Have you **ever** been camping?*
- *never* (negative meaning)
  *Claire has **never** tried Thai food before.*
  *We have **never** flown first class.*
- *for* (over a period of time)
  *She has dreamed about hiking on the Appalachians **for** years.*
- *since* (from a starting point in the past)
  *Lisa has been in bed with the flu **since** Monday.*
- *recently* (normally in affirmative or interrogative sentences)
  *He has **recently** passed his driving test.*
  *Have you travelled abroad **recently**?*
- *so far* (normally in affirmative sentences)
  *She has uploaded three videos from her trip **so far**.*

---

## *have gone (to)/have been (to)/have been in*

- *Chris **has gone to** the museum.* (He's on his way to the museum or he's there now. He hasn't come back yet.)
- *We **have been to** Ireland.* (We went to Ireland but we aren't there now. We've come back.)
- *Samantha **has been in** Rome for three days.* (She is still in Rome.)

## Present perfect continuous

**Form:** subject + *have/has been* + main verb + *-ing*

| Affirmative | Negative |
|---|---|
| I/You/We/They **have/'ve been sleeping**. He/She/It **has/'s been sleeping**. | I/You/We/They **have not/ haven't been sleeping**. He/She/It **has not/hasn't been sleeping**. |
| Interrogative | Short answers |
| **Have** I/you/we/they **been sleeping**? **Has** he/she/it **been sleeping**? | **Yes**, I/you/we/they **have**./ **No**, I/you/we/they **haven't**. **Yes**, he/she/it **has**./ **No**, he/she/it **hasn't**. |

### Use
We use the **present perfect continuous**:
- to place **emphasis** on **the duration of an action** which started in the past and continues up to the present. *We **have been walking** around the city for four hours.*
- for an action that **started in the past** and lasted for some time. It may still be continuing or has finished, but its **results are visible in the present**. *It **has been raining** all day and the streets are flooded.*
- to express **anger**, **irritation**, **annoyance** or **criticism**. *I can't believe you**'ve been holding** the map the wrong way up all this time!* (annoyance)

---

**Time words/phrases used with the *present perfect continuous*:** since, for, how long (to place emphasis on duration)

---

# Unit 2

## Past simple

**Form:** regular verb + *-ed*
The **past simple** affirmative of regular verbs is formed by adding *-ed* to the verb. Some verbs have an irregular past form (See Irregular Verbs list at the back of the book).

| Affirmative | Negative |
|---|---|
| I/You/He/She/It/We/ They **walked/took**. | I/You/He/She/It/We/They **did not/ didn't walk/take**. |
| Interrogative | Short answers |
| **Did** I/you/he/ she/it/we/they **walk/take**? | **Yes**, I/you/he/she/it/we/they **did**. **No**, I/you/he/she/it/we/they **didn't**. |

### Spelling
- We add *-d* to verbs ending in *-e*. *I smile – I smiled*
- For verbs ending in consonant + *-y*, we drop the *-y* and add *-ied*. *I carry – I carried*
- For verbs ending in vowel + *-y*, we add *-ed*. *I enjoy – I enjoyed*

- For verbs ending in one stressed vowel between two consonants, we double the last consonant and add **-ed**. *I prefer – I prefer**red***

**Use**

We use the **past simple** for:
- actions which happened at **a specific time** (stated, implied or already known) **in the past**.
  *He **attended** the International Kite Festival last year.* (When? Last year.)
  *His **took** lots of photos.* (When? The time is implied/ already known, last year.)
- **past habits**. *He **collected** coins when he was younger.*
- past actions which happened **one immediately after the other**.
  *He **boarded** the bus, **found** a seat and **sat** down.*
- past actions which **won't take place again**.
  *Pam **celebrated** her 21st birthday last April.*

| Time words/phrases used with the *past simple*: yesterday, yesterday morning/evening etc, last night/ week etc, two weeks/a month ago, in 2020, etc |
| --- |

---

## Past continuous

**Form:** *was/were* + main verb + **-ing**

| Affirmative | Negative |
| --- | --- |
| I/He/She/It **was running**. <br><br> We/You/They **were running**. | I/He/She/It **was not/wasn't running**. <br> We/You/They **were not/ weren't running**. |
| **Interrogative** | **Short answers** |
| **Was** I/he/she/it **running**? <br><br> **Were** we/you/they **running**? | **Yes**, I/he/she/it **was**./ **No**, I/he/she it **wasn't**. <br> **Yes**, we/you/they **were**./ **No**, we/you/they **weren't**. |

We use the **past continuous** for:
- an action which was **in progress** at a stated time in the past. We do not know when the action started or finished. *Anna **was watching** the parade at 11:00 am.*
- a past action which was **in progress** when another action **interrupted** it. We use the past continuous for the action in progress (longer action) and the past simple for the action which interrupted it (shorter action). *They **were watching** the fireworks display on TV when the lights **went out**.*
- two or more actions which were happening at the same time in the past **(simultaneous actions)**.
  *While Olga **was dancing** on the stage, her sister **was taking photos** of her.*
- to give **background information** in a story. *It was a cold morning. It **was snowing** and a freezing wind **was blowing**.*

| Time words/phrases used with the *past continuous*: while, when, as, at 7pm yesterday, etc |
| --- |

## Past simple vs Past continuous

| Past simple | Past continuous |
| --- | --- |
| actions which happened at a **stated time** in the past *Henry **participated** in the parade last year.* | actions **in progress** at a stated time in the past *She **was sleeping** at midnight last night.* |
| actions which happened **one after the other** in the past *I **had** dinner, **cleared** the table and **did** the dishes.* | two or more actions which were happening **at the same time** in the past *While Ian **was driving**, Penny **was giving** him directions.* |

## Past simple vs Present perfect

| Past simple | Present perfect |
| --- | --- |
| an action which happened at a **stated time** in the past *He **left** an hour ago.* (When? An hour ago. The time is mentioned.) | an action which happened at an **unstated time** in the past *He **has left**.* (We don't know when.) |
| an **action which started and finished in the past** *John Wills **was** the town mayor for two years.* (He is not the mayor now.) | an **action which started in the past and is still continuing** in the present *John Wills **has been** the town mayor for two years.* (He is still the mayor.) |

---

## *used to/would – be/get used to*

- We use *used to/would*/**past simple** to talk about past habits or actions that happened regularly in the past, but no longer happen.
  *She **used to take/would take/took** part in the parade every year.* (She doesn't do that anymore.)
- We use *would/used to* for repeated actions or routines in the past. We don't use *would* with **stative verbs**.
  *Harry **used to drive/would drive** to work every day.* **BUT** *Lia **used to** love parades.* (NOT: ~~Lia would love parades.~~)
- We use the **past simple** for an action that happened at a definite time in the past.
  *She **visited** the Tower of London two weeks ago.* (NOT: ~~She used to visit/would visit the Tower of London two weeks ago.~~)
- We use *be used to* to show that we **are accustomed to** or **are in the habit of (doing) sth**.
- *Be used to* can be followed by a **noun**, a **pronoun** or an **-ing** form. *He grew up in a small village so he wasn't used to large crowds.* (past) *I don't like sugar in my coffee. I'm not used to it.* (present) *She is used to working long hours.* (present)

# Grammar Reference

- We use **get used to** to express the idea of **becoming accustomed to** (doing) something (gradually).
- **Get used to** can be followed by a **noun**, a **pronoun** or an **-ing** form. *He found it strange at first, but he is getting used to her sense of humour now.* (present) *As a child he was scared of the dark, but he got used to it.* (past) *Don't be nervous, you will soon get used to performing in public.* (future)

## Unit 3

### Past perfect

**Form:** subject + *had* + past participle of the main verb

| Affirmative | Negative |
|---|---|
| I/You/He, etc **had seen.** | I/You/He, etc **had not/hadn't seen.** |
| **Interrogative** | **Short answers** |
| **Had** I/you/he, etc **seen?** | **Yes**, I/you/he, etc **had.**/ **No**, I/you/he, etc **hadn't.** |

We use the **past perfect**:
- for an action which **finished before another past action** or **before a stated time in the past.** *We had packed our suitcases by the time the taxi came.* (past perfect [**had packed**] before another past action [**came**]) *The sightseeing tour had finished by 2:00 pm.* (before a stated time in the past [**by 2:00 pm**])
- for an action which **finished in the past** and whose **result was visible at a later point in the past.** *They were upset because they had lost their way back to their hotel.*

**Note:** The **past perfect** is the past equivalent of the **present perfect.** *Pete couldn't travel because he had lost his passport.* (present perfect: *Pete can't travel because he has lost his passport.*)

**Time words/phrases used with the *past perfect*:** before, already, after, for, since, just, till/until, by, by the time, never, etc

### Past perfect continuous

**Form:** subject + *had been* + main verb + *-ing*

| Affirmative | Negative |
|---|---|
| I/You/He/She/It/ We/They **had been eating.** | I/You/He/She/It/We/They **had not/hadn't been eating.** |
| **Interrogative** | **Short answers** |
| **Had** I/you/he, etc **been eating?** | **Yes**, I/you/he/she/it/we/they **had.**/ **No**, I/you/he/she/it/we/they **hadn't.** |

We use the **past perfect continuous**:
- to put emphasis on the **duration** of an action which started and finished in the past, before another action or stated time in the past, usually with *for* or *since*. *Paula had been waiting for the bus for over an hour before it finally came.*
- for an action which **lasted for some time** in the past and whose **result was visible** in the past. *He had been training for the race for months, so he did it in good time.*

**Note:** The **past perfect continuous** is the past equivalent of the **present perfect continuous.** *Gordon was tired because he had been hiking for five hours.* (present perfect continuous: *Gordon is tired because he has been hiking for five hours.*)

**Time words/phrases used with the *past perfect continuous*:** for, since, how long, before, until, etc

### Past simple vs Past perfect

| Past simple | Past perfect |
|---|---|
| actions which happened **at a stated time** or **one after the other** in the past *Susan returned from her trip on Sunday.* *Nick got into bed, turned off the light and fell asleep immediately.* | an action which **finished before another past action** or **before a stated time in the past** *He had left for the airport before I got up.* *We had reached the station by 6:00 am.* |

### A/An

- We use **a/an** with singular countable nouns when we mention something for the first time. *We went on a trip to Hawaii. The trip was amazing.*
- We use **a** before singular countable nouns which begin with a consonant sound *(a boat, a guide)*. We use **an** before singular countable nouns which begin with a vowel sound *(an honour, an island)*.
- We don't use **a/an** with uncountable or plural nouns. In these cases, we use **some** in affirmative sentences. *There is some sand in my shoes. We brought back some souvenirs.*

### The/–

The definite article is used with singular and plural nouns. *the book – the books*
We use **the**:
- with **nouns when we are talking about something specific**, that is, when the noun is mentioned for a second time or is already known. *Ethan bough a map of the city. The map was very useful when we went sightseeing.*

- with nouns which are **unique** (the Northern Lights, the sky, **the** moon, etc).
- before the names of **rivers** (the Seine), **seas** (the Adriatic Sea), **oceans** (the Pacific Ocean), **mountain ranges** (the Rocky Mountains), **deserts** (the Kalahari), **groups of islands** (the Azores), **countries** when they include words such as 'state', 'kingdom', etc (the Kingdom of Bahrain) and nouns with **of** (the Acropolis of Athens).
- with **historical periods/events** the Middle Ages, the Second World War **BUT** World War II.
- before the names of **musical instruments** (the violin, the trumpet, etc).
- before the names of **hotels** (the Hyatt Hotel), **theatres/cinemas** (the View), **ships** (the Santa Maria), **organisations** (the WHO), **newspapers** (the Herald) and **museums** (the Louvre Museum).
- before **nationalities** (the Australians) and **families** (the Andersons).
- before **titles when the person's name is not mentioned** (the mayor, the prince).
- before the words **morning**, **afternoon** and **evening**. We often watch TV in **the** evening.
- with **only**, **last**, **first** used as adjectives. This is **the first** time I've tried kayaking.
- with **adjectives** in the **superlative** form. This is one of **the coldest** winters for decades.

We don't use **the**:
- with **plural nouns when we talk about them in general**. Sports are popular with young people.
- before **proper names**. Kelly was born in Canada.
- before the names of **countries** (Belgium), **cities/towns** (New York), **streets** (Nicholson Street), **parks** (Stanley Park), **squares** (Federation Square), **stations** (Northcote Station), **mountains** (Mount Fuji), **islands** (Fraser Island), **lakes** (Lake Como) and **continents** (Asia).
- with **two-word names** when the first is the name of a person. Charles de Gaulle Airport
- before the names of **meals** (lunch, supper, etc) and **games/sports** (football, rugby, etc). Volleyball is a team sport.
- with the words **this/that/these/those**. These souvenirs are very expensive.
- with **possessive adjectives** or the **possessive case**. This isn't **your** backpack. It's Roger's.
- before **means of transport**. She loves travelling **by** train.
- before **titles when the person's name is mentioned**. President Johnson, King Edward **BUT** the President, the King
- with the words **school**, **church**, **bed**, **hospital**, **prison** or **home** when we refer to the purpose for which they exist. Alex studies Law at university. (Alex is a student.)

**BUT** Alex went to **the** university to use the Law library. (Alex visited the university building.)
- with **languages**. Lisa is fluent in Spanish. **BUT** The Spanish language has very easy grammar.

**NOTE:** We use **the** + adjective to refer to a group of people, usually with the following adjectives: **poor**, **rich**, **sick**, **old**, **dead**, **blind**, **young**, etc. There are a lot of charities that help **the poor**.

# Unit 4

## Comparisons

- We use the **comparative** to compare one person or thing with another. We use the **superlative** to compare one person or thing with others of the same group.
  Their garden is **prettier** than ours.
  They have **the prettiest** garden in our street.
- We often use **than** after a comparative.
  Jake's new flat is bigger **than** his old one.
- We normally use **the** before a superlative. We can use **in** or **of** after superlatives. We often use **in** with places.
  Umberto is **the kindest of** all my neighbours.
  He lives in **the tallest** building **in** the city.

**Formation of comparatives and superlatives**

| Adjectives of **one syllable** take *-(e)r/-(e)st* to form their comparative and superlative forms. | | |
|---|---|---|
| **Adjective** | **Comparative** | **Superlative** |
| short | short**er** (than) | **the** short**est** (of/in) |
| large | larg**er** (than) | **the** larg**est** (of/in) |

| Adjectives of **one syllable** that end in **a single vowel + a single consonant** double the last consonant and add *-er/-est*. | | |
|---|---|---|
| **Adjective** | **Comparative** | **Superlative** |
| thin | thin**ner** (than) | **the** thin**nest** (of/in) |

| Adjectives of **one** or **two syllables** ending in *-ly* or *-y*, drop the *-y* and add *-ier/-iest* | | |
|---|---|---|
| **Adjective** | **Comparative** | **Superlative** |
| silly | sill**ier** (than) | **the** sill**iest** (of/in) |
| healthy | health**ier** (than) | **the** health**iest** (of/in) |

| Adjectives of **two or more syllables** take *more/the most* | | |
|---|---|---|
| **Adjective** | **Comparative** | **Superlative** |
| modern | **more** modern (than) | **the most** modern (of/in) |
| exciting | **more** exciting (than) | **the most** exciting (of/in) |

# Grammar Reference

Note: *clever, common, cruel, friendly, gentle, narrow, pleasant, polite, quiet, shallow, simple, stupid* form their comparatives and superlatives either with *-er/-est* or with *more/the most*.

*clever – clever**er**/**more** clever – clever**est**/**the most** clever*

## Adverbs

- Adverbs that have **the same form** as their adjectives *(hard, fast, free, late, high, early, low, deep, long, near, straight)* take *-er/-est*.
  *high – high**er** – **the** high**est***
- Adverbs formed by adding *-ly* to the adjective take *more* in the comparative and *the most* in the superlative form.
  *kindly – **more** kindly – **the most** kindly*

| Adverbs | | Comparative | Superlative |
|---|---|---|---|
| adverbs having the same form as their adjectives add *-er/-est* | *low* | *low**er*** | *the low**est*** |
| *early* drops the *-y* and adds *-ier/-iest* | *early* | *earl**ier*** | *the earl**iest*** |
| two-syllable adverbs and those formed by adding *-ly* to their adjectives take *more/the most* | *seldom* | ***more** seldom* | *the most seldom* |
| | *sadly* | ***more** sadly* | *the most sadly* |

| Irregular forms | | |
|---|---|---|
| Adjective/Adverb | Comparative | Superlative |
| *good/well* | *better* | *the best* |
| *bad/badly* | *worse* | *the worst* |
| *little* | *less* | *the least* |
| *a lot of/much/many* | *more* | *the most* |
| *far* | *farther/further* | *the farthest/furthest* |

### Notes:
- We can use *elder/eldest* for people in the same family.
  *Freya's **elder/eldest** sister has bought her own house.*
- *further/farther* (adv) = longer (in distance)
  *The train station is **further/farther** away from my house than the bus stop.*
  *further* (adj) = more
  *If you have any **further** questions, I'll be happy to answer them.*

## Types of comparisons

- *as* + **adjective** + *as* (to show that two people or things are similar/different in some way). In negative sentences we use *not as/so ... a*s.
  *Kathy's flat is **as big as** mine.*
  *Our new sofa is **not as/so comfortable as** our old one.*

- *less* + **adjective** + *than* (expresses the difference between two people or things). The opposite is *more ... than*. *James is **less excited than** Lily about the idea of moving to the countryside.*
- *the least* + **adjective** + *of/in* (compares one person or thing with two or more people or things of the same group). The opposite *is the most ... of/in*.
  *Sharon is **the least experienced** assistant in the shop.*
- **comparative** + *and* + **comparative** (to show that something is increasing or decreasing).
  *The prices of flats in the city centre are growing **higher and higher**.*
  *It's becoming **more and more** difficult to drive in early morning traffic.*
- *the* + **comparative** ... , *the* + **comparative** (shows that two things change together, or that one thing depends on another thing).
  ***The bigger** the house, **the more** furniture you'll need for it.*
- *the same as*
  *Her bedroom looks exactly **the same as** her twin sister's.*
- *twice/three times/half* etc *as* + **adjective** + *as*
  *The price of my grandparents' house is **three times as high as** the original price.*
  *George's little sister is **half as tall as** him.*
- *too* + **adjective/adverb** + *to*-infinitive (to show that something is more, or at a higher degree, than necessary).
  *They don't like the area because it's **too crowded**.*
- **adjective/adverb** + *enough* + *to*-infinitive (to show that there is as much of something as is wanted, or at the necessary degree).
  *Ryan **was kind enough** to help us move house.*
- *very* + **adjective/adverb**:
  *Houses in this area are **very expensive**.*
- *much/a lot/even/a bit/a little/far/slightly* + **comparative form of adjective/adverb**:
  *We want to move **a bit closer** to the city centre.*
- *by far* + **superlative form of adjective/adverb**:
  *This is **by far the strangest** building I've ever seen.*

## Impersonal sentences (*There – It*)

**Impersonal sentences** have no natural subject and the words *there* or *it* can be used in the subject position.

We use *there* + *be*:
- to say **where** or **when** sth is. *There's a new shopping centre in the area. There's a concert at the park on Sunday.*
- to refer to a **number** or **amount**. *There are two schools close to my house. There are lots of beautiful villas along the coast.*
- to say that **sth exists or happens**. *There is an easier way to solve the problem. There's a party happening next door.*

We use *it* + *be*:
- to refer to **times/dates**. *It's half past seven. It's my sister's birthday on 3rd November.*

- to talk about the weather/temperatures. *It's snowing. It's quite warm today.*
- to begin a sentence followed by an adjective.
  *It's obvious that he's angry about something.*
  *It's hard to find a flat for a large family in this area.*
- for identification. *There's someone on the phone for you. It's your lawyer.*

# Unit 5

## Future simple

**Form:** subject + ***will*** + main verb

| Affirmative | Negative |
|---|---|
| I/You/He/She/It/We/They **will/'ll stay.** | I/You/He/She/It/We/They **will not/won't stay.** |
| **Interrogative** | **Short answers** |
| **Will** I/you/he/she/it/ we/they **stay?** | **Yes**, I/you/he/she/it/we/they **will./** **No**, I/you/he/she/it/we/they **won't.** |

### Use
We use the **future simple:**
- for **on-the-spot decisions.** *I'm cold. I'll put on a jumper.*
- for **predictions based on what we believe or imagine will happen** (usually with the verbs: ***think***, ***believe***, ***expect***, ***imagine***, etc; with the expressions: ***I'm sure***, ***I'm afraid***, etc; with the adverbs: ***probably***, ***perhaps***, etc).
  *I expect you**'ll apologise** to Jenny for your rudeness. Perhaps Clarence **won't come** to the technology exhibition tomorrow.*
- for **promises** (usually with the verbs ***promise***, ***swear***, etc) *I promise I**'ll email** you the details of the trip tonight.*; **threats** *Read my personal emails again and I**'ll be** furious.*; **warnings** *Don't run on the icy pavement! You **will slip** and fall.*; **hopes** *Sam hopes **he will get** a new smartphone for his birthday.*; **offers** *Don't take a taxi home, I**'ll drive** you.*; **requests** *Will you help me with my essay?*
- for actions/events/situations which will **definitely happen** in the future and which **we cannot control.** *It **will be** spring soon.*

> **Time words/phrases used with the *future simple*:** tomorrow, the day after tomorrow, next week/month/ year, tonight, soon, in a week/month/year, etc

## Present simple/Present continuous (future meaning)

- We can use the **present simple** to talk about **schedules** or **timetables**. *Shops **open** at 9:00.*

- We use the **present continuous** for **fixed arrangements** in the near future. *I'm leaving for school in half an hour.*

## be going to

**Form:** subject + verb ***to be*** *(am/is/are)* + ***going to*** + base form of the main verb

| Affirmative | I am/'m<br>He/She/It is/'s<br>We/You/They are/'re | going to play. |
|---|---|---|
| Negative | I am not/ I'm not<br>He/She/It is not/isn't<br>We/You/They are not/aren't | going to play. |
| Interrogative | Am I<br>Is he/she/it<br>Are we/you/they | going to play? |
| Short answers | Yes, I am./No, I'm not.<br>Yes, he/she/it is./<br>No, he/she/it isn't.<br>Yes, we/you/they are./<br>No, we/you/they aren't. | |

### Use
We use ***be going to:***
- to talk about **future plans** and **intentions.**
  *John **is going to study** robotics. (He's planning to.)*
- to make predictions based on what we see or know.
  *Hurry up! We **are going to miss** the bus.*
- to talk about **things we are sure about**, or **we have already decided to do** in the near future.
  *They **are going to get** married in two weeks. (They have already decided to do it.)*

## Future continuous

**Form:** subject + ***will be*** + main verb + ***-ing***

| Affirmative | Negative |
|---|---|
| I/You/He/She/It/We/They **will/'ll be coming.** | I/You/He/She/It/We/They **will not/won't be coming.** |
| **Interrogative** | **Short answers** |
| **Will** I/you/he/she/it/ we/they **be coming?** | **Yes**, I/you/he/she/it/we/they **will./** **No**, I/you/he/she/it/we/they **won't.** |

We use the **future continuous:**
- for actions which will be **in progress** at a **stated future time.**
  *This time next Monday, I **will be starting** my new job.*
- for actions which will **definitely happen** in the future as a result of a routine or **arrangement.** *George **will be doing** a course in IT this autumn.*

- when we **ask politely** about someone's **plans for the near future** (to see if they can do sth for us or because we want to offer to do sth for them).
  *Will you be going to the shops later?*

## Future perfect

**Form:** subject + *will have* + past participle of the main verb

| Affirmative | Negative |
|---|---|
| I/You/He/She/It/We/They **will/'ll have started.** | I/You/He/She/It/We/They **will not/won't have started.** |
| **Interrogative** | **Short answers** |
| **Will** I/you/he/she/it/ we/they **have started?** | **Yes**, I/you/he/she/it/we/they **will.**/ **No**, I/you/he/she/it/we/they **won't.** |

We use the **future perfect** for actions that will have **finished before a stated time in the future**.
*The seminar will have finished by 11:00 o'clock.*

> **Time words/phrases used with the *future perfect*:** before, by, by then, by the time, until/till, etc
> **Note:** *until/till* are normally used with the future perfect only in **negative sentences**.

## Time clauses

- **Time clauses** are introduced by: *after, as, as soon as, before, by the time* (= before, not later than), *every time, just as, once, the moment (that), until/till* (= up to the time when), *when, while*, etc.
  *I'll call you as soon as I get dinner on the table.*
- **Time clauses** follow the rule of the sequence of tenses.

| Main clause | Time clause |
|---|---|
| present simple/ present continuous/ future/imperative | present simple/present continuous/present perfect |
| *I'll send you a text message before I leave work.* (NOT: ~~to leave~~) | |
| **Main clause** | **Time clause** |
| past simple/past perfect | past simple/past continuous/past perfect |
| *She started her essay after she had completed her research.* | |

- When the time clause precedes the main clause, a comma is used. When the time clause follows, no comma is used.
  *As soon as he goes to work, he checks his emails.* **BUT** *He checks his emails as soon as he goes to work.*

**Note:** We use future forms with **'when'** when it is used as a question word. *When will you get a new laptop?* (**Compare:** *I'll help you update your profile when I have some free time.* [time word])

# Unit 6

## Modals

**Modal verbs:**
- don't take *-s*, *-ing* or *-ed* suffixes.
- are followed by the bare infinitive (infinitive without *to*).
- come before the subject in questions and are followed by *not* in negations.
- don't have tenses in the normal sense. When followed by a **present infinitive**, they often refer to an action or state in the **present** or **future**. *You could ask a colleague to help you.* When followed by a **perfect infinitive**, they often refer to an **action** or **state** in the **past**. *You could have asked a colleague to help you.*

**Note:** The forms of the infinitive are the following:

> **Present:** (to) work
> **Present continuous:** (to) be working
> **Perfect:** (to) have worked
> **Perfect continuous:** (to) have been working

> **Obligation/Duty/Necessity**
> *(must, have to, need to, should/ought to)*

- *Must* expresses a **duty/strong obligation** to do sth, and shows that sth is essential. We generally use *must* when the speaker has decided that sth is necessary to do. *We must be on time for work.* (**It's our duty. We are obliged to do it.**) *Lucy must learn how to make presentations.*
- *Need to/Have to* express **strong necessity/obligation.** *You need to ask permission if you want to take a day off work.* We usually use *have to* when somebody other than the speaker has decided that sth is necessary to do. *My supervisor says that I have to attend tomorrow's meeting.* (**It's necessary. My supervisor says so.**)
- *Had to* is the past form of both *must* and *have to*.
- *Should/Ought to* express a **duty/weak obligation.** *Employees should suggest ways to improve the company.* (**It's their duty.** – less emphatic than *must*)

> **Absence of necessity**
> *(don't have to/don't need to/needn't)*

- *Don't have to/Don't need to/Needn't:* it **isn't necessary** to do sth in the present/future. *You don't have to finish the report today. Pam doesn't need to go to the office today; she's going to work from home. You needn't send your job application by post; you can apply online.*

- *Didn't need to/Didn't have to:* it wasn't necessary to do sth. We don't know if it was done or not. *Ben didn't have to stay back at work.* (We don't know whether he stayed back or not.)
- *Needn't have* + past participle: it wasn't necessary to do sth, but it was done. An action happened in the past even though it wasn't necessary. *I needn't have ordered a printer, as Jackson had already done it.*

> **Permission/Prohibition**
> *(can, could, may, be allowed to, mustn't, can't)*

- *Can/Could/May* are used to **ask for/give permission**. *Can/Could/May I leave earlier today?* (**Is it OK if ...?**) *May* and *could* are more formal than *can*.
- *Can/May* are used to give permission. *You can/may use my office to have your meeting.*
- *Be allowed to* is used to ask/state what **the rule** is. *Are employees allowed to take their work laptops home?*
- *Mustn't/Can't:* it is **forbidden** to do sth; it is **against the rules/law; you are not allowed to** do sth. *You mustn't/can't wear shorts and sandals at work.*

> **Advice (should/ought to/must/shouldn't/ oughtn't to/mustn't)**

- *Should:* general advice – *Patrick should try to get on with his colleagues better.* (**It's my advice./I advise him to do so.**)
- *Ought to:* general advice – *You ought to put in your request in writing.* (**It's a good idea/thing to do.**)
- *Must:* strong advice – *You mustn't ignore your colleagues' advice.* (**It shows a lack of cooperation.**)

> **Possibility (can, could, may, might)**

- *Can* + present infinitive: **general/theoretical possibility**; not usually used for a specific situation. *Starting a new job can be stressful.* (**It is theoretically possible.**)
- *Could/May/Might* + present infinitive: **possibility** in a **specific situation**. *Bill might get a promotion.* (**It is possible./It is likely./Perhaps.**)

**Note:** We can use *can/could/might* in questions but **not 'may'**. *How could we solve this problem?*
- *Could/Might* + perfect infinitive refers to **sth in the past that was possible but didn't happen.** *He could have accepted the job, but he didn't want to move to another city.* (**It was possible but he didn't do it.**)

> **Ability/Inability (can, could, was able to)**

- *Can('t)* expresses **(in)ability in the present/future.** *Stella can develop web applications.* (**She is able to ...**)
- *Could(n't)* expresses general repeated **(in)ability in the past.** *Nigel could run long distances when he was younger.* (**He was able to ...**)

- *Was able to* expresses **ability** on a **specific occasion** in the **past.** *Sarah was able to finish her report with the help of her colleague.* (**She managed to ...**)
- *Couldn't/Wasn't able to* may be used to express **inability in the past, repeated or specific** *Jerry couldn't/wasn't able to speak French when he was young.* (**wasn't able to**; general repeated action in the past) *Sharon couldn't/wasn't able to find her notes for her presentation.* (**didn't manage to**; past single action)

> **Offers/Suggestions/Requests**
> *(can, would, shall, could)*

- *Can* (offer): *Can I help you carry this box?* (**Would you like me to ...?**)
- *Would* (offer): *Would you like me to call a taxi for you?* (**Do you want me to ...?**)
- *Shall* (suggestion): *Shall we order lunch?* (**What about ordering lunch ...?**)
- *Can/Could* (suggestion): *We can hire another graphic designer. We could present our ideas to the manager.* (**Let's ...**)
- *Can/Could/Would/Will* (request): *Can/Could/Would/ Will you come to the office on Saturday?* (**Are you willing to ...?**)

## Modals of deduction

- *Must:* **almost certain** that sth is/was **true** (positive logical assumption). *Mr Thomas must be the new Human Resources officer. She is late; she must have missed her bus.* (**I'm almost sure that sth is/was true.**)
- *May/Might/Could:* maybe, it's possible. *She may/ might/could quit her job if she doesn't get a pay rise. Hayley may/might/could have sent the email to the wrong address.* (**It is possible./It is likely./Perhaps.**)
- *Can't/Couldn't:* be sure that sth is/was **impossible** (negative logical assumption). *It can't/couldn't be easy for him to study while having a full-time job. Martha can't/couldn't have got the job; she doesn't have the qualifications.* (**I'm sure that sth isn't/wasn't true.**)

| | | |
|---|---|---|
| • *Perhaps she is right.*<br>• *I'm sure he runs the company.*<br>• *It's likely that she will get a work visa.* | **present infinitive** | • *She may be right.*<br>• *He must run the company.*<br>• *She may get a work visa.* |
| • *It's possible that he is working now.*<br>• *It's likely that Jo is leaving her job next month.* | **present continuous infinitive** | • *He could be working now.*<br>• *Jo may be leaving her job next month..* |

| | |
|---|---|
| • I'm sure he **didn't finish** the report.<br>• **It's likely that** she **has made** a mistake. | **perfect infinitive** |
| • Perhaps I **had heard** wrong. | |
| • He **can't have finished** the report.<br>• She **might have made** a mistake.<br>• I **may have heard** wrong. | |

| | |
|---|---|
| • Perhaps he **was having** a meeting when I called him.<br>• Perhaps she **has been thinking** of quitting. | **perfect continuous infinitive** |
| • I'm sure Amy **had been trying** for months to get an interview. | |
| • He **may have been having** a meeting when I called him.<br>• She **may have been thinking** of quitting.<br>• Amy **must have been trying** for months to get an interview. | |

## Unit 7

### The passive

**Form**

We form the **passive** with the verb **to be** in the appropriate tense and the **past participle** of the main verb. Study the table:

| | Active | Passive |
|---|---|---|
| **Present simple** | Ian **develops** apps. | Apps **are developed** by Ian. |
| **Present continuous** | Ian **is developing** apps. | Apps **are being developed** by Ian. |
| **Past simple** | Ian **developed** apps. | Apps **were developed** by Ian. |
| **Past continuous** | Ian **was developing** apps. | Apps **were being developed** by Ian. |
| **Present perfect** | Ian **has developed** apps. | Apps **have been developed** by Ian. |
| **Past perfect** | Ian **had developed** apps. | Apps **had been developed** by Ian. |
| **Future simple** | Ian **will develop** apps. | Apps **will be developed** by Ian. |
| **Future perfect** | Ian **will have developed** apps. | Apps **will have been developed** by Ian. |
| **Infinitive** | Ian **has to develop** apps. | Apps **have to be developed** by Ian. |
| **-ing form** | We saw Ian **developing** apps. | We saw apps **being developed** by Ian. |
| **Modal verbs** | Ian **can develop** apps. | Apps **can be developed** by Ian. |

**Note:** The **present perfect continuous**, the **past perfect continuous** and the **future continuous** are not normally used in the **passive**.

We use the **passive**:

• when the agent (the person/people doing the action) is **unknown**, **unimportant** or **obvious from the context**. *The technology exhibition **was cancelled**. (We don't know who cancelled it.) These laptops are **made** in Germany. (Who makes them is unimportant.) She **has been fired** from her job. (It's obvious that her employer has fired her.)*

• when the **action** is **more important** than the **agent**, as in **news headlines**, **newspaper articles**, **advertisements**, **instructions**, **formal notices**, **processes**, etc. *New medical software **was demonstrated** in last night's science exhibition.*

• when we want to **avoid taking responsibility** for an action, or when we refer to an unpleasant event and we do not want to say who or what is to blame. *The files **were deleted** by accident.*

• to **emphasise** the agent. *The experiment **was carried out** by university students.*

• to make statements **more formal** or **polite**. *The smartphone **has been damaged**. (More polite than saying "You have damaged the smartphone.")*

**Changing from the active into the passive:**

• The **object** of the active sentence becomes the **subject** in the passive sentence.

• The active verb remains in the same tense but changes into the passive form.

• The **subject** of the active sentence becomes the **agent**, and is either introduced with the preposition **by** or is omitted.

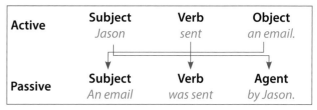

| Active | **Subject**<br>*Jason* | **Verb**<br>*sent* | **Object**<br>*an email.* |
|---|---|---|---|
| Passive | **Subject**<br>*An email* | **Verb**<br>*was sent* | **Agent**<br>*by Jason.* |

Only transitive verbs (verbs that take an object) can be changed into the passive. *The clouds **disappeared** from the sky.* (intransitive verb; **no passive form**)

**Note:** Some transitive verbs (*have, fit* [= be the right size], *suit, resemble,* etc) cannot be changed into the passive. *Nia **resembles** a famous actress.* (NOT: ~~A famous actress is resembled by Nia.~~)

• **Let** becomes **be allowed to** in the passive. *He **lets** me use his tablet. I **am allowed to use** his tablet.*

• We can use the verb **to get** instead of the verb **to be** in everyday speech, when we talk about things that happen by accident or unexpectedly. *My suitcases **got lost** at the airport.*

• **By** + **agent** is used to say who or what carries out an action. **With** + **instrument/material/ingredient** is used to say what the agent used. *The sculpture was made **by** a local artist. It was made **with** clay.*

- The agent can be **omitted** when the subject is **they**, **(s)he**, **someone/somebody**, **people**, **one**, etc. *Our Internet connection has been upgraded. (= They have upgraded our Internet connection.)*
- The agent is **not omitted** when it is a **specific** or **important person**, or when it is **essential** to the meaning of the sentence. *The announcement was made by Mayor West.*
- With verbs which can take two objects, such as **bring**, **tell**, **send**, **show**, **teach**, **promise**, **sell**, **read**, **offer**, **give**, **lend**, etc, we can form two different passive sentences. *Mr Benson teaches computer skills to senior citizens. (active) Senior citizens are taught computer skills by Mr Benson. (passive, more common) Computer skills are taught to senior citizens by Mr Benson. (passive, less common)*
- In passive questions with **who**, **whom** or **which**, we do not omit **by**. *Who wrote the email? Who was the email written by?*
- The verbs **hear**, **help**, **see** and **make** are followed by a bare infinitive in the active, but a **to**-infinitive in the passive. *She made the shop replace the faulty laptop. (active) The shop was made to replace the faulty laptop.*

## Personal – Impersonal constructions

The verbs **think**, **believe**, **say**, **report**, **know**, **expect**, **consider**, **understand**, etc are used in the following passive patterns in personal – impersonal constructions.
**Active:** *People say (that) technology improves our lives.*

**Passive: a) subject of *that*-clause + passive form of main verb + *to*-infinitive** (personal construction)
*Technology is said to improve our lives.*

**b) *It* + passive form of main verb + *that*-clause** (impersonal construction) *It is said (that) technology improves our lives.*

## The causative

- We use **have + object** (thing) + **past participle** to say that we have arranged for someone to do something for us. *Mark had anti-virus software installed. (He didn't install it himself.)*
- Questions and negations in the causative are formed with **do/does** (present simple) or **did** (past simple) + **have + object + past participle**. *How often do you have your computer serviced?*

|  | Active | Causative |
|---|---|---|
| **Present simple** | They **fix** PCs. | They **have** PCs **fixed**. |
| **Present continuous** | They **are fixing** PCs. | They **are having** PCs **fixed**. |
| **Past simple** | They **fixed** PCs. | They **had** PCs **fixed**. |
| **Past continuous** | They **were fixing** PCs. | They **were having** PCs **fixed**. |
| **Future simple** | They **will fix** PCs. | They **will have** PCs **fixed**. |
| **Future continuous** | They **will be fixing** PCs. | They **will be having** PCs **fixed**. |
| **Present perfect simple** | They **have fixed** PCs. | They **have had** PCs **fixed**. |
| **Present perfect continuous** | They **have been fixing** PCs. | They **have been having** PCs **fixed**. |
| **Past perfect simple** | They **had fixed** PCs. | They **had had** PCs **fixed**. |
| **Past perfect continuous** | They **had been fixing** PCs. | They **had been having** PCs **fixed**. |
| **-ing form** | They like **fixing** PCs. | They like **having** PCs **fixed**. |
| **Infinitive** | They have **to fix** PCs. | They have **to have** PCs **fixed**. |
| **Modal verbs** | They **may fix** PCs. | They **may have** PCs **fixed**. |

- We also use **the causative form** to say that something unpleasant or unexpected happened to somebody. *The scientist had his lab destroyed in the fire.*
- We can use **get** instead of **have** only in informal conversation.
  *Emily will get her research published.*
- **Make/Have + object (person) + bare infinitive** are used to express that someone causes someone else to do something, but the meaning is slightly different.
  *He made the students turn off their phones. (He insisted that the students turn off their phones.)*
  *My mum had me write an email for the gas company. (She asked me to write an email.)*
- **Get + object (person) + to-infinitive** shows that someone persuades someone else to do something.
  *She got her brother to help her with her Science homework. (She persuaded him to help her.)*

## Reflexive/Emphatic pronouns

| | | |
|---|---|---|
| I – **myself** | he – **himself** | we – **ourselves** |
| you – **yourself** | she – **herself** | you – **yourselves** |
| | it – **itself** | they – **themselves** |

We use **reflexive pronouns**:
- with verbs such as **burn**, **cut**, **hurt**, **introduce**, **kill**, **look at**, **teach**, etc, or with prepositions, when the subject and the object of the verb are the same person.
  *Tina (subject) taught herself (object) how to write simple computer programs.*

# Grammar Reference

- in the following expressions: *enjoy yourself* (have a good time), *behave yourself* (be good), *help yourself* (you are welcome to take sth if you want) *by yourself* (on your own). *Andrew went to the science and technology show by himself.*
- We use **emphatic pronouns** to emphasise the subject or the object of a sentence.
  *The shop owner himself delivered the laptop to my house.* (No one else delivered it.)
  *She spoke to the President himself.* (She didn't speak to anyone else.)

**Notes:**
- We do not normally use reflexive pronouns with the verbs *concentrate*, *feel*, *meet* and *relax*.
  *Dennis feels confident that his new app will be a success.*
- Reflexive pronouns are used with the verbs *dress*, *wash* and *shave* when we want to show that someone did something with a lot of effort.
  *Part of her job as a nurse it to help weak patients wash themselves.*

## Unit 8

### Conditionals: types 0 & 1

**Conditional clauses** consist of two parts: the *if*-clause (hypothesis) and the **main clause** (result).
When the *if*-clause comes before the **main clause**, the two clauses are separated with a comma.
*If the factory closes, a lot of people will lose their jobs.*
When the **main clause** comes before the *if*-clause, no comma is needed.
*A lot of people will lose their jobs if the factory closes.*

| | if-clause (hypothesis) | Main clause (result) |
|---|---|---|
| **0 conditional:** general truth or scientific fact | *if/when* + present simple | present simple |
| | *If you have the flu, your muscles ache.* | |
| **1st conditional:** • real situation, likely to happen in the present/future | *if/when* + present simple | simple future – *can/must/may*, etc + bare infinitive |
| | *If the charity asks for help, I'll volunteer.* | |
| • instructions | *if/when* + present simple | imperative |
| | *If you find a stray animal in the street, take it to an animal shelter.* | |

**Notes:**
- With type 1 conditionals we can use *unless* + **affirmative verb** or *if* + **negative verb**.
  *Unless we all make an effort, global warming will continue to be a problem.*

- We use *if* to show that something might happen, whereas we use *when* to show that something will definitely happen. *If you go to the cinema, I will come with you.* (= You might go to the cinema.) *When you go to the cinema, I will come with you.* (= I know that you will definitely go to the cinema.)
- We do not normally use *will*, *would* or *should* in an *if*-clause. However, we can use *will* or *would* after *if* to make a polite request, or express insistence or uncertainty (usually with expressions such as *I don't know*, *I doubt*, *I wonder*, etc). In this case, *if* means *whether*. We can also use *should* after *if* to talk about something which is possible, but not very likely to happen. *If you will give me your address, I will email you the information.* (Will you please give me your address? – polite request) *If you will keep overeating, you'll become overweight.* (If you insist on overeating ... – insistence) *I wonder if she will tell me what's bothering her.* (I wonder whether ... – uncertainty) *If I should stay back at work, I'll let you know.* (I don't really expect that I'll stay back at work.)

### Conditionals: types 2 & 3

| | if-clause (hypothesis) | Main clause (result) |
|---|---|---|
| **2nd conditional:** • imaginary, unreal, or highly unlikely situations in the present/ future | *If* + past simple | *would/could/might* + bare infinitive |
| | *If we had better public transport, fewer people would drive to work.* (but we don't – unreal in the present) | |
| • advice | *If I were you, I would see a doctor about that cough.* | |
| **3rd conditional:** | *If* + past perfect | *would/could/might have* + past participle |
| • unreal situations in the past | *If Stephen hadn't watched the documentary, he wouldn't have learnt so much about illiteracy.* (but he did – unreal in the past) | |
| • regrets | *If I had known he had lost his job, I would have lent him the money he asked for.* | |
| • criticism | *If you hadn't ignored my advice, you wouldn't have got into trouble.* | |

**Note:** We can use *were* instead of *was* for all persons in the *if*-clause of type 2 conditionals.
*If Judy were/was free tonight, she would visit her friend.*
We use *if I were* you ... in the *if*-clause of type-2 conditionals when we want to give advice.
*If I were you, I'd talk to my parents about the problem.*

## Wishes

We can use *I wish/if only* to express a wish.

| I wish/If only | | Use |
|---|---|---|
| + past simple/ past continuous | *I wish I **didn't feel** ill.* (but I do) *If only it **wasn't/ weren't** snowing today.* (but it is) | to express what we would like to be different about a present situation |
| + could + bare infinitive | *Beth wishes she **could run** in the charity race.* (but she can't) | to express regret in the present concerning lack of ability |
| + past perfect | *I wish I **hadn't missed** my appointment.* (but I did) *If only the shelter **hadn't closed** down.* (but it did) | to express regret about something that happened or didn't happen in the past |
| + subject + would + bare infinitive | *I wish **you would help** out around the house.* *If only **he wouldn't complain** all the time.* | to express: • a polite imperative • a desire for a situation or a person's behaviour to change |

**Notes:**
- **If only** is used in exactly the same way as *I wish*, but it is more emphatic or more dramatic.
  *If only Patrick had accepted our help!*
- We can use *were* instead of *was* after *wish* and *if only*.
  *She wishes she **were/was** more confident.*

## Question tags

- **Question tags** are short questions at the end of statements.
- We use them in speech **to confirm something**, or to find out if something is true or not.
- We form them with the **auxiliary** or **modal** verb from the main sentence and the appropriate subject pronoun. *You didn't forget to call Adam, **did you**? Helen can help out at the shelter, **can't she**?*

### Use
- A positive statement takes a negative question tag.
  *He has lost his job, **hasn't he**?*
- A negative statement takes a positive question tag.
  *You aren't going to the meeting, **are you**?*
- When the verb of the sentence is in the present simple, we use *do (not)/does (not)* in the question tag.
  *Paul teaches at the local secondary school, **doesn't he**?*
- When the verb of the sentence is in the past simple, we use *did (not)*.
  *Penny took part in the beach clean-up, **didn't she**?*
  Some verbs/expressions form question tags differently:

| I am → aren't I? | *I am next in line, **aren't' I**?* |
|---|---|
| Imperative → **will you/ won't you?** | *Put this in the recycling bin, **will you/won't you**?* |
| **Don't** → **will you?** | *Don't close the window, **will you**?* |
| **Let's** → **shall we?** | *Let's take the dog for a walk, **shall we**?* |
| **You've got** → **haven't you?** | *You've got a big house, **haven't you**?* |
| **You have** (idiomatically) → **don't you?** | *You always have tea for breakfast, **don't you**?* |
| **This/That is** → **isn't it?** | *This is Sam's car, **isn't it**?* |
| **No one** → **do/did they** | *No one missed the seminar, **did they**?* |

### Intonation
- When we are sure of the answer and expect agreement, the voice goes down in the question tag.
  *You haven't seen Tim today, **have you**? (↘)*
- When we are not sure of the answer and want to check information, the voice goes up in the question tag.
  *He'll keep his promise, **won't he**? (↗)*

# Unit 9

## (*to*-) infinitive

The **to-infinitive** is used:
- to express **purpose**. *Anna uses a dictionary **to look up** unknown words.*
- after certain verbs that refer to the future (**agree, appear, decide, expect, hope, plan, promise, refuse**, etc). *Alan **has decided to do** a course in IT.*
- after **would like, would prefer, would love**, etc to express a specific preference. *I **would prefer to do** my research at the university library.*
- after adjectives which describe feelings/emotions (**happy, glad, sad**, etc), express willingness/ unwillingness (**eager, reluctant, willing**, etc) or refer to a person's character (**clever, kind**, etc), and the adjectives **lucky, fortunate**. *My little brother is **eager to start** school next year.*
- after **too/enough**. *The lecture hall is big **enough to seat** 300 students.*
- to talk about an unexpected event, usually with **only**. *He rushed to the lecture theatre **only to find out** that the professor had cancelled his lecture.*
- after **it** + **be** + **adjective/noun**. *It was **kind** of Olga to help me study.*
- in the expressions **to tell you the truth, to be honest, to sum up, to begin with**, etc. ***To begin with**, let's select a title for our presentation.*

# Grammar Reference

The **infinitive without *to*** (bare infinitive) is used:
- after **modal verbs**. *You must ask Professor Betts for help with your term paper.*
- after the verbs *let*, *make*, *see*, *hear* and *feel*. *Someone heard him admit he had lied.* **BUT** we use the ***to*-infinitive** after *be made*, *be heard*, *be seen*, etc (passive form). *He was heard to admit he had lied.*
- after *had better* and *would rather*. *You had better renew your library card.*

**Note:**
- *Help* can be followed by the ***to*-infinitive**, but in American English it is normally followed by the **infinitive without *to***. *My brother helped me (to) do my Maths homework.*
- If two ***to*-infinitives** are linked by *and* or *or*, the *to* of the second infinitive can be omitted. *Lucy decided to take a break from studying and go for a walk.*

## *-ing* form

The ***-ing* form** is used:
- as a **noun**. *Studying abroad can cost a lot of money.*
- after certain verbs: *admit*, *appreciate*, *avoid*, *consider*, *continue*, *deny*, *fancy*, *finish*, *start*, *go* (for activities), *imagine*, *mind*, *miss*, *quit*, *save*, *suggest*, *practise*, *prevent*, etc. *Celia has finished typing up her essay.*
- after *love*, *like*, *enjoy*, *prefer*, *dislike*, *hate*, to express general preference. *Sophie prefers studying at the library because it's quiet there.* **BUT** for a specific preference (*would like/ would prefer/would love*) we use ***to*-infinitive**. *Sophie would prefer to study at her friend's house tonight so that they can work on their project.*
- after expressions such as *be busy*, *it's no use*, *it's no good*, *it's (not) worth*, *what's the use of*, *can't help*, *there's no point (in)*, *can't stand*, *have difficulty (in)*, *have trouble*, etc. *Althea is busy correcting her students' tests.*
- after *spend*, *waste* or *lose* (time, money, etc). *Dinah spent two weeks preparing her presentation.*
- after the preposition *to* with verbs and expressions such as *look forward to*, *be/get used to*, *in addition to*, *object to*. *Denise looks forward to starting university in autumn.*
- after other **prepositions**. *David is keen on studying Archaeology.*
- after the verbs *hear*, *listen to*, *notice*, *see*, *watch* and *feel* to describe an incomplete action. *I watched the technician setting up the projector for the lecture.* (I watched part of it.) **BUT** we use the **bare infinitive** with these verbs to describe the complete action. *I watched the technician set up the projector for the lecture.* (I watched the whole thing.)

| Forms of the infinitive | | |
|---|---|---|
| | **Active voice** | **Passive voice** |
| **Present** | (to) take | (to) be taken |
| **Present continuous** | (to) be taking | – |
| **Perfect** | (to) have taken | (to) have been taken |
| **Perfect continuous** | (to) have been taking | – |

| Forms of the *-ing* form | | |
|---|---|---|
| | **Active voice** | **Passive voice** |
| **Present** | seeing | being seen |
| **Perfect** | having seen | having been seen |

| Forms of the infinitive/*-ing* form corresponding to verb tenses |
|---|
| present simple/*will* → **present infinitive/*-ing* form** |
| present continuous/future continuous → **present continuous infinitive** |
| past simple/present perfect/past perfect/ future perfect → **perfect infinitive/*-ing* form** |
| past continuous/present perfect continuous/ past perfect continuous → **perfect continuous infinitive** |

| Difference in meaning between the *to*-infinitive and the *-ing* form |
|---|
| Some verbs can take either the ***to*-infinitive** or the ***-ing* form** with a change in meaning. |
| • *forget* + ***to*-infinitive** = not remember *Ian forgot to put his name on the exam paper.* <br> • *forget* + ***-ing* form** = not recall *Katy will never forget teaching her first class.* |
| • *remember* + ***to*-infinitive** = not forget *Did you remember to call Diane?* <br> • *remember* + ***-ing* form** = recall *Pete doesn't remember taking his phone to the library with him.* |
| • *mean* + ***to*-infinitive** = intend to *They mean to study for the test together.* <br> • *mean* + ***-ing* form** = involve *Studying away from home usually means renting a place to live.* |
| • *regret* + ***to*-infinitive** = be sorry to (normally used in the present simple with verbs such as *say*, *tell* and *inform*) *We regret to inform you that your application was rejected.* <br> • *regret* + ***-ing* form** = feel sorry about *Maya regrets not going to college.* |

- **try** + **to**-infinitive = attempt, do one's best
  *He **tried to download** a book from the Internet.*
- **try** + **-ing** form = do sth as an experiment
  *Try practising your speech in front of a mirror.*
- **stop** + **to**-infinitive = stop temporarily in order to do sth else. *After studying for three hours, Ben **stopped to have** lunch.*
- **stop** + **-ing** form = finish doing sth
  *Mrs Lee **stopped teaching** at the age of 62.*
- **would prefer** + **to**-infinitive (specific preference)
  *I **would prefer to do** an online course.*
- **prefer** + **-ing** form (general preference)
  *Amanda **prefers walking** to school.*

## Relatives

We use relative pronouns (***who, whose, which, that***) and relative adverbs (***where, when, why***) to introduce relative clauses. We use relative clauses to identify/describe the person/place/thing in the main clause.

Relative clause

*The lady **who** works at the library is very helpful.*

## Relative pronouns

| | subject of the relative clause (cannot be omitted) | object of the relative clause (can be omitted) |
|---|---|---|
| people | who/that *The girl **who/that** sits next to me is a new student.* | who/whom/that *The man (**who/ whom/that**) you saw is my Maths teacher.* |
| things/animals | which/that *I bought some books **which/that** were on sale.* | which/that *The test (**which/that**) we had yesterday was easy.* |
| possession | whose (never omitted) *Ian is the student **whose** article appeared in the local paper. This is a book **whose** characters/the characters of which are very interesting.* | |

## Relative adverbs

- We use ***where*** to refer to places. *The classroom **where** we do ICT has new computers.*
- We use ***why*** to give a reason. *She didn't tell us the reason **why** she decided to change schools.*
- We use ***when*** to refer to time. *This is the period **when** students are studying for their final exams.*

**Note:** When using ***where*** or ***when***, we do not need a preposition. *The school **where** I go is next to a park.* (NOT: ~~The school where I go to is next to a park.~~)

## Defining & Non-defining relative clauses

- A **defining relative clause** gives necessary information, essential to the meaning of the main sentence. It is not put in commas and is introduced with ***who, which, that, whose, where, when*** or ***the reason (why)***. The relative pronoun can be omitted when it is the object of the relative clause.
  *The professor **who** teaches Economics at my university is a published author. The class (**which/that**) I enjoy most is English Literature.*
- A **non-defining relative clause** gives extra information and is not essential to the meaning of the main sentence. It is put in commas and is introduced with ***who, which, whose, where*** or ***when*** but never ***that***, which is only used in defining relative clauses. The relative pronoun cannot be omitted.
  *The staffroom, **where** teachers take their break, is on the second floor.*
- ***Whose*** is never omitted.
  *Georgia wants to study at a college **whose** courses are available online.*
- ***That*** can be used instead of ***who, whom*** or ***which***, but it is never used after commas or prepositions.
  *Andrea tutors students **who/that** have difficulty in Maths.*
  *Mr Sinclair, **who** teaches us Physics, is a very funny person.*

## Prepositions in relative clauses

- We usually avoid using prepositions before relative pronouns. When we do, we use ***whom***, not ***who***. Compare: *The woman **to whom** I sent the email is the college secretary.* **(formal)** *The woman **who** I sent the email **to** is the college secretary.* **(less usual)** *The woman I sent the email **to** is the college secretary.* **(everyday English)**
- We don't use a preposition with ***where*** or ***when***.
  *The school **where** I go has a recycling programme.* NOT: ~~The school where I go to has a recycling programme.~~
- We can replace ***where/when*** with a preposition followed by ***which***. In informal English, this preposition is placed at the end of the sentence and ***which*** is omitted.
  *That's the classroom **where/in which** we have our Music lessons. That's the classroom we have our Music lessons in.*
  *Mondays and Thursdays are the days **when/on which** we have PE. Mondays and Thursdays are the days we have PE on.*
- ***Which*** and ***whom*** can be used in expressions of quantity with ***of*** (***some of, many of, half of, both of, a few of, several of, none of***, etc.).

# Grammar Reference

*The exam had a lot of questions. A few of them were quite difficult. The exam had a lot of questions, **a few of which** were quite difficult.*
*Thirty students went on the school trip to the History Museum. A lot of them had been there before. Thirty students went on the school trip to the History Museum, **a lot of whom** had been there before.*

## Unit 10

### Reported speech

**Direct speech** is the exact words someone said. We use quotation marks in direct speech.
**Reported speech** is the exact meaning of what someone said, but not the exact words. We do not use quotation marks in reported speech. The word **'that'** can either be used or omitted after the introductory verb (*say, tell*, etc).

#### Say – Tell
- ***say*** + no personal object
  *Pam **said (that)** there was a storm coming.*
- ***say*** + ***to*** + personal object
  *Pam **said to me (that)** there was a storm coming.*
- ***tell*** + personal object
  *Pam **told me (that)** there was a storm coming.*
- We use ***say*** + ***to*-infinitive**, but never ***say about***. We use ***tell sb/speak/talk about* sth**.
  *Mum **said to stay** inside because it was too cold.*
  *He **told us/spoke/talked about** the town's new recycling scheme.*

| | |
|---|---|
| **Say** | hello, good morning/afternoon, etc, something/nothing/anything, so, a few words, no more, for certain/sure, sorry, etc |
| **Tell** | the truth, a lie, a story, a secret, a joke, the time, the difference, one from another, someone one's name, someone the way, someone so, someone's fortune, etc |
| **Ask** | a question, a favour, the price, about someone, the time, around, for something/someone, etc |
| **Speak** | to someone, your mind, for yourself, up, slowly, a language, out, up for somebody |
| **Talk** | sense, nonsense, to yourself, someone into/out of (doing) something, talk your way out of something |

### Reported statements

- In reported speech, personal/possessive pronouns and possessive adjectives change according to the meaning of the sentence. *Susan said, "I've lost my umbrella."* (direct speech) *Susan said (that) **she** had lost **her** umbrella.* (reported speech)

- We can report someone's words either a long time after they were said (out-of-date reporting), or a short time after they were said (up-to-date reporting).

#### Up-to-date reporting
The tenses can either change or remain the same in reported speech.
**Direct speech:** *Ben said, "I'm working on my project."*
**Reported speech:** *Ben said (that) he is working/was working on his project.*

#### Out-of-date reporting
The introductory verb is in the past simple, and the tenses change as follows:

| Direct speech | Reported speech |
|---|---|
| **Present simple → Past simple** | |
| *"I **recycle** old papers," he said.* | *He said (that) he **recycled** old papers* |
| **Present continuous → Past continuous** | |
| *"We **are going** to the beach clean-up," she said.* | *She said (that) **they were going** to the beach clean-up.* |
| **Present perfect → Past perfect** | |
| *"I **have adopted** a tiger," he said.* | *He said (that) he **had adopted** a tiger.* |
| **Past simple → Past simple or Past perfect** | |
| *"The snowstorm **lasted** for an hour," they said.* | *They said (that) the snowstorm **lasted/had lasted** for an hour.* |
| **Past continuous → Past continuous or Past perfect continuous** | |
| *"It **was raining** all day," he said.* | *He said (that) it **was raining/had been raining** all day.* |
| **Will → Would** | |
| *"We **will install** solar panels," they said.* | *They said (that) they **would install** solar panels.* |

- Certain words and time expressions change according to the meaning, as follows:

| | | |
|---|---|---|
| now | → | then, immediately |
| today | → | that day |
| yesterday | → | the day before, the previous day |
| tomorrow | → | the next/following day |
| this week | → | that week |
| last week | → | the week before, the previous week |
| next week | → | the week after, the following week |
| ago | → | before |
| here | → | there |
| this | → | that |

- Verb tenses **change** in reported speech when we consider what the speaker said to be untrue.
  *"Kangaroos live in Antarctica," he said. → He said (that) Kangaroos **lived** in Antarctica.* (We know they don't.)

- Verb tenses can **either change or remain the same** in reported speech when reporting a **general truth** or **law of nature**.
  *"The Earth rotates on its axis every 24 hours," the teacher said. → The teacher said that the Earth rotated/rotates on its axis every 24 hours.*
- Verb tenses **remain the same** in reported speech:
  **a)** when the introductory verb is in the **present**, **future** or **present perfect**. *She says, "I want to join an environmental organisation." She says (that) she wants to join an environmental organisation.*
  **b)** in **type 2** and **3 conditionals**. *"If the weather was warmer, we would go for a swim," she said. She said (that) if the weather was warmer, they would go for a swim. "If I had known about tree planting event, I would have taken part," I said. I said (that) If I had known about tree planting event, I would have taken part.*

## Reported questions

- Reported questions are usually introduced with the verbs **ask**, **enquire**, **wonder**, or the phrase **want to know**.
- When the direct question begins with a question word (**who**, **where**, **how**, **when**, **what**, etc), the reported question is introduced with the same question word.
  *"Where is the recycling centre?" he asked. (direct question) He asked where the recycling centre was. (reported question)*
- When the direct question begins with an auxiliary (**be**, **do**, **have**) or a modal verb (**can**, **may**, etc), then the reported question is introduced with **if** or **whether**.
  *"Does your school have recycling bins?" she asked me. (direct question) She asked me if/whether my school had recycling bins. (reported question)*
- In reported questions, the word order is the same as in statements. The question mark and words such as **please**, **well**, **oh**, etc are omitted. The verb tenses, pronouns, possessive adjectives and time phrases change as in reported statements.
  *"What are you doing now?" he asked her. (direct question) He asked her what she was doing then. (reported question).*

## Modals in reported speech

Certain modal verbs change in reported speech as follows:
- **can → could** (present reference) / **would be able to** (future reference)
  *"I can't find my raincoat," Leyla said. Leyla said (that) she couldn't find her raincoat. (present reference) "I can drive you to school tomorrow," John said. John said (that) he would be able to drive me to school the following day. (future reference)*

- **may → might/could**
  *"It may snow tonight," Patrick said. Patrick said (that) it might/could snow that night.*
- **shall → should** (asking for advice) / **offer** (offering to do sth) *"What shall I do with these empty jars?" he asked me. He asked me what he should do with those empty jars. (asking for advice) "Shall I make us some tea?" she asked. She offered to make us some tea. (offering to do sth)*
- **must → had to** (obligation) / **must** (logical assumption)
  *"You must take the rubbish out," my mum said. My mum said (that) I had to take the rubbish out. (obligation) "The snow must be a metre deep," Frank told me. Frank told me (that) the snow must be a metre deep. (logical assumption)*
- **needn't → didn't need to/didn't have to** (present reference) / **wouldn't have to** (future reference) *"You needn't pay to see the exhibition," said Maria. Maria said (that) I didn't need to/didn't have to pay to see the exhibition. (present reference) "We needn't take anything with us to the beach clean-up tomorrow," James told me. James told me (that) we wouldn't have to take anything with us to the beach clean-up the following day. (future reference)*

## Special introductory verbs for reported commands/requests/suggestions/orders/ instructions, etc

- **Reported commands/requests/suggestions/ orders/instructions** are introduced with a special **introductory verb** that is appropriate to the situation (see the list below) followed by a **to-infinitive**, an **-ing** form or a **that-clause**, depending on the introductory verb.
  *"Pick up your litter now," the police officer told him. → The police officer commanded him to pick up his litter immediately. (command)*
  *"Please help me clear away the flood water," Sam told his sister. → Sam asked his sister to help him clear away the flood water. (request)*
  *"Why don't we plant some flowers?" she said. → She suggested planting some flowers. (suggestion)*
  *"We can buy separate bins for the recyclables," he told me. → He suggested (that) we (should) buy separate bins for the recyclables. (suggestion)*
- To report **orders** or **instructions**, we can use the verbs **order** or **tell** + **sb** + **(not) to-infinitive**.
  *"Don't step on the grass," the park keeper told them. (direct order) The park keeper told them not to step on the grass. (reported order) "Stop making noise," my teacher said. (direct order) My teacher ordered me to stop making noise. (reported order)*

# Grammar Reference

| Special Introductory Verbs | | | |
|---|---|---|---|
| **Introductory verb** | **Direct speech** | | **Reported speech** |
| *+ to -inf* | | | |
| **agree** | *"OK, I will go to the shops with you."* | → | *He **agreed to go** to the shops with me.* |
| **demand** | *"I want to talk to the manager."* | → | *She **demanded to talk** to the manager.* |
| **offer** | *"Would you like me to take you to the doctor?"* | → | *He **offered to take** me to the doctor.* |
| **promise** | *"I'll be by your side the whole time."* | → | *She **promised to be** by my side the whole time.* |
| **refuse** | *"No, I will not lend you my laptop."* | → | *He **refused to lend** me his laptop.* |
| **threaten** | *"Study harder or I'll take away your games console."* | → | *She **threatened to take away** his games console if he didn't study harder.* |
| **claim** | *"I finished my chores."* | → | *He **claimed to have finished** his chores.* |
| *+ sb + to-inf* | | | |
| **advise** | *"You shouldn't go out in the rain."* | → | *She **advised me not to go** out in the rain.* |
| **allow/permit** | *"You can leave earlier."* | → | *He **allowed/permitted me to leave** earlier.* |
| **ask** | *"Please, close the door!"* | → | *She **asked me to close** the door.* |
| **beg** | *"Please, tell me the truth!"* | → | *He **begged me to tell** him the truth.* |
| **command** | *"Arrest him, officer!"* | → | *He **commanded the officer to arrest** him.* |
| **encourage** | *"Go on, share your story!"* | → | *She **encouraged me to share** my story.* |
| **forbid** | *"You mustn't take photos in the museum!"* | → | *He **forbade me to take** photos in the museum.* |
| **instruct** | *"Fill in the form and leave it with the secretary."* | → | *She **instructed me to fill in** the form and leave it with the secretary.* |
| **invite** | *"Would you like to stay over?"* | → | *She **invited me to stay over**.* |
| **order** | *"Stop talking!"* | → | *She **ordered us to stop** talking.* |
| **remind** | *"Don't forget to call the plumber."* | → | *He **reminded me to call** the plumber.* |
| **urge** | *"Start exercising more!"* | → | *She **urged me to start** exercising more.* |
| **warn** | *"Don't swim in this lake!"* | → | *He **warned us not to swim** in that lake.* |
| **want** | *"I'd like you to give me more details."* | → | *She **wanted me to give** her more details.* |
| *+ -ing form* | | | |
| **accuse sb of** | *"You left the door unlocked."* | → | *He **accused me of leaving** the door unlocked.* |
| **apologise (to sb) for** | *"I'm so sorry I called you a liar."* | → | *She **apologised to me for calling me** a liar.* |
| **admit (to)** | *"Yes, I lost your camera."* | → | *He **admitted (to) losing** my camera.* |
| **boast about** | *"We sell the freshest products in the market."* | → | *They **boasted about selling** the freshest products in the market.* |
| **complain (to sb) about** | *"You are constantly making fun of me."* | → | *He **complained to me about** my constantly **making** fun of him.* |
| **deny** | *"I didn't cheat in the test."* | → | *She **denied cheating** in the test.* |
| **insist on** | *"You must water the plants."* | → | *He **insisted on** me/my **watering** the plants.* |

| Introductory verb | Direct speech | | Reported speech |
|---|---|---|---|
| suggest | "Let's make our own compost." | → | She **suggested making** their own compost. |
| | **+ that-clause** | | |
| agree | "Yes, a homeless shelter is necessary in our town." | → | She **agreed that** a homeless shelter was necessary in their town. |
| boast | "I do great work for the charity." | → | He **boasted that** he did great work for the charity. |
| claim | "The President called to congratulate me." | → | She **claimed that** the President had called to congratulate her. |
| complain | "There are not enough litter bins in the park." | → | He **complained that** there were not enough litter bins in the park. |
| deny | "I didn't delete the file." | → | She **denied that** she deleted/had deleted the file. |
| exclaim | "What a good idea!" | → | He **exclaimed that** it was a good idea. |
| explain | "Sea levels are rising because of global warming." | → | She **explained that** sea levels are/were rising because of global warming. |
| inform sb | "The bottle bank is further down the street." | → | He **informed me that** the bottle bank was further down the street. |
| promise | "I will do the shopping for you." | → | She **promised that** she would do the shopping for me. |
| suggest | "You should ask Kim for advice." | → | He **suggested that** I should ask Kim for advice. |
| | **to sb + how + to-infinitive** | | |
| explain to sb + *how* + *to*-infinitive | "And that's how you change the ink in the printer." | → | She **explained to me how to change** the ink in the printer. |
| wonder (when the subject of the introductory verb is **not** the same as the subject in the reported question) | He asked himself, "When did they install new bins?" <br> She asked herself, "How did he get here?" <br> He asked himself, "Why does Ken want to talk to me?" | → <br><br> → <br> → | He **wondered when** they had installed new bins. <br><br> She **wondered how** he had got there. <br><br> He **wondered why** Ken wanted to talk to him. |
| | **+ where/what/why/how + to-inf or clause** | | |
| wonder (when the subjects are the same) | She asked herself, "Who will I invite to my graduation?" | → | She **wondered who to invite** to her graduation. <br> She **wondered who she should invite** to her graduation. |

# Unit 11

## Determiners

- *every – each*
- *Every* and *each* are used with singular countable nouns. We normally use *each* when we talk about two people or things. We use *every/each* when we talk about three or more people or things. *He left the house wearing different socks on each foot!* (NOT: ...on every foot...) *She tried on each/every dress in the shop.*
- *Every one* and *each (one)* can be followed by *of*. *Mrs Thomas bought a small gift for each one of her students.*
- We use *every* when we are thinking of people or things together, in a group, to mean 'all', 'everybody/everything'. *Every shop in the shopping centre has sales.* (all shops)

We use *each* when we are thinking of people or things separately, one at a time. *Each sales assistant in the shop will meet with the new manager.*
- We use *every* to show how often something happens. *The local supermarket announces new offers every Thursday.*
- We use *every*, but not *each*, with words and expressions such as *almost*, *nearly*, *practically* and *without exception*. *Almost every appliance I've bought from this shop has turned out to be faulty.* (NOT: almost each appliance)

**Note:**
- *each other* = one another *The two managers work well with each other.*
- *every other* = alternate *He works at the supermarket every other day.*

# Grammar Reference

- ***another*** = one more part from those already mentioned. ***Another*** can also be used with expressions of distance, money and time. *I'm sure there's **another** bookshop in the area, not just the one in Smith Street. He couldn't buy the camera because he needed **another** £50.*

### both/neither – all/whole/none – either

- ***Both*** refers to two people, things or groups. It has a positive meaning and is followed by a plural verb. *Both brothers **are** business owners.*
- ***Neither*** refers to two people, things or groups, and has a negative meaning. ***Neither of*** + **plural noun phrase** can be followed by either a singular or plural verb in the affirmative. *Neither of the two shopping centres in my town **has/have** a pet shop.* **BUT** *Neither skirt **fits** me.*
- ***All*** refers to more than two people, things or groups. It has a positive meaning and is followed by a plural verb. *All big companies **want** to increase their sales. All of them **have** marketing departments.*
- ***Both/All*** can go:
  a) after the verb **to be**. *They are **both/all** interested in a career in advertising.*
  b) after a modal/auxiliary verb, but before the main verb. *We should **all/both** do our shopping online.*
- ***Whole*** is used with singular countable nouns. We use **a/the/this/my**/etc + ***whole*** + **noun**. *Jessica does the shopping for **the whole family**.* **ALSO:** *Jessica does the shopping for **all the family**.* We don't use ***whole*** with uncountable nouns. *He spent **all the money** he had left on a game.* (NOT: ~~... the whole money ...~~) ***All*** + **day/morning/week/year** = **the whole** + **day/morning/week/year** *She has been looking forward to her day off all week/the whole week.*
- ***None of*** refers to more than two people, things or groups, and has a negative meaning. It is used with nouns or object pronouns, and is followed by either a singular or plural verb. *None of the local shops **sells/sell** the brand I'm looking for.* **BUT** *'How much sugar did you put in my coffee?' 'None.'*
- ***Either*** refers to two people, things or groups, and is followed by a singular countable noun. ***Either of*** + **plural noun phrase** can be followed by either a singular or plural verb. *Either of the two T-shirts **looks/look** good on you.* **BUT** *Either T-shirt **fits** you perfectly.* We can use ***not ... either of*** instead of ***neither of***. ***Either*** can also be used at the end of a negative sentence. *She has two grocery shops close to her house, but she **doesn't** shop at **either of them**.* (= She has two grocery shops close to her house, but she shops at neither of them.) *James **doesn't** like TV adverts and Lily **doesn't either**.*
- ***Both ... and ...*** is followed by a plural verb. *Both Karen and Elias buy organic vegetables only.*
- ***Neither ... nor/Either ... or*** take either a singular or plural verb, depending on the subject which follows

nor or or. *Neither the shop assistant nor the manager **has** agreed to give me my money back. **Either** I or my parents **are** going to do grandmas' shopping tomorrow.*

## Countable/Uncountable nouns – Quantifiers & Partitives

### Quantifiers

- We use ***a/an*** with singular countable nouns when we mention something for the first time. *Lydia has bought **a shirt**. The shirt is for her brother.*
- We use ***a*** before singular countable nouns which begin with a consonant sound. *(a card, a bike)* We use ***an*** before singular countable nouns which begin with a vowel sound. *(an onion, an heirloom)*
- We don't use ***a/an*** with uncountable or plural nouns. In these cases, we use ***some*** in affirmative sentences. *I need **some help** with the instructions. There are **some problems** with the phone I bought.*
- We use ***any*** in interrogative and negative sentences with uncountable nouns and plural countable nouns. *Is there **any coffee** in the pot? There **aren't any nuts** in the cake.*
- We use ***no*** instead of ***not any*** in sentences to make them negative. *There is **no flour** left.* (= There isn't any flour.)
- ***Much*** and ***many*** are usually used in negative or interrogative sentences. ***Much*** is used with uncountable nouns and ***many*** is used with countable nouns. *He **doesn't** put **much sauce** on his pasta. Is there **much cheese** left? There **aren't many shoe shops** in my town. Are there **many eggs** in the carton?*
- ***Too many*** is used with countable nouns and too much is used with uncountable nouns to show that there is more than the required quantity of something. *You bought **too many** apples. There is **too much salt** in the salad.*
- ***How much/many*** is used in interrogative sentences. *How much water do you drink every day? How many students bring lunch from home?*
- ***Enough*** is used with countable and uncountable nouns in the affirmative, negative and interrogative to show that there is as much of something as required. *We **have enough bags** to put all our groceries in. He **doesn't** have **enough petrol** to drive to the market. Did you buy **enough bread** for everyone?*
- ***A couple of/Hundreds of/Three of***, etc are used with countable nouns. They are normally used in affirmative sentences. The ***of*** is omitted when ***a couple/hundred/plenty/three***, etc are not followed by a noun. *Let's get **a couple of things** from the grocer's. How many bread rolls have we got? **A couple**.*
- ***A bit of*** is used with uncountable nouns. It is normally used in affirmative sentences or interrogatives. The ***of*** is omitted when ***a bit*** is not followed by a noun. *She ate **a bit of chocolate** after dinner. Shall I put **a bit of oil** in the salad? Yes, just add **a bit**.*

- **A lot of/Lots of/Plenty of** are used with both plural countable and uncountable nouns. They are normally used in affirmative sentences. The **of** is omitted when **a lot/lots/plenty** are not followed by a noun. *He drinks a lot of/lots of coffee. I hope you eat plenty of fresh fruit and vegetables. I certainly eat lots.*
- **A few** means not many, but enough. It is used with plural countable nouns. *I'm leaving for the supermarket in a few minutes.*
- **A little** means not much, but enough. It is used with uncountable nouns. *She likes putting a little honey in her tea.* **Note:** *few/little* mean hardly any, not enough and can be used with **very** for emphasis. *Few shops in my town sell organic vegetables so it's not easy for me to find any. We can't make custard because we have very little milk.*
- **Several (of)** (= more than three but not many) is used with countable nouns. *They invited several people to their dinner party. Several of the guests were from out of town.*
- **Both** (= two) and **all** (= the whole quantity) are used with countable and uncountable nouns. *Both bread and rice are starchy food. All the products on this shelf are gluten-free.*

**Partitives**

We cannot use **a/an** or a number before an uncountable noun. If we want to say how much of something there is, we use a phrase of quantity, called a **partitive**, followed by **of**. Partitives can be used with **uncountable nouns** or **plural countable nouns**. *a cup of tea, a carton of cream, a tin of baked bins, a bag of oats, a bottle of oil, a can of ginger ale, a packet of crisps, a glass of juice, a slice of bread, a bowl of porridge, a jar of peanut butter, a tube of glue, a pot of coffee, a box of washing powder, a bar of gold*

## some/any/no/every & compounds

- **Some**, **any** and **no** are used with uncountable nouns and plural countable nouns.

| | Affirmative | Interrogative | Negative |
|---|---|---|---|
| **Countable/ Uncountable** | some | any | no/not any |
| **People** | someone/ somebody everyone/ everybody | anyone/ anybody | no one/ not anyone nobody/ not anybody |
| **Things** | something/ everything | anything | nothing/not anything |
| **Places** | somewhere everywhere | anywhere | nowhere/ not anywhere |

- **Some** and its compounds are used in interrogative sentences when we make an offer or a request. *Shall I pour you some juice?* **(offer)** *Can someone drive me to the supermarket?* **(request)**

- When **any** and its compounds are used in affirmative sentences, there is a difference in meaning. Study the following examples:
  a) *You can use any fruit to make the dessert.* (It doesn't matter which.)
  b) *Anyone/Anybody in the staff can deal with customers' complaints.* (It doesn't matter who.)
  c) *I'll have anything you make for dinner.* (It doesn't matter what.)
  d) *Leave the mail anywhere on my desk.* (It doesn't matter where.)
- **Every** is used with singular countable nouns. *Every table in the restaurant is reserved.*
- The pronouns **everyone/everybody**, **everything** and the adverb **everywhere** are used in affirmative, interrogative and negative sentences, and are followed by a singular verb. *Everything in this section is on special offer. Everyone at this checkout pays by credit card. Everywhere in the park is a good place to have a picnic.*

# Unit 12

## Clauses of concession

**Clauses of concession** are used to express contrast. They are introduced with the following words/phrases:
- **but** – *Liam joined a gym but he rarely goes.*
- **although/even though/though** + **clause** – *Even though* is more emphatic than *although*. *Though* is informal and is often used in everyday speech. It can also be put at the end of a sentence. *Although/Even though/Though Adam didn't feel very well, he went to work. Adam went to work although/even though/though he didn't feel very well. Adam went to work. He didn't feel very well, though.*
- **in spite of/despite** + **noun/-ing form** – *In spite of/Despite his doctor's advice, Jim didn't cut down on fatty foods. In spite of/Despite being advised by his doctor, Jim didn't cut down on fatty foods.*
- **in spite of/despite** + **the fact that** + **clause** – *In spite of/Despite the fact that it was raining heavily, she went jogging.*
- **however/nevertheless** – A comma is always used after 'however/nevertheless'. *Avocados contain lots of vitamins. However/Nevertheless, they are high in calories.*
- **while/whereas** – *Chris is a fitness fanatic while/whereas his brother hardly ever exercises.*
- **yet** (formal)/**still** – *Doctors warn us of the dangers of smoking, yet millions around the world continue to smoke. There is no cure for the common flu. Still/Yet, there are many ways to ease the symptoms.*
- **on the other hand** – *Gyms offer lots of ways to exercise. On the other hand, gym membership can be expensive.*

# Grammar Reference

## Clauses of result

**Clauses of result** are used to express result. They are introduced with the following words/phrases:

- **as a result/therefore/consequently/as a consequence** *Stephen didn't follow his doctor's advice. As a result/ Therefore/ Consequently/As a consequence, he delayed his recovery.* **OR** *Stephen didn't follow his doctor's advice and as a result/therefore/ consequently/as a consequence he delayed his recovery.*
- **such a/an + adjective + singular countable noun + that** *It is such a nice day that I 've decided to walk to work.*
- **such + adjective + plural/uncountable noun + that** *She had such mild symptoms that she didn't need to go to the hospital. He takes such good care of his health that he rarely falls ill.*
- **such a lot of + plural/uncountable noun + that** *Dr Stewart saw such a lot of patients that he was exhausted by the end of the day. The leaflet had such a lot of information that it answered all my questions.*
- **so + clause** *His arm was broken, so the doctor put it in plaster.*
- **so + adjective/adverb + that** *The medicine was so effective that he started feeling better immediately. She gets up so early that she has time to go jogging before work.*
- **so much/little + uncountable noun + that** *There is so much sugar in fizzy drinks that it's bad for your health. He gets so little sleep that he feels tired all the time.*
- **so many/few + plural noun + that** *There were so many patients waiting to see the doctor that she waited two hours for her turn. The hospital has so few nurses that it's difficult to provide adequate care.*

## Clauses of purpose

**Clauses of purpose** are used to explain why somebody does something.
We can express **positive purpose** using:

- **to + infinitive** *David went to the shop to buy some vegetables.*
- **in order (not) to/so as (not) to + infinitive** *Stella put on her trainers in order to/so as to go for a run.*
- **so that/in order that + can/will** (present/future reference) *I'll buy a recipe book so that/in order that I can learn how to make vegetarian dishes.*
- **so that/in order that + could/would** (past reference) *She took up yoga so that/in order that she could get in shape.*
- **in case + present tense** (present/future reference) *I'll give you my doctor's number in case you want to get a second opinion.*
- **in case + past tense** (past reference) *She didn't make any meat dishes in case any of the guests were vegetarians.* **Note: in case** is never used with **will** or **would**. *I called her in case she wanted to come swimming with me.* (NOT: *...in case she would want ...*)
- **for + noun** (expresses the purpose of an action) *He called the dentist for an appointment.*
- **for + -ing form** (expresses the purpose of sth or its function) *This exercise machine is for training the upper part of the body.*
- **with a view to + -ing form** *Matt is training hard with a view to competing in the marathon.*

We can express **negative purpose** using:

- **in order not to/so as not to + infinitive** *We should warm up before exercising in order not to/so as not to hurt ourselves.* **Note:** We never use **not to** to express negative purpose.
- **prevent + noun/pronoun (+ from) + -ing form** *Regular visits to the dentist prevent you from having problems with your teeth.*
- **avoid + -ing form** *Patricia watches her calorie intake to avoid putting on weight.*
- **so that + can't/won't** (present/future reference) *I'll take some water with me so that we won't get thirsty during our hike.*
- **so that + couldn't/wouldn't** (past reference) *He wrote down the time of his doctor's appointment so that he wouldn't forget it.*

**Notes:**
- **Clauses of purpose** should not be confused with **clauses of result**.
- **Clauses of purpose** are introduced with **so that/in order that**. *Ryan went online so that he could find a gym close to him.* (this shows purpose)
- **Clauses of result** are introduced with **so/such ... that**. *He plays tennis so well that I'm sure he'll play professionally one day.* (this shows result)
- **Clauses of purpose** follow the rule of the sequence of tenses. *She is studying hard so that she gets into Medical School. He bought a stationary bike so that he could exercise at home.*

## Clauses of reason

**Clauses of reason** are adverbial clauses and are used to express the reason for something. They are introduced by:

- **because** *He didn't try the shrimp pasta because he's allergic to seafood.*
- **as/since** (= because) *Susan walks five kilometres a day as/since she enjoys the exercise.*
- **the/a reason for + noun/-ing form + is/was + noun/ -ing form** *The reason for the popularity of his training video is the fact that the exercises are easy to do.*
- **the/a reason why ... is/was + noun/-ing form/ that-clause** *The reason why she missed her morning class was that she overslept.*

- *because of/on account of/due to* + **noun/-*ing* form**
  *He stopped training for the race because of/on account of/due to an injury.*
- *due to the fact that* + **clause**
  *The gym closed down due to the fact that it didn't have enough members.*
- *now (that)* + **clause**
  *Now (that) the weather is warm, we can start swimming again.*
- *for* = **because** (in formal written style)
  *Drink plenty of water for your body needs to stay hydrated.*
  **Note:** a clause of reason introduced with *for* always comes after the main clause.

## Intensifiers

- We use words like *very*, *really*, *extremely*, to make adjectives stronger.
  *Our new yoga instructor is really nice.*
- We do not normally use *very* with strong adjectives e.g. *awful*, *brilliant*, *amazing*, *delicious*, *disgusting*, *excellent*, *huge*, *enormous*, *ideal*, *wonderful*, etc. Instead, we can use intensifiers such as *absolutely*, *completely*, *exceptionally*, *utterly*, *really*, *quite*, *totally*.
  *Your idea to build a home gym is absolutely brilliant!*
- We can use *a lot*, *a great deal of*, *a good deal*, *much*, *far* etc with comparative adjectives.
  *Honey is a much healthier sweetener than sugar.*

# Word List

## Unit 1 –
## On the map

### 1a

**achievement** /əˈtʃiːvmənt/
(n) = the state of having
succeeded in sth difficult

**blaze** /bleɪz/ (n) = a brightly
coloured mark

**bridge** /brɪdʒ/ (n) = a
structure over water for
people and vehicles to
cross

**campsite** /ˈkæmpsaɪt/ (n) =
a place where
holidaymakers can put
up their tents

**canal** /kəˈnæl/ (n) = an
artificially made passage
for water to run through,
or for boats to travel
along

**capture** /ˈkæptʃə/ (v) = to
represent sth accurately
through images or
photographs

**catch** /kætʃ/ (v) = to locate
and stop an animal such
as a fish that is trying to
escape

**catch on** /ˌkætʃ ˈɒn/
(phr v) = to become
more and more popular

**complete** /kəmˈpliːt/ (v) = to
manage to finish sth

**drop out** /ˌdrɒp ˈaʊt/
(phr v) = to quit an effort

**dry (sb/sth) off** /ˌdraɪ ˈɒf/
(phr v) = to remove
water from sb/sth

**dry out** /ˌdraɪ ˈaʊt/ (phr v) =
to lose all water and
harden

**dry up** /ˌdraɪ ˈʌp/ (phr v) = (of
lakes, rivers) to become
dry by being exposed to
a heat source

**encounter** /ɪnˈkaʊntə/ (n) = a
meeting/interaction with
sth/sb

**entire** /ɪnˈtaɪə/ (adj) = whole;
complete

**epic** /ˈepɪk/ (adj) = quite
difficult and vast in
scope

**equivalent** /ɪˈkwɪvələnt/
(n) = sth of the same
amount as sth else

**eventually** /ɪˈventʃuəli/
(adv) = in the end

**exhaustion** /ɪgˈzɔːstʃən/
(n) = extreme tiredness

**footpath** /ˈfʊtpɑːθ/ (n) =
a narrow track in the
country for people to
walk along

**grab the opportunity**
(phr) = to take advantage
of a possibility

**hill** /hɪl/ (n) = an area of land
that is higher than the
surrounding area

**hold** /həʊld/ (v) = to keep
sth in your hand(s)

**hostel** /ˈhɒstl/ (n) = a
cheap place for young
travellers to stay

**humid** /ˈhjuːmɪd/ (adj) =
uncomfortably hot and
wet

**main road** /ˌmeɪn ˈrəʊd/
(n) = one of the biggest
roads in an area

**mainly** /ˈmeɪnli/ (adv) =
mostly

**majority** /məˈdʒɒrəti/ (n) =
the bigger number of a
group of people/things

**moose** /muːs/ (n) = an
animal like a deer

**mountain range** /ˈmaʊntɪn
ˌreɪndʒ/ (n) = a number
of mountains in a line

**on average** (phr) = usually;
generally

**peak** /piːk/ (n) = the top of a
mountain

**pond** /pɒnd/ (n) = a small
lake

**rack up** /ˌræk ˈʌp/ (phr v) =
to manage to collect a
number of points, goals,
etc

**record** /ˈrekɔːd/ (n) = the
best or fastest time in
which sth has been
done

**roughly** /ˈrʌfli/ (adv) =
approximately; almost

**route** /ruːt/ (n) = the way
between two places

**soar** /sɔː/ (v) = (of birds) to
fly upwards into the sky

**spectacular** /spekˈtækjʊlə/
(adj) = very exciting to
look at; impressive

**station** /ˈsteɪʃən/ (n) = a
place where trains
and buses stop for
passengers to get on
or off

**stream** /striːm/ (n) = a small
river

**sunbeam** /ˈsʌnbiːm/ (n) = a
ray of sunlight

**troublesome** /ˈtrʌbəlsəm/
(adj) = causing
difficulties and pain

**woods** /wʊdz/ (pl n) = a
small forest

**worn-out** /ˌwɔːn ˈaʊt/ (adj) =
damaged by continued
use

### 1b

**cliff** /klɪf/ (n) = the steep
face of a rock area next
to the sea

**coast** /kəʊst/ (n) = the place
where the land joins the
sea

**countless** /ˈkaʊntləs/ (adj) =
too many; numerous

**due to** /ˈdjuː tu/ (prep) =
because of

**insect bite** /ˈɪnsekt baɪt/
(n) = the fact that a small
animal such as a bee or
mosquito injures your
skin

**selfie** /ˈselfi/ (n) = a photo
of yourself that you take
with your mobile

**travel diary** /ˈtrævəl ˌdaɪəri/
(n) = a notebook in
which you take down
your thoughts and
feelings while visiting
different places

### 1c

**basement** /ˈbeɪsmənt/ (n) =
the floor of a building
under the surface of the
earth

**bunk beds** /ˈbʌŋk bedz/
(pl n) = two beds one on
top of the other

**crossroads** /ˈkrɒsrəʊdz/
(pl n) = the place where
two roads go across
each other

**cycle lane** /ˈsaɪkəl leɪn/
(n) = the part of a road
for bicycles

**dead end** /ˌded ˈend/ (n) = a
street without an exit

**junction** /ˈdʒʌŋkʃən/ (n) =
the place where a road
meets another one but
doesn't cross it

**line** /laɪn/ (n) = a railway
track and the route it
follows

**lounge** /laʊndʒ/ (n) = a living
room in a hostel for all
the guests

**pedestrian crossing**
/pəˌdestriən ˈkrɒsɪŋ/
(n) = a place on a road,
marked with lines like
a zebra's, for people to
walk across

**roundabout** /ˈraʊndəbaʊt/
(n) = a circular place
where three or more
roads join

**speed limit** /ˈspiːd ˌlɪmɪt/
(n) = the maximum
speed at which a vehicle
is allowed to move

**stop and give way (sign)**
(phr) = the instruction to
stop a vehicle in order to
allow other vehicles to
pass first (via a sign)

**stroll** /strəʊl/ (n) = a walk

**the underground** /ðə
ˈʌndəgraʊnd/ (n) = a
rail network under the
surface of the Earth

**traffic lights** /ˈtræfɪk ˌlaɪts/
(pl n) = each of a set of
lights which control the
movement of vehicles
on the road

**twin room** /ˈtwɪn ruːm/ (n) =
a hotel room with two
single beds

## Culture 1

**amphibious** /æmˈfɪbiəs/
(adj) = (of a tour) taking
place on both land and
water

**choosy** /'tʃuːzi/ (adj) = accepting only the best

**cityscape** /'sɪtiskeɪp/ (n) = the image of a city

**commentary** /'kɒməntəri/ (n) = an oral description during an event

**crawl** /krɔːl/ (n) = a speed that is very slow

**gentle** /'dʒentl/ (adj) = calm and pleasant

**kingfisher** /'kɪŋfɪʃə/ (n) = a type of small, bright blue and orange bird that feeds on fish

**on board** (phr) = on the ship (during the cruise)

**outing** /'aʊtɪŋ/ (n) = a short trip for pleasure for a group

**route** /ruːt/ (n) = the way you follow to go from one place to another

**splash** /splæʃ/ (v) = to move into water and send drops of it all around

**splendid** /'splendɪd/ (adj) = impressive

**steadily** /'stedɪli/ (adv) = very gradually

**thrilling** /'θrɪlɪŋ/ (adj) = very exciting

## Unit 2 – Legends & Festivals

### 2a

**blow sb away** /ˌbləʊ ə'weɪ/ (phr v) = to impress sb very much

**blow into (a place)** /ˌbləʊ ɪntu/ (phr v) = to arrive somewhere unexpectedly

**blow sb off** /ˌbləʊ 'ɒf/ (phr v) = to not meet sb at an arranged meeting

**blow up** /ˌbləʊ 'ʌp/ (phr v) = 1) to enlarge a photograph; 2) to fill (a balloon, etc) with air

**blow sth out** /ˌbləʊ 'aʊt/ (phr v) = to extinguish (a candle, etc) using your breath

**bring sth to life** (phr) = to make sth real or exciting

**burst** /bɜːst/ (v) = to explode

**cattle** /'kætl/ (pl n) = bulls and cows on a farm

**cave** /keɪv/ (n) = a large, natural, underground hole

**celebrate** /'seləbreɪt/ (v) = to remember or honour the importance of a nation or an event

**come up with** /ˌkʌm 'ʌp wɪð/ (phr v) = to think of a plan, an idea, etc

**contest** /'kɒntest/ (n) = a competition

**culture** /'kʌltʃə/ (n) = all the beliefs and customs of a particular nation

**custom** /'kʌstəm/ (n) = a well-established way of behaviour that you should respect

**feature** /'fiːtʃə/ (v) = (of a show) to include sth as an important part

**flame** /fleɪm/ (n) = each of the bright sharp points rising from sth on fire

**highlight** /'haɪlaɪt/ (n) = the most exciting part or event of sth

**juggler** /'dʒʌglə/ (n) = sb who entertains people by throwing objects into the air and catching them quickly

**juggling** /'dʒʌglɪŋ/ (n) = entertaining people by throwing objects into the air and catching them quickly

**legend** /'ledʒənd/ (n) = a well-known story from the past

**march** /mɑːtʃ/ (v) = to walk with regular steps as part of a parade

**open-air show** /ˌəʊpən eə 'ʃəʊ/ (n) = a performance held outdoors

**parade** /pə'reɪd/ (n) = a number of people and vehicles going along the streets to celebrate sth

**performer** /pə'fɔːmə/ (n) = an actor, a dancer, a musician, etc

**resident** /'rezɪdənt/ (n) = a person who lives in a place

**sculpture** /'skʌlptʃə/ (n) = a piece of art made of stone, wood, clay, etc

**set off** /ˌset 'ɒf/ (phr v) = to start a journey or an attempt at sth

**soar** /sɔː/ (v) = to fly upwards into the sky

**stall** /stɔːl/ (n) = each of the tables or enclosed areas in an open-air market where goods are sold

**sth roars into life** (phr) = sth suddenly becomes active with a lot of noise

**sulphur** /'sʌlfə/ (n) = a type of chemical burning with an unpleasant smell and a blue flame

**tradition** /trə'dɪʃən/ (n) = a belief or way of behaviour that a community has been following for a long time

### 2b

**audience** /'ɔːdiəns/ (n) = all the people who watch a show, a concert, etc

**bench** /bentʃ/ (n) = a long seat in a public place, e.g. a park

**blacksmith** /'blæksmɪθ/ (n) = sb whose job is to make and repair iron items

**exchange** /ɪks'tʃeɪndʒ/ (v) = to give sb sth and receive sth else from them

**light a bonfire** (phr) = to make a large fire in an open space

**pour** /pɔː/ (v) = to rain heavily

**procession** /prə'seʃən/ (n) = a parade

**rehearse** /rɪ'hɜːs/ (v) = (of a performer) to do some practice to prepare for a show

**sea serpent** /ˌsiː 'sɜːpənt/ (n) = a big mythical snake that people believe might live in the sea

**shelter** /'ʃeltə/ (n) = anything that protects you from the rain, hot sun, etc

**sighting** /'saɪtɪŋ/ (n) = the occasion when sth rare appears or becomes visible

**soaking wet** (phr) = totally covered with water

**spicy** /'spaɪsi/ (adj) = (of food) having a strong and often hot flavour

**wrap** /ræp/ (v) = to cover all of sth with paper, cloth, etc

### 2c

**archery** /'ɑːtʃəri/ (n) = the art of shooting arrows at targets

**bagpipes** /'bægpaɪps/ (pl n) = a traditional wind instrument consisting of a bag and a pipe

**count sb in** /ˌkaʊnt 'ɪn/ (phr v) = to include sb in an activity

**demonstration** /ˌdemən'streɪʃən/ (n) = an event in which sb shows their special skills or qualities

**gather** /'gæðə/ (v) = to pick (flowers, fruit, etc)

**haggis** /'hægɪs/ (n) = a Scottish dish made from a sheep's organs and cooked in a sheep's stomach

**highlight** /'haɪlaɪt/ (n) = the most exciting part or event of sth

**hold a two-minute silence** (phr) = (of a group of people) to stop talking for two minutes in order to honour sb dead

**let off** /ˌlet 'ɒf/ (phr v) = to make (fireworks, etc) explode

# Word List

**medieval** /ˌmediˈiːvəl/ (adj) = of the Middle Ages (between AD 500 and AD 1500)

**memorable** /ˈmemərəbəl/ (adj) = that is worth remembering

**outlaw** /ˈaʊtlɔː/ (n) = sb who has committed a crime but has not been arrested

**poppy** /ˈpɒpi/ (n) = a plant with red flowers and black seeds

**present** /prɪˈzent/ (v) = to introduce sb to sb else in a formal way

**present** /ˈprezənt/ (n) = a gift

**refund** /ˈriːfʌnd/ (n) = money returned to sb because they're not satisfied with an item/service they've bought

**refund** /rɪˈfʌnd/ (v) = to return sb's money because they're not satisfied with an item/ service they've bought

**root** /ruːt/ (n) = the part of a plant that supports it and grows under the soil

**toffee apple** /ˈtɒfi ˌæpl/ (n) = an apple on a stick, covered with a sticky sweet substance

**update** /ʌpˈdeɪt/ (v) = to give sb the latest information

**update** /ˈʌpdeɪt/ (n) = the latest information about sth

**wealth** /welθ/ (n) = the fact that sb has a huge amount of money

## Culture 2

**admit** /ədˈmɪt/ (v) = to accept the fact that sth is true

**cautious** /ˈkɔːʃəs/ (adj) = careful

**common** /ˈkɒmən/ (adj) = ordinary

**interesting** /ˈɪntrəstɪŋ/ (adj) = fascinating

**occasional** /əˈkeɪʒənəl/ (adj) = infrequent

**path** /pɑːθ/ (n) = the way along which you move

**penny** /ˈpeni/ (n) = (pl pence) a cash value that is one hundredth of a British pound; the coin of this value

**playwright** /ˈpleɪraɪt/ (n) = sb who writes theatrical plays

**recite** /rɪˈsaɪt/ (v) = to say a poem, etc by heart

**saying** /ˈseɪɪŋ/ (n) = a proverb

**spin around** /ˌspɪn əˈraʊnd/ (phr v) = to turn around quickly

**stored** /stɔːd/ (pp) = kept

**unique** /juːˈniːk/ (adj) = one of a kind

## Unit 3 – Adventures

### 3a

**abseiling** /ˈæbseɪlɪŋ/ (n) = the sport of climbing down a rock using a rope

**admit** /ədˈmɪt/ (v) = to accept the fact that sth is true

**anxious** /ˈæŋkʃəs/ (adj) = worried and nervous

**apparently** /əˈpærəntli/ (adv) = being likely based on what you know or see

**appreciate** /əˈpriːʃieɪt/ (v) = to realise sth

**beforehand** /bɪˈfɔːhænd/ (adv) = happening before sth else happens

**breathtaking** /ˈbreθˌteɪkɪŋ/ (adj) = amazing

**come face to face with sb/sth** (phr) = to meet sb/sth in person

**course** /kɔːs/ (n) = the route followed during an event, tour or sporting activity

**descend** /dɪˈsend/ (v) = to go down a place

**dizziness** /ˈdɪzinəs/ (n) = a feeling that you're going to fall down

**downstream** /ˌdaʊnˈstriːm/ (adv) = moving towards the mouth of a river or stream

**exhausted** /ɪgˈzɔːstɪd/ (adj) = very tired

**experience** /ɪkˈspɪəriəns/ (v) = to have sth happen to you; to feel sth

**explore** /ɪkˈsplɔː/ (v) = to go around a place in order to learn about it

**extraordinary** /ɪkˈstrɔːdənəri/ (adj) = unusual and impressive; remarkable

**feel** /fiːl/ (v) = to have an emotion or physical feeling

**ferocious** /fəˈrəʊʃəs/ (adj) = wild and dangerous

**fully-trained** /ˌfʊli ˈtreɪnd/ (adj) = having been taught all the necessary skills

**hire** /haɪə/ (v) = to pay money in order to use (a car, a bike, etc)

**ill** /ɪl/ (adj) = unwell; sick

**incredible** /ɪnˈkredəbəl/ (adj) = unbelievable

**interact (with sb)** /ˌɪntərˈækt/ (v) = to communicate with and affect each other

**leading** /ˈliːdɪŋ/ (adj) = the most important

**leafless** /ˈliːfləs/ (adj) = (of a tree) without any leaves on

**look around** /ˌlʊk əˈraʊnd/ (phr v) = to explore an area

**look back** /ˌlʊk ˈbæk/ (phr v) = to think about sth from the past

**look out for** /ˌlʊk ˈaʊt fə/ (phr v) = to try to avoid sth dangerous

**look over** /ˌlʊk ˈəʊvə/ (phr v) = to examine sth

**look through sth** /ˌlʊk θruː/ (phr v) = to look at the different parts of sth

**of a lifetime** (phr) = the best or most important thing (surprise, chance, opportunity, etc) you have ever experienced

**plain** /pleɪn/ (n) = a huge flat area

**pool** /puːl/ (n) = an enclosed area with water where you can go swimming

**sight** /saɪt/ (n) = sth that you can see

**site** /saɪt/ (n) = an important or interesting place

**slide** /slaɪd/ (n) = a sloping surface where you can go down without using your feet

**snap a picture** (phr) = to take a photo

**surface** /ˈsɜːfɪs/ (n) = the uppermost part of sth

**thrilling** /ˈθrɪlɪŋ/ (adj) = very exciting

**track** /træk/ (v) = to look for and find sth

**trained** /treɪnd/ (adj) = having been given all the necessary knowledge and skills to do a job, etc

### 3b

**backpacker** /ˈbækˌpækə/ (n) = a tourist who travels with little money and a rucksack on his/ her back

**cancel** /ˈkænsəl/ (v) = to call sth off

**change my mind** (phr) = to have a second opinion, different from the one I had before

**convince** /kənˈvɪns/ (v) = to persuade sb (to do sth)

**delta** /ˈdeltə/ (n) = an area where a river splits into smaller ones before it flows into the sea

**destination** /ˌdestɪˈneɪʃən/ (n) = the place where you want to go

**flood** /flʌd/ (v) = (of water) to fully cover a place

**river bank** /ˈrɪvə bæŋk/ (n) = each of the two sides of a river

**set off** /set ˈɒf/ (phr v) = to start a trip, journey, etc

**storm** /stɔːm/ (n) = very bad weather with strong winds and rain

**stunning** /ˈstʌnɪŋ/ (adj) = very impressive

**tough** /tʌf/ (adj) = difficult

### 3c

**agritourism holiday** /ˈæɡrɪtʊərɪzəm ˌhɒlədeɪ/ (n) = holidaymaking on a farm or ranch

**allergic (to sth)** /əˈlɜːdʒɪk/ (adj) = getting ill when you eat or touch a particular substance

**bang** /bæŋ/ (v) = to hit a part of the body with a loud noise

**board** /bɔːd/ (n) = a long flat piece of wood or plastic for sports

**burn (-burnt-burnt)** /bɜːn/ (v) = to injure yourself with fire

**city break** /ˈsɪti breɪk/ (n) = a short holiday in which you visit a big city abroad

**dig (-dug-dug)** /dɪɡ/ (v) = to make a hole by removing earth or snow

**drag** /dræɡ/ (v) = to pull sb/sth

**drown** /draʊn/ (v) = to lose your life when you stay underwater too long

**ecotourism holiday** /ˈiːkəʊtʊərɪzəm ˌhɒlədeɪ/ (n) = an environmentally friendly holiday that doesn't affect the natural landscape in a negative way

**get seasick** (phr) = to get ill when travelling by sea

**get stuck** (phr) = to be unable to move from a point

**hiking trip** (phr) = a trip during which you go for long walks in the country

**infection** /ɪnˈfekʃən/ (n) = an illness caused by viruses or bacteria

**injection** /ɪnˈdʒekʃən/ (n) = putting a medicine into sb's body through a needle

**light (-lit-lit)** /laɪt/ (v) = to make sth start burning

**paddle** /ˈpædl/ (v) = to move across water in a boat using a short pole with a flat end

**paddle boarding** /ˈpædl ˌbɔːdɪŋ/ (n) = the sport of moving across water standing on a long piece of wood or plastic and using an oar to push the water

**pick** /pɪk/ (v) = to gather fruits from trees, flowers from plants, etc

**poisonous** /ˈpɔɪzənəs/ (adj) = (of a snake) having a toxic substance that can kill people

**scream in pain** (phr) = to shout loudly because a part of your body hurts

**sore** /sɔː/ (adj) = (of a part of the body) painful

**sting (-stung-stung)** /stɪŋ/ (v) = (of an insect) to bite sb

**tangled** /ˈtæŋɡəld/ (adj) = caught in a place and trapped

**throw up** /θrəʊ ˈʌp/ (phr v) = to vomit

**track** /træk/ (v) = to look for and find sth

**twist** /twɪst/ (v) = to injure a part of your body, such as your ankle, knee or wrist, by turning it very suddenly

**weed** /wiːd/ (n) = a water plant without flowers

### Culture 3

**access (to sth)** /ˈækses/ (n) = the fact that you're allowed to enter a place

**action-packed** /ˈækʃən ˈpækt/ (adj) = full of exciting things

**adrenaline-filled** /əˈdrenəlɪn ˈfɪld/ (adj) = very exciting

**crawl** /krɔːl/ (v) = to move slowly and with difficulty on your hands and knees

**gust** /ɡʌst/ (n) = a sudden and strong movement of wind

**on your doorstep** (phr) = very near you

**purchase** /ˈpɜːtʃəs/ (v) = to buy sth

**range** /reɪndʒ/ (v) = to vary between an upper and a lower limit

**squeeze** /skwiːz/ (v) = to try to get through a very small space

**stick to sth** /stɪk tu/ (phr v) = to keep doing sth and not decide to change it

**tailor** /ˈteɪlə/ (v) = to prepare sth so that it suits sb's needs

**the basics** /ðə ˈbeɪsɪks/ (pl n) = the essentials; the most important and necessary things

**(the) tip of the iceberg** (idm) = a small amount of sth much larger that's unknown or not yet shown

**whizz** /wɪz/ (v) = to move very fast making a sound

### Values A: Curiosity

**admire** /ədˈmaɪə/ (v) = to like and respect sb very much

**boredom** /ˈbɔːdəm/ (n) = the state of being unhappy because sth is not interesting enough

**curiosity** /ˌkjʊəriˈɒsəti/ (n) = the strong desire to want to know about things

**daily routine** (phr) = the activities that sb normally does every day, such as eating, sleeping, etc

**empathy** /ˈempəθi/ (n) = the state of understanding sb's feelings and problems; compassion

**inspire (sb to do sth)** /ɪnˈspaɪə/ (v) = to influence sb to do sth new; to motivate sb

**likeable** /ˈlaɪkəbəl/ (adj) = (of a person) nice and easy to like

**on the go** (phr) = while being busy doing sth else; while doing another activity

**passionately** /ˈpæʃənətli/ (adv) = enthusiastically

**satisfied (with sth/sb)** /ˈsætɪsfaɪd/ (adj) = feeling happy with sth/sb; content

**selfish** /ˈselfɪʃ/ (adj) = caring only about yourself and not anybody else; self-centred

**social life** /ˈsəʊʃəl ˈlaɪf/ (n) = sb's daily activities with friends or other company

**whiskers** /ˈwɪskəz/ (pl n) = the long thick hairs that grow near the mouth of a cat, mouse, etc

**wonder** /ˈwʌndə/ (n) = a feeling of admiration and excitement caused by experiencing sth interesting and new

### Public Speaking Skills A

**anecdote** /ˈænɪkdəʊt/ (n) = a short story describing sb's personal experiences

**approach** /əˈprəʊtʃ/ (v) = to go near sb/sth

**broaden your horizons** (phr) = to increase your knowledge or to experience various new things

**encourage** /ɪnˈkʌrɪdʒ/ (v) = to give sb the confidence and support to do sth

139

# Word List

**gap year** /gæp jɪə/ (n) = a year that a high school graduate takes off studying before continuing studies at university or college

**grasshopper** /ˈɡrɑːsˌhɒpə/ (n) = an insect that has got long back legs and can jump high into the air

**independent** /ˌɪndəˈpendənt/ (adj) = not needing help, money, support, advice, etc from sb else; self-sufficient

**inspire** /ɪnˈspaɪə/ (v) = to influence sb's decisions or plans, or give sb a desire to do sth

**mature** /məˈtʃʊə/ (adj) = behaving like a sensible and reasonable adult

**path** /pɑːθ/ (n) = a course of action; the choice of what you want to do in your life

**reflect** /rɪˈflekt/ (v) = to think about sth carefully

**ruin** /ˈruːɪn/ (v) = to destroy or spoil sth

## Unit 4 – There's no place like home!

### 4a

**avoid** /əˈvɔɪd/ (v) = to stop sth bad from happening

**bumpy** /ˈbʌmpi/ (adj) = (of a surface) with many raised parts; not flat

**bungalow** /ˈbʌŋɡələʊ/ (n) = a small one-level house, usually in the country

**castle** /ˈkɑːsəl/ (n) = a big and strong building of the past where kings and rulers lived; a fortress

**comfort** /ˈkʌmfət/ (n) = the condition of feeling pleasant and relaxed

**comfortable** /ˈkʌmftəbəl/ (adj) = helping you feel relaxed

**complex** /ˈkɒmpleks/ (n) = a group of buildings

**concrete cube** /ˈkɒnkriːt ˈkjuːb/ (n) = a building material in the form of an object with six sides made from cement, sand, water, etc

**convenient** /kənˈviːniənt/ (adj) = easy to reach or use

**convenient access** (phr) = the fact that you are able to reach and use sth easily

**cottage** /ˈkɒtɪdʒ/ (n) = a small house in the country

**detached house** /dɪˌtætʃt ˈhaʊs/ (n) = an individual house that is not joined to the houses next to it

**dull** /dʌl/ (adj) = boring

**enormous** /ɪˈnɔːməs/ (adj) = huge

**express** /ɪkˈspres/ (v) = to show (a feeling, an idea, etc)

**facilities** /fəˈsɪlətiz/ (pl n) = services provided for the public

**farmhouse** /ˈfɑːmhaʊs/ (n) = a house on a farm

**fate** /feɪt/ (n) = the power that is believed to control our lives

**flat** /flæt/ (n) = each of the apartments in a block of flats

**functional** /ˈfʌŋkʃənəl/ (adj) = practical and useful

**get on like a house on fire** (idm) = to become friends in a short period of time

**hang (-hung-hung)** /hæŋ/ (v) = to fix sth (a coat, a curtain, etc) somewhere at the upper part of it so that its lower part is free to move

**home** /həʊm/ (n) = the place where sb lives and the people they live with

**hook** /hʊk/ (n) = a bent piece of metal for hanging things on

**house** /haʊs/ (n) = the building where a family, usually, lives

**houseboat** /ˈhaʊsbəʊt/ (n) = a boat on a river or canal that people can live in

**lack (of sth)** /læk/ (n) = a shortage of sth

**level** /ˈlevəl/ (adj) = (of a surface) flat

**live** /lɪv/ (v) = to spend your life in a place

**located** /ləʊˈkeɪtɪd/ (pp) = situated

**make yourself at home** (idm) = to become very comfortable in another person's house

**mobile home** /ˌməʊbaɪl ˈhəʊm/ (n) = a small house on wheels

**move away** /ˌmuːv əˈweɪ/ (phr v) = to leave your area/town and go to live in another area/town

**move in** /ˌmuːv ˈɪn/ (phr v) = to begin to live somewhere as your home

**move into (a house)** /ˈmuːv ɪntə/ (phr v) = to start living in a new house

**move on** /ˌmuːv ˈɒn/ (phr v) = to progress; to go on

**move up** /ˌmuːv ˈʌp/ (phr v) = 1) to increase; 2) to get a better job

**nothing to write home about** (idm) = not very interesting or special

**odd** /ɒd/ (adj) = strange

**office** /ˈɒfɪs/ (n) = a room or a building where employees work at desks

**physical challenge** (phr) = a difficulty in performing actions

**pole** /pəʊl/ (n) = each of the wooden or metal sticks that support a ceiling

**put your own house in order** (idm) = to deal with your own problems before commenting on the problems of others

**remind (sb of sth)** /rɪˈmaɪnd/ (v) = to make sb think that sth is similar (to sth else)

**resident** /ˈrezɪdənt/ (n) = sb who lives in a certain place

**semi-detached house** /ˌsemi dɪˈtætʃt ˈhaʊs/ (n) = each of two houses that are joined on only one side

**soundproof** /ˈsaʊndpruːf/ (adj) = (of a building) not allowing sound to enter or leave

**stay** /steɪ/ (v) = to remain in a place for a certain period of time

**stretch** /stretʃ/ (v) = to straighten your body in order to reach sth

**study** /ˈstʌdi/ (n) = a quiet room in a house where you can read and write

**stunning** /ˈstʌnɪŋ/ (adj) = very exciting

**swing** /swɪŋ/ (n) = a board hanging from two ropes on which children sit and move forwards and backwards

**terraced house** /ˌterəst ˈhaʊs/ (n) = each of a number of similar houses in a long row under the same roof

**townhouse** /ˈtaʊnhaʊs/ (n) = a modern house in a town or city

**uninviting** /ˌʌnɪnˈvaɪtɪŋ/ (adj) = (of a place) not pleasant or attractive

**villa** /ˈvɪlə/ (n) = a large house near the sea or in the country that holidaymakers usually rent to stay in

### 4b

**eco-friendly** /ˌiːkəʊ ˈfrendli/ (adj) = that does not pollute the environment

**efficiently** /ɪˈfɪʃəntli/ (adv) = without wasting energy, money, etc

**fetch** /fetʃ/ (v) = to go to a place in order to bring sth back

**guest** /gest/ (n) = sb who pays to stay in a hotel, hostel, etc

**heating system** /ˈhiːtɪŋ ˈsɪstəm/ (n) = a mechanical system that provides heat for a building

**nevertheless** /ˌnevəðəˈles/ (adv) = even so; regardless

**queue** /kjuː/ (v) = to wait in a line

**rattle** /ˈrætəl/ (v) = (of the wind) to cause sth to make a series of repeated knocks

**rent** /rent/ (n) = an amount of money that you pay monthly in order to live in sb's house, room, etc

**run** /rʌn/ (v) = to operate and live in (a home)

**sensible** /ˈsensəbəl/ (adj) = reasonable; logical

**stuff** /stʌf/ (n) = various things

### 4c

**access (to a place)** /ˈækses/ (n) = the ability to get into a place

**air conditioning** /ˈeə kənˈdɪʃənɪŋ/ (n) = the system that provides a house, building, etc with cool air

**amenities** /əˈmiːnətiz/ (pl n) = desirable facilities or features that make a place more pleasant

**basement flat** /ˈbeɪsmənt ˌflæt/ (n) = an apartment on the lowest level of a building

**central heating** /ˌsentrəl ˈhiːtɪŋ/ (n) = a mechanical system that provides heat for all the rooms or flats in a building

**clothes dryer** /ˈkləʊðz draɪə/ (n) = a machine that dries wet clothes by spinning them and using hot air

**dissatisfied** /dɪˈsætɪsfaɪd/ (adj) = not pleased with sth that has happened

**en-suite bathroom** /ɒn ˌswiːt ˈbɑːθrʊm/ (n) = a bathroom within a bedroom

**gorgeous** /ˈɡɔːdʒəs/ (adj) = fabulous

**heated towel rail** (phr) = a metal rail to hang towels on that becomes warm to the touch

**in the heart of (a place)** (phr) = within the central part of a place

**king-size bed** (phr) = a very large bed

**light fittings** /ˈlaɪt fɪtɪŋz/ (pl n) = all the electric lights and lamps

**official** /əˈfɪʃəl/ (adj) = for people in authority

**open fireplace** /ˌəʊpən ˈfaɪəpleɪs/ (n) = an area in a wall for a fire where smoke can be sent up a chimney

**open plan kitchen and dining area** (phr) = a large room that includes a kitchen area and a large space to sit and eat meals

**pottery** /ˈpɒtəri/ (n) = items made of wet soil which is baked and dried

**private entrance** (phr) = an individual point of entry to a place that can only be used by certain people

**residence** /ˈrezɪdəns/ (n) = the place where sb lives

**ride** /raɪd/ (n) = the act of travelling in a vehicle

**roof garden** /ˈruːf ɡɑːdən/ (n) = a garden on the top of a building

**sarcastic** /sɑːˈkæstɪk/ (adj) = making remarks that mean the opposite of what you say in order to criticise sb/sth

**sights** /saɪts/ (pl n) = places of interest that are worth seeing

**solar water heater** /ˌsəʊlə ˈwɔːtə hiːtə/ (n) = a device that stores and heats water using energy from the sun

**spare** /speə/ (adj) = extra

**storage space** /ˈstɔːrɪdʒ speɪs/ (n) = an empty space for putting in things that are not in use

**studio flat** /ˈstjuːdiəʊ ˌflæt/ (n) = a small one-room apartment

**train station** /ˈtreɪn ˌsteɪʃən/ (n) = a railway station

**walk-in shower** /ˌwɔːk ɪn ˈʃaʊə/ (n) = a shower in a large open space that you can easily enter and move around in

## Culture 4

**barbershop** /ˈbɑːbəʃɒp/ (n) = a place where men can have their hair cut

**be going strong** (phr) = to continue being successful after a long period of time

**celebrity** /səˈlebrəti/ (n) = a very famous person; a star

**designer boutique** /dɪˈzaɪnə buːˈtiːk/ (n) = a small elegant shop that only sells clothes made by famous people in the fashion industry

**feature** /ˈfiːtʃə/ (v) = to present sb famous to the public

**gourmet bistro** (phr) = a small restaurant serving high quality food and drink

**graffiti** /ɡrəˈfiːti/ (n) = illegal writings and drawings on buildings, buses, etc

**have your/its share of sth** (phr) = to have a lot of sth (often too much)

**hotspot** /ˈhɒtspɒt/ (n) = a very popular point in an area

**in the heart of (a place)** (phr) = within the central part of a place

**ornate** /ɔːˈneɪt/ (adj) = heavily decorated

**trendy** /ˈtrendi/ (adj) = fashionable

**unique** /juːˈniːk/ (adj) = being the only example of sth, usually in a special way

**vegan kiosk** (phr) = a stall in the street which only sells food that doesn't come from animals

**well developed** /ˌwel dɪˈveləpt/ (adj) = fully grown and functional

## Unit 5 – Let's talk

### 5a

**at risk** (phr) = in a potentially harmful situation

**come up with (sth)** /ˌkʌm ˈʌp wɪð/ (phr v) = to think of an idea

**commit crimes** (phr) = to do sth illegal

**communicate** /kəˈmjuːnɪkeɪt/ (v) = to share information via talking, writing or gestures

**communication breakdown** (phr) = a lack of understanding between people

**element** /ˈelɪmənt/ (n) = a part of a specific thing

**expert** /ˈekspɜːt/ (n) = a highly qualified person

**express** /ɪkˈspres/ (v) = to show feelings or ideas

**eye contact** /ˈaɪ kɒntækt/ (n) = the act of two people both looking into each other's eyes

# Word List

**facial expression** (phr) = the look on your face that shows how you feel or what you are thinking (e.g. a smile or a frown)

**gesture** /ˈdʒestʃə/ (n) = a body movement, such as a movement of the hands, that shows emotions or ideas

**get (the/our) message across** (phr) = to allow sb to understand sth

**govern** /ˈɡʌvən/ (v) = to control (especially in an official capacity)

**impact** /ˈɪmpækt/ (n) = a strong effect that sth has on sb/sth

**interact** /ˌɪntərˈækt/ (v) = to communicate or engage with others

**keep down** /kiːp ˈdaʊn/ (phr v) = to make less noise

**keep from** /kiːp frɒm/ (phr v) = to prevent sb from doing sth; to prevent sth from happening

**keep on** /kiːp ˈɒn/ (phr v) = to continue (to employ sb)

**keep out** /kiːp ˈaʊt/ (phr v) = to prevent sb from entering

**keep up** /kiːp ˈʌp/ (phr v) = to maintain sth

**language barrier** /ˈlæŋɡwɪdʒ ˌbæriə/ (n) = the fact that two people can't communicate because they don't share a common language

**non-verbal communication** (phr) = forms/methods of interaction that don't use words

**paralysed** /ˈpærəlaɪzd/ (adj) = unable to move due to injury

**say** /seɪ/ (v) = to pronounce words or give an instruction

**session** /ˈseʃən/ (n) = a period of arranged activity

**speak** /spiːk/ (v) = to talk to sb

**talk** /tɔːk/ (v) = to speak with sb

**tell** /tel/ (v) = to say sth to sb else

**tone of voice** (phr) = the pitch or quality of sb's voice that shows the speaker's feelings

**verbal communication** (phr) = forms/methods of spoken interaction

**video chat** /ˈvɪdiəʊ ˌtʃæt/ (n) = an online service that lets you talk to people over the Internet via video

**visual communication** (phr) = forms/methods of visual interaction (e.g. pictures, video)

**written communication** (phr) = forms/methods of printed or handwritten interaction

## 5b

**body language** /ˈbɒdi ˌlæŋɡwɪdʒ/ (n) = gestures or acts with the body that express your feelings

**communication skills** /kəˌmjuːnɪˈkeɪʃən ˌskɪlz/ (pl n) = the abilities needed to express yourself and interact with others

**conference** /ˈkɒnfərəns/ (n) = a large meeting that discusses business matters

**current** /ˈkʌrənt/ (adj) = of the present moment

**digital communication** (phr) = means/methods of interacting via computers

**end-of-year assessment** (phr) = the process of judging a student's performance at the end of an academic year

**frown** /fraʊn/ (v) = to push the eyebrows downwards to show that you are annoyed about sth or worried

**initial** /ɪˈnɪʃəl/ (adj) = first

**install** /ɪnˈstɔːl/ (v) = to put sth in place to be used

**launch** /lɔːntʃ/ (v) = to release sth

**optical fibre** /ˌɒptɪkəl ˈfaɪbə/ (n) = a glass rod that carries large amounts of digital data

**phone charger** /fəʊn ˌtʃɑː dʒə/ (n) = the accessory that connects a phone to an electrical source in order to power the battery

**podcast** /ˈpɒdkɑːst/ (n) = a radio episode that is broadcast over the Internet

**public speaking** (phr) = the act of talking to large groups of people

**sales figures** /seɪlz ˌfɪɡəz/ (pl n) = the statistics that show how well a product has sold

**temporarily disrupt** (phr) = to affect the proper functionality of sth for a short period of time

**video call function** (phr) = the part of software that enables video calls over the Internet

**wonder** /ˈwʌndə/ (v) = to consider sth or ask yourself sth

## 5c

**affect** /əˈfekt/ (v) = to influence sth

**agreement** /əˈɡriːmənt/ (n) = a situation in which people share an opinion about sth

**clue** /kluː/ (n) = sth that tells you sth about sth

**comfort (sb)** /ˈkʌmfət/ (v) = to make sb feel better about sth

**effective** /ɪˈfektɪv/ (adj) = successful

**enthusiasm** /ɪnˈθjuːziæzəm/ (n) = the feeling of being positive about sth

**exclude** /ɪkˈskluːd/ (v) = to stop sb from being a part of sth

**face to face** /ˌfeɪs tə ˈfeɪs/ (adv) = in person

**in person** (phr) = by seeing sb in the flesh rather than speaking over the phone or via the Internet

**irritation** /ˌɪrɪˈteɪʃən/ (n) = the feeling of being annoyed

**misspelling** /ˌmɪsˈspelɪŋ/ (n) = the act of writing a word incorrectly

**mode of communication** (phr) = a method of interacting with sb

**spelling** /ˈspelɪŋ/ (n) = the ability to write words correctly

**textspeak** /ˈtekstspiːk/ (n) = Internet abbreviations and slang

**uncertainty** /ʌnˈsɜːtənti/ (n) = a situation in which sth is not known for sure

## Culture 5

**appropriate** /əˈprəʊpriət/ (adj) = suitable

**awkward** /ˈɔːkwəd/ (adj) = uncomfortable or embarrassing

**balance** /ˈbæləns/ (n) = a state in which things maintain equal importance

**bow** /baʊ/ (n) = a sign of respect in which sb bends their body and lowers their head

**crucial** /ˈkruːʃəl/ (adj) = very important

**fluent** /ˈfluːənt/ (adj) = able to speak a language very well

**glance** /ɡlɑːns/ (v) = to look quickly

**globetrotter** /ˈgləʊbtrɒtə/ (n) = sb who travels the world

**greatly** /ˈgreɪtli/ (adv) = very much

**greet** /griːt/ (v) = to welcome sb

**lean** /liːn/ (v) = to bend your body in one direction

**nod** /nɒd/ (v) = to shake your head up and down in agreement

**non-verbal** /ˌnɒn ˈvɜːbəl/ (adj) = without using words

**seasoned** /ˈsiːzənd/ (adj) = experienced

**stare** /steə/ (v) = to look at sb/sth intensely

**tend** /tend/ (v) = to be likely to happen or act in a particular fashion

**typical** /ˈtɪpɪkəl/ (adj) = displaying the expected characteristics of sth

**variety is the spice of life** (phr) = doing lots of different things makes life enjoyable

## Unit 6 – Challenges

### 6a

**alive** /əˈlaɪv/ (adj) = full of energy

**art director** /ɑːt dəˌrektə/ (n) = sb who is in charge of a business that produces theatrical plays, TV and radio programmes, advertisements, graphics, etc

**audience** /ˈɔːdiəns/ (n) = all the people who watch a play, show, etc at the same time

**bank clerk** /ˈbæŋk klɑːk/ (n) = a bank teller

**blank** /blæŋk/ (adj) = empty

**citizen** /ˈsɪtɪzən/ (n) = sb who lives in a city or country

**client** /ˈklaɪənt/ (n) = sb who pays a professional or a company for their services

**code** /kəʊd/ (n) = the language used for computer programming

**contact** /ˈkɒntækt/ (n) = sb in a senior position in society who can help

**creativity** /ˌkriːeɪˈtɪvəti/ (n) = the ability to use your imagination and produce original ideas

**crew** /kruː/ (n) = all the people who work together on the same thing

**deadline** /ˈdedlaɪn/ (n) = the time by which you are expected to complete a task you've been given

**delegate** /ˈdelɪgeɪt/ (v) = to give work to people in a lower position than you

**design** /dɪˈzaɪn/ (v) = to create sth new

**explore** /ɪkˈsplɔː/ (v) = to go around a place in order to learn about it

**fill in** /fɪl ˈɪn/ (phr v) = 1) to complete a form or document (also: to fill out); 2) to give details to sb about sth

**fill out** /fɪl ˈaʊt/ (phr v) = to gain weight

**fill up** /fɪl ˈʌp/ (phr v) = 1) to put sth in a container so that there's no more space; 2) to eat enough so that you don't feel hungry

**fitness trainer** /ˈfɪtnəs ˌtreɪnə/ (n) = sb who helps to coach people during exercise or explains exercises to them

**flight attendant** /ˈflaɪt əˌtendənt/ (n) = sb whose job is to serve food and drinks during a flight and ensure passenger safety

**goal** /gəʊl/ (n) = whatever you're trying to achieve

**hang out (with sb)** /hæŋ ˈaʊt/ (phr v) = to spend pleasant time with sb

**independent** /ˌɪndɪˈpendənt/ (adj) = not controlled by external groups or people; not part of a larger company

**inspirational** /ˌɪnspəˈreɪʃənəl/ (adj) = giving you hope and new ideas

**list** /lɪst/ (n) = a number of things you write one under the other so that you'll not forget them

**listing** /ˈlɪstɪŋ/ (n) = an official catalogue; each of the items included in an official catalogue

**live** /laɪv/ (adj) = (of a TV/ radio programme) broadcast at the same time as it is happening

**local** /ˈləʊkəl/ (n) = sb who was born and lives in the same place

**marketing assistant** /ˈmɑːkɪtɪŋ əˌsɪstənt/ (n) = sb whose job is to help the person running the marketing department of a business

**marketing manager** /ˈmɑːkɪtɪŋ ˌmænɪdʒə/ (n) = sb whose job is to run the marketing department of a business

**multimedia developer** /ˌmʌltiˈmiːdiə dɪˌveləpə/ (n) = sb whose job is to create applications or software for the computer and entertainment industries

**passionate (about sth)** /ˈpæʃənət/ (adj) = liking sth very much

**podcast** /ˈpɒdkɑːst/ (n) = a digital broadcast

**requirement** /rɪˈkwaɪəmənt/ (n) = whatever is necessary for you to do sth

**rock star** /ˈrɒk stɑː/ (n) = a very famous and popular rock and roll musician

**sales assistant** /ˈseɪlz əˌsɪstənt/ (n) = sb who serves customers in a shop

**sales manager** /ˈseɪlz ˌmænɪdʒə/ (n) = sb who is in charge of the sales department of a business

**share** /ʃeə/ (v) = to let sb enjoy sth along with you

**spectator** /spekˈteɪtə/ (n) = sb who watches a sports event

**spice** /spaɪs/ (n) = whatever adds excitement and interest to sth

**squeeze (sth) in** /ˌskwiːz ˈɪn/ (phr v) = to find time to do sth in spite of your tight schedule

**step into** /ˈstep ɪntə/ (phr v) = to start learning more things about sth

**street artist** /ˈstriːt ˌɑːtɪst/ (n) = sb who draws pictures on the walls of a town or city

**suit** /suːt/ (v) = to be the most appropriate for sb

**supermarket cashier** /ˈsuːpəmɑːkɪt kæˌʃɪə/ (n) = sb who works at the checkout of a supermarket where he/ she receives money and gives change

**supermarket manager** /ˈsuːpəmɑːkɪt ˌmænɪdʒə/ (n) = sb who is in charge of a supermarket

**tour guide** /ˈtʊə gaɪd/ (n) = sb whose job is to show tourists around a place

**weather reporter** /ˈweðə rɪˌpɔːtə/ (n) = a reporter who informs the public about the weather conditions in the near future

**wonder** /ˈwʌndə/ (v) = to ask yourself

# Word List

## 6b

**applicant** /ˈæplɪkənt/ (n) = sb who asks, in writing, for a job, a place on a course, etc

**citizen** /ˈsɪtɪzən/ (n) = sb who was born in a country and is a legal member of this country; sb who has acquired that status

**corridor** /ˈkɒrɪdɔː/ (n) = a long passage in a building with doors on either side

**crash** /kræʃ/ (v) = (of a computer) to stop working

**decline** /dɪˈklaɪn/ (v) = to legally refuse to accept a document, an application, etc

**employee** /ɪmˈplɔɪiː/ (n) = sb who gets paid to work for sb else

**experience** /ɪkˈspɪəriəns/ (v) = to get to know sth with your senses

**immigration** /ˌɪmɪˈgreɪʃən/ (n) = the process of going into a foreign country to live and work there

**job offer** /dʒɒb ˌɒfə/ (n) = the fact that an employer has stated that they will offer you a job

**obtain** /əbˈteɪn/ (v) = to manage to be given sth

**pressure** /ˈpreʃə/ (n) = a feeling of worry and anxiety because you have to do a lot of work

**progress report** /ˈprəʊgres rɪˌpɔːt/ (n) = a piece of writing in which an employee mentions how far they've gone with their task

**recover** /rɪˈkʌvə/ (v) = to manage to get a computer file back that you thought was lost

**retail** /ˈriːteɪl/ (n) = the practice of shops selling goods to customers

**submit** /səbˈmɪt/ (v) = to officially give a document, an application, etc to sb in authority

**valid** /ˈvælɪd/ (adj) = (of a document, ticket, etc) legal and acceptable

**working holiday visa** (phr) = an official permit that allows a traveller to work in the foreign country they are visiting

## 6c

**achieve** /əˈtʃiːv/ (v) = to try and manage to get sth

**appreciate** /əˈpriːʃieɪt/ (v) = to express your gratitude to sb for sth they've done for you

**autonomous** /ɔːˈtɒnəməs/ (adj) = able to make decisions on your own; working without direct instructions

**caregiver** /ˈkeəgɪvə/ (n) = sb whose job is to take care of old or sick people

**come up with** /kʌm ˈʌp wɪð/ (phr v) = to produce an original idea, a plan, etc

**cooperative** /kəʊˈɒpərətɪv/ (adj) = able and willing to work well with others

**creative** /kriˈeɪtɪv/ (adj) = able to come up with original ideas

**current** /ˈkʌrənt/ (adj) = present

**delight** /dɪˈlaɪt/ (n) = satisfaction and happiness

**delight** /dɪˈlaɪt/ (v) = to give pleasure to sb

**flexible** /ˈfleksəbəl/ (adj) = adaptable

**in harmony** (phr) = in peaceful agreement with others

**influential** /ˌɪnfluˈenʃəl/ (adj) = able to change people's mind or affect their performance positively

**junior manager** /ˌdʒuːniə ˌmænɪdʒə/ (n) = sb in control of a company who is at the lowest level

**leadership skills** /ˈliːdəʃɪp ˌskɪlz/ (pl n) = the ability to be in charge of a group of people in an effective way

**medication** /ˌmedɪˈkeɪʃən/ (n) = medicine for sick people

**outlook** /ˈaʊtlʊk/ (n) = your opinion of, and attitude towards, sth

**punctual** /ˈpʌŋktʃuəl/ (adj) = on time

**reliable** /rɪˈlaɪəbəl/ (adj) = trustworthy

**rely on (sb)** /rɪˈlaɪ ɒn/ (phr v) = to consider sb trustworthy and depend on them

**resident** /ˈrezɪdənt/ (n) = a person living in a place

**respectful** /rɪˈspektfəl/ (adj) = showing appreciation and good manners to others

**responsible** /rɪˈspɒnsəbəl/ (adj) = carefully doing your job or duty

**retire** /rɪˈtaɪə/ (v) = to stop working because of old age

**shift** /ʃɪft/ (n) = the period of time during which a factory worker, a hospital doctor, etc works

**suit** /suːt/ (v) = (of a job, etc) to be the most appropriate for sb

**tolerant** /ˈtɒlərənt/ (adj) = accepting others as they are

**work under pressure** (phr) = to work efficiently when you feel anxious and stressed

**work values** /ˈwɜːk ˌvæljuːz/ (pl n) = the most important features in any type of work

## Culture 6

**be on first-name terms** (phr) = to know people so well that you call each other by your first names

**bone-crushing** /ˈbəʊn krʌʃɪn/ (adj) = extremely strong as if breaking a bone

**business casual** /ˈbɪznəs ˌkæʒuəl/ (n) = clothes which are not formal but are acceptable in the workplace

**code of conduct** (phr) = a set of behavioural rules laid down by a company

**crush** /krʌʃ/ (v) = to squeeze sth very hard

**divider** /dɪˈvaɪdə/ (n) = a thin flat surface for separating a room into parts

**etiquette** /ˈetɪket/ (n) = a set of acceptable behavioural rules

**flip-flops** /ˈflɪp flɒps/ (pl n) = a pair of rubber summer shoes with a V-shaped strap at the front

**gaze** /geɪz/ (n) = a steady look expressing surprise, admiration, etc

**immigrant** /ˈɪmɪgrənt/ (n) = sb who goes to a foreign country to live and work there

**open plan** /ˌəʊpən ˈplæn/ (adj) = without being divided into separate parts

**punctuality** /ˌpʌŋktʃuˈæləti/ (n) = the quality of always being on time

**receptive** /rɪˈseptɪv/ (adj) = showing that you're willing to listen to sb else

**rock up** /ˌrɒk ˈʌp/ (phr v) = to arrive at a place very casually

**stateside** /ˈsteɪtsaɪd/ (adv) = in the United States of America

## Values B: Productivity

**capable (of sth/of doing sth)** /ˈkeɪpəbəl/ (adj) = having the ability to do sth

**challenging** /ˈtʃælɪndʒɪŋ/ (adj) = difficult; testing your skills and abilities

**commute** /kəˈmjuːt/ (n) = the daily travelling from your home to work, school, college, etc

**goal** /ɡəʊl/ (n) = sth you want to achieve; an aim

**guilty (about sth/about doing sth)** /ˈɡɪlti/ (adj) = feeling unhappy because you have not done sth or you have done sth wrong; ashamed

**motivated** /ˈməʊtɪveɪtɪd/ (adj) = feeling inspired

**productivity** /ˌprɒdʌkˈtɪvəti/ (n) = the amount of work you can do in a specific period of time

**specific** /spəˈsɪfɪk/ (adj) = particular

**stay on track** (phr) = to continue to do the things you have planned

**time waster** /ˈtaɪm weɪstə/ (n) = an activity that uses up a lot of time without any useful result

**treat** /triːt/ (n) = a small luxury as a reward for sth

## Public Speaking Skills B

**ban** /bæn/ (v) = to prohibit sth; to not allow sth

**elect** /ɪˈlekt/ (v) = to choose sb for an official post in the government, a council, etc by voting for them

**passionate** /ˈpæʃənət/ (adj) = having very strong feelings about sb/sth; enthusiastic about sb/sth

## Unit 7 – High-tech

### 7a

**access** /ˈækses/ (v) = to be able to obtain (information from a computer)

**artificial intelligence** /ˌɑːtɪfɪʃəl ɪnˈtelɪdʒəns/ (n) = the ability of computers to make decisions and perform tasks

**automatically** /ˌɔːtəˈmætɪkli/ (adv) = without human involvement

**command** /kəˈmɑːnd/ (n) = an instruction to perform a specific action given to a computer

**compose** /kəmˈpəʊz/ (v) = to write sth (music, poetry, formal writing)

**consist (of sth)** /kənˈsɪst/ (v) = to be made up of two or more parts

**customer behaviour** /ˈkʌstəmə bɪˌheɪvjə/ (n) = the trends and patterns in what customers do and order

**device** /dɪˈvaɪs/ (n) = a gadget

**digital assistant** /ˌdɪdʒɪtl əˈsɪstənt/ (n) = a computer program that answers questions and performs basic tasks

**drop by** /ˌdrɒp ˈbaɪ/ (phr v) = to visit sb informally

**drop off** /ˌdrɒp ˈɒf/ (phr v) = 1) to fall asleep; 2) to decrease

**drop out** /ˌdrɒp ˈaʊt/ (phr v) = to leave a college/university course without having finished it

**for sale** (phr) = (of a house, car, etc) available for people to buy

**go off** /ˌɡəʊ ˈɒf/ (phr v) = (of an alarm clock) to start ringing

**high-speed broadband** (phr) = a system that enables users to access the Internet very fast

**in the sale** (phr) = included as part of a special offer during a period when things are sold at a lower price

**independently** /ˌɪndɪˈpendəntli/ (adv) = separately

**industrial equipment** /ɪnˌdʌstriəl ɪˈkwɪpmənt/ (n) = all the machinery used in manufacturing and other businesses

**lightbulb** /ˈlaɪtbʌlb/ (n) = a rounded glass object that produces light when connected to electricity

**maintain** /meɪnˈteɪn/ (v) = to keep machines, buildings, etc in good condition

**manage** /ˈmænɪdʒ/ (v) = to control sth efficiently

**memory** /ˈmeməri/ (n) = sth that sb remembers from the past

**microchip** /ˈmaɪkrəʊtʃɪp/ (n) = a very small piece of silicon used in computers and other digital devices that performs specific operations

**monitor** /ˈmɒnɪtə/ (v) = to watch the progress of sth for a period of time

**offender** /əˈfendə/ (n) = sb who breaks the law

**powerful** /ˈpaʊəfəl/ (adj) = effective

**predict** /prɪˈdɪkt/ (v) = to use information and say what will happen in the future

**reminder** /rɪˈmaɪndə/ (n) = any type of message that helps sb remember sth

**remotely** /rɪˈməʊtli/ (adv) = (operating a device) from a distance

**revolutionise** /ˌrevəˈluːʃənaɪz/ (v) = to totally change sth and make it much better

**run out of (sth)** /ˌrʌn ˈaʊt əv/ (phr v) = to have none of sth left because you've used it all

**sensor** /ˈsensə/ (n) = a device used for discovering any heat, light, movement, etc

**smart device** /ˌsmɑːt dɪˈvaɪs/ (n) = a digital gadget, such as a smartphone, laptop, tablet, etc

**stationary** /ˈsteɪʃənəri/ (adj) = not moving

**stationery** /ˈsteɪʃənəri/ (n) = the materials needed for writing (pens, pencils, paper, etc)

**straightaway** /ˌstreɪtəˈweɪ/ (adv) = immediately

**the authorities** /ði ɔːˈθɒrətiz/ (pl n) = the officials who are in charge of an area, city or country

**the Internet of Things (IoT)** (phr) = the interconnection of digital devices

**virtual reality** /ˌvɜːtʃuəl riˈæləti/ (n) = the ability of computers to create lifelike environments with which the user can interact

**wearable** /ˈweərəbəl/ (n) = a digital gadget that we can wear

### 7b

**activate** /ˈæktɪveɪt/ (v) = to make a device start working

**addiction** /əˈdɪkʃən/ (n) = the fact that sb is unable to stop doing sth harmful

**attach** /əˈtætʃ/ (v) = to connect sth to sth else

**award** /əˈwɔːd/ (v) = to give sb/sth a prize or title

# Word List

**broadcast** /ˈbrɔːdkɑːst/ (v) = to air a TV or radio programme

**coding** /ˈkəʊdɪŋ/ (n) = programming to activate an application or software

**come out** /kʌm ˈaʊt/ (phr v) = (of a product) to become available for people to buy

**dust** /dʌst/ (n) = a dry dirt powder that covers surfaces

**faulty** /ˈfɔːlti/ (adj) = (of a device, etc) not working properly

**HDMI cable** /ˌeɪtʃ diː em ˈaɪ keɪbəl/ (n) = a wire that is connected to multimedia devices and improves the quality of pictures and sound

**in a row** (phr) = happening one after the other

**queue** /kjuː/ (n) = a line of people waiting at a counter, station, etc

**screwdriver** /ˈskruːdraɪvə/ (n) = a tool for turning a pointed piece of metal into an object in order to join things together

**tech fair** /tek feə/ (n) = a large exhibition with products of modern technology

**virus** /ˈvaɪərəs/ (n) = a very tiny living organism that causes diseases

## 7c

**accurate** /ˈækjərət/ (adj) = exact and correct

**assist** /əˈsɪst/ (v) = to help sb with sth

**book** /bʊk/ (v) = to make a reservation

**browse** /braʊz/ (v) = to search for goods on the Internet

**chat** /tʃæt/ (v) = to talk to friends over the Internet

**converse (with sb)** / kənˈvɜːs/ (v) = to talk with sb

**create** /kriˈeɪt/ (v) = to make a new thing

**drop (sb) off** /drɒp ˈɒf/ (phr v) = to take sb to a place in your vehicle on your way to somewhere else

**excel (at/in sth)** /ɪkˈsel/ (v) = to be or do sth better than anyone else

**get (a taxi)** /get/ (v) = to find and take (a taxi)

**mimic** /ˈmɪmɪk/ (v) = to imitate sb

**monitor** /ˈmɒnɪtə/ (v) = to watch the progress of sth for a period of time

**music streaming app** /ˈmjuːzɪk striːmɪŋ ˌæp/ (n) = a piece of software that allows you to listen to music as it is being broadcast on the Internet

**order** /ˈɔːdə/ (v) = to request food, drink, a product, etc (through the Internet)

**set up** /ˌset ˈʌp/ (phr v) = to get a computer program ready for use

**share** /ʃeə/ (v) = to let people watch or listen to sth through the Internet

**stream** /striːm/ (v) = to watch a video or listen to music as they are being broadcast on the Internet

**upload** /ʌpˈləʊd/ (v) = to transfer data to the Internet so that anyone can access it

## Culture 7

**CGI** /siː dʒiː ˈaɪ/ (abbrev) = (Computer-Generated Imagery) the process of creating pictures and images through computer software; the visual outcomes of that process

**colonise** /ˈkɒlənaɪz/ (v) = to go, in large numbers, to live in another place

**combine** /kəmˈbaɪn/ (v) = to join two or more different things together to create sth

**depict** /dɪˈpɪkt/ (v) = to show sth in pictures

**founded** /ˈfaʊndɪd/ (pp) = established

**in advance** (phr) = (occurring) before an event

**intellectual** /ˌɪntəˈlektʃuəl/ (adj) = relating to the mind

**mission** /ˈmɪʃən/ (n) = the result that an organisation is trying to achieve via its actions

**multimedia** /ˌmʌltiˈmiːdiə/ (n) = the use of words, pictures and sound in digital technology

**narrate** /nəˈreɪt/ (v) = to tell a story

**play a role** (phr) = to have an effect on sb/sth

**renowned** /rɪˈnaʊnd/ (adj) = well-known for sth

**resource** /rɪˈzɔːs/ (n) = sth that you can get valuable information from

**spread the word** (idm) = to let more and more people know about sth

**state-of-the-art** /ˌsteɪt əv ði ˈɑːt/ (adj) = using the most modern technology

**the public** /ðə ˈpʌblɪk/ (n) = all the ordinary people in a society

**venue** /ˈvenjuː/ (n) = the place for an event

**vital** /ˈvaɪtl/ (adj) = very important

## Unit 8 – Better societies

### 8a

**access (to sth)** /ˈækses/ (n) = the right or ability to make use of sth

**action** /ˈækʃən/ (n) = the process of doing sth

**activity** /ækˈtɪvəti/ (n) = the fact that a lot of things are taking place

**affect** /əˈfekt/ (v) = to have an impact on sb/sth

**apply** /əˈplaɪ/ (v) = to make a formal request in writing

**border** /ˈbɔːdə/ (n) = the official line that separates one country from another

**child labour** /tʃaɪld ˌleɪbə/ (n) = the use of children to do physical work illegally

**climate change** /ˈklaɪmət ˌtʃeɪndʒ/ (n) = changes in global weather and climate as a result of human or natural activity

**common** /ˈkɒmən/ (adj) = shared by a lot of people

**dean** /diːn/ (n) = a university/college official who is in charge of a department

**estimated** /ˈestɪmeɪtɪd/ (adj) = not exact

**fall apart** /ˌfɔːl əˈpɑːt/ (phr v) = 1) to break into pieces; 2) to be unable to think calmly

**fall behind** /ˌfɔːl bɪˈhaɪnd/ (phr v) = to make no progress

**fall in with** /ˌfɔːl ˈɪn wɪð/ (phr v) = 1) to accept (an idea/plan, etc); 2) to become friends with sb

**fall out** /ˌfɔːl ˈaʊt/ (phr v) = to have an argument

**fall through** /ˌfɔːl ˈθruː/ (phr v) = to fail to happen

**famine** /ˈfæmɪn/ (n) = the situation in which a large number of people don't have food for a certain period of time

**gear** /gɪə/ (n) = each of the devices in a vehicle which control the power that the moving parts get from the engine

**generate** /ˈdʒenəreɪt/ (v) = to create sth

**healthy** /ˈhelθi/ (adj) = (of food) very good for your body

**homelessness** /ˈhəʊmləsnəs/ (n) = the state of not having a home

**illiteracy** /ɪˈlɪtərəsi/ (n) = a lack of reading and writing ability

**income** /ˈɪŋkəm/ (n) = the money that sb earns from their job

**inequality** /ˌɪnɪˈkwɒləti/ (n) = the unfair situation where not all people have the same opportunities, living conditions, etc

**miserable** /ˈmɪzərəbəl/ (adj) = very unhappy

**neighbouring** /ˈneɪbərɪŋ/ (adj) = nearby

**NGO** /ˌen dʒiː ˈəʊ/ (abbrev) = (Non-Governmental Organisation) an independent organisation that helps people in need, protects the environment, etc

**ordinary** /ˈɔːdənəri/ (adj) = average; nothing special

**overpopulation** /ˌəʊvəpɒpjʊˈleɪʃən/ (n) = the fact that too many people live in a certain area

**poverty** /ˈpɒvəti/ (n) = the state of having very little or no money at all

**real** /rɪəl/ (adj) = not imaginary or invented

**reason** /ˈriːzən/ (v) = to make a judgement based on facts

**refugee** /ˌrefjʊˈdʒiː/ (n) = sb who escapes his/her country because of a war or poverty

**relatively** /ˈrelətɪvli/ (adv) = comparatively

**remember** /rɪˈmembə/ (v) = to not forget sth

**remind (sb of sth)** /rɪˈmaɪnd/ (v) = to help sb think of sth from the past

**special** /ˈspeʃəl/ (adj) = not ordinary

**specialised** /ˈspeʃəlaɪzd/ (adj) = having expert skill in or knowledge of sth

**true** /truː/ (adj) = correct

**war** /wɔː/ (n) = armed fighting between two or more opposing groups or countries

## 8b

**affect** /əˈfekt/ (v) = to have an impact on sb/sth

**channel** /ˈtʃænl/ (n) = a passage for water to run through

**conference** /ˈkɒnfərəns/ (n) = a formal meeting for discussing important matters

**donate** /dəʊˈneɪt/ (v) = to offer money and goods to organisations which help people in need

**escape** /ɪˈskeɪp/ (v) = to get away from a danger

**give sb a lift** (phr) = to take sb somewhere in your car

**illiteracy rate** /ɪˈlɪtərəsi ˌreɪt/ (n) = the percentage of people in an area/country who don't know how to read or write

**resources** /rɪˈzɔːsɪz/ (pl n) = water, wood, oil, gas, etc

**vaccinate** /ˈvæksɪneɪt/ (v) = to protect sb from a disease by giving them a substance containing the virus that causes that disease

**wages** /ˈweɪdʒɪz/ (pl n) = the money that sb earns from their job on a weekly basis

## 8c

**accent** /ˈæksənt/ (n) = the specific way that sb or a group of people pronounce words

**addiction** /əˈdɪkʃən/ (n) = the fact that sb is unable to stop doing sth harmful

**animal abuse** /ˈænɪməl əˌbjuːs/ (n) = cruel treatment of animals

**bullying** /ˈbʊliɪŋ/ (n) = the practice of older and more powerful students threatening and/or hurting younger or weaker ones

**concentrate** /ˈkɒnsəntreɪt/ (v) = to be able to focus on sth

**depression** /dɪˈpreʃən/ (n) = a serious condition in which you feel very sad and unhappy

**fat** /fæt/ (n) = a substance under the skin of humans' and animals' bodies that stores energy and keeps them warm

**food intake** /fuːd ˌɪnteɪk/ (n) = the amount of food that sb eats

**high-pressure** /haɪ ˌpreʃə/ (adj) = causing a lot of stress and anxiety

**intelligence** /ɪnˈtelɪdʒəns/ (n) = the mind's ability to learn, think and make decisions

**lack** /læk/ (v) = to have none or not enough of sth necessary

**obese** /əʊˈbiːs/ (adj) = unhealthily overweight

**obesity** /əʊˈbiːsəti/ (n) = the condition of being unhealthily overweight

**overweight** /ˌəʊvəˈweɪt/ (adj) = being heavier than you should be for your height or age

**pick on sb** /ˈpɪk ɒn/ (phr v) = to choose sb and treat them unfairly

**racism** /ˈreɪsɪzəm/ (n) = the conviction that your ethnic group is superior to others

**stress** /stres/ (n) = mental or emotional pressure

**struggle** /ˈstrʌgəl/ (v) = to experience difficulty when trying to achieve sth

**unemployment** /ˌʌnɪmˈplɔɪmənt/ (n) = the state of being jobless

## Culture 8

**campaign** /kæmˈpeɪn/ (v) = to organise a number of activities in order to achieve a goal

**clean** /kliːn/ (adj) = (of water) free of dirt and drinkable

**define** /dɪˈfaɪn/ (v) = to describe the meaning of sth clearly

**improve** /ɪmˈpruːv/ (v) = to become better

**intern** /ɪnˈtɜːn/ (n) = a university/college graduate who is working in order to gain experience

**launch** /lɔːntʃ/ (v) = to start (an ambitious project)

**major** /ˈmeɪdʒə/ (adj) = highly important

**mission** /ˈmɪʃən/ (n) = a goal that an organisation is trying to reach through its actions

**power** /paʊə/ (n) = political strength

**reduce** /rɪˈdjuːs/ (v) = to decrease sth

**regularly** /ˈregjʊləli/ (adv) = often

**spread** /spred/ (v) = to cause sth to reach a larger number of things or people

## Unit 9 – Live & Learn

### 9a

**abandon** /əˈbændən/ (v) = to stop using sth

**attend** /əˈtend/ (v) = to go to a class or lecture

# Word List

**beat** /biːt/ (v) = (of the heart) to make a regular sound as it pumps blood

**campus** /ˈkæmpəs/ (n) = a large area that includes university buildings, students' halls of residence and other facilities

**check in** /ˌtʃek ˈɪn/ (phr v) = 1) to report your arrival (at a hotel, clinic, etc) (Opp.: check out); 2) to arrive at an airport and show your ticket before getting on a plane

**check off** /ˌtʃek ˈɒf/ (phr v) = to tick off items on a list

**check out** /ˌtʃek ˈaʊt/ (phr v) = to look at sth to see if you like it

**check up on (sb/sth)** /ˌtʃek ˈʌp ɒn/ (phr v) = to find out how sth is progressing, or if sb is doing what they're supposed to be doing

**concept** /ˈkɒnsept/ (n) = an idea

**constellation** /ˌkɒnstəˈleɪʃən/ (n) = a group of stars forming a specific pattern

**course** /kɔːs/ (n) = a programme of university studies

**creature** /ˈkriːtʃə/ (n) = an imaginary life form

**do** /duː/ (v) = to take part in an activity such as a course

**effect** /ɪˈfekt/ (n) = an artificially produced image

**experience** /ɪkˈspɪəriəns/ (v) = to get to know sth with your senses

**follow** /ˈfɒləʊ/ (v) = to do what sb tells you

**identification** /aɪˌdentɪfɪˈkeɪʃən/ (n) = recognising sb/sth

**interactive** /ˌɪntərˈæktɪv/ (adj) = (of a computer program) that the user can communicate with

**lecture hall** /ˈlektʃə hɔːl/ (n) = each of the university rooms where professors teach their students

**make** /meɪk/ (v) = to create sth

**mark** /mɑːk/ (n) = a grade given to a student's work

**nutritionist** /njuːˈtrɪʃənɪst/ (n) = a scientist who is an expert at how foods affect our health

**overpowering** /ˌəʊvəˈpaʊərɪŋ/ (adj) = too strong; overwhelming

**passive** /ˈpæsɪv/ (adj) = not changing a situation, and allowing others to be in control

**review** /rɪˈvjuː/ (v) = to consider sth again before making a decision

**revise** /rɪˈvaɪz/ (v) = to study again what you've learnt before taking an exam

**school grounds** /ˈskuːl graʊndz/ (pl n) = a large area that includes a school, its playground and facilities

**score** /skɔː/ (n) = the total number of points that a student gets in an exam

**stimulating** /ˈstɪmjuleɪtɪŋ/ (adj) = causing interest and excitement

**undergraduate** /ˌʌndəˈgrædʒuət/ (n) = a university student studying for their first degree

**visual learner** /ˌvɪʒuəl ˈlɜːnə/ (n) = sb who finds learning easier through images than other methods

## 9b

**announce** /əˈnaʊns/ (v) = to formally inform a number of people about sth

**assignment** /əˈsaɪnmənt/ (n) = a piece of homework that a teacher gives his/her students

**challenge** /ˈtʃælɪndʒ/ (v) = to encourage sb to develop their abilities and skills

**cheat (in sth)** /tʃiːt/ (v) = to behave dishonestly during a test/exam

**degree** /dɪˈgriː/ (n) = the qualification you get when you graduate from a university or college

**failure** /ˈfeɪljə/ (n) = a lack of success

**lab** /læb/ (n) = (short for 'laboratory') a school/university room where students do experiments

**lend** /lend/ (v) = to give sb sth to use for a certain period of time

**roommate** /ˈruːmmeɪt/ (n) = sb that you share a room with in university accommodation

**sth is due** (phr) = sth is expected to have finished (by a particular time)

**strict** /strɪkt/ (adj) = very hard on those who do not obey

**submit** /səbˈmɪt/ (v) = to hand sth in to sb

**wage** /weɪdʒ/ (n) = the amount of money that sb earns on a daily or weekly basis

## 9c

**advanced** /ədˈvɑːnst/ (adj) = (of a course) at a higher level

**certificate** /səˈtɪfɪkət/ (n) = an official document which verifies that you have successfully completed a course

**equip** /ɪˈkwɪp/ (v) = to provide the necessary items for an activity

**fees** /fiːz/ (pl n) = an amount of money that you pay in order to attend a course

**flexible** /ˈfleksəbəl/ (adj) = that you can easily adapt to your needs

**grateful** /ˈgreɪtfəl/ (adj) = thankful

**mature** /məˈtʃʊə/ (adj) = being an older adult

**register** /ˈredʒɪstə/ (v) = to enrol for a course

**school facility** /ˈskuːl fəˌsɪləti/ (n) = a place that provides a service for all pupils and students

**upcoming** /ˈʌpˌkʌmɪŋ/ (adj) = that is going to happen

## Culture 9

**achieve** /əˈtʃiːv/ (v) = to manage to obtain sth

**attitude** /ˈætɪtjuːd/ (n) = an opinion about sth

**background** /ˈbækgraʊnd/ (n) = the family and environment that sb comes from

**drop out (of school, etc)** /ˌdrɒp ˈaʊt/ (phr v) = to quit school, etc before finishing it

**financial** /faɪˈnænʃəl/ (adj) = having to do with money

**focus** /ˈfəʊkəs/ (n) = sth that is the centre of your attention

**impressive** /ɪmˈpresɪv/ (adj) = admirable

**longer** /ˈlɒŋgə/ (adj) = more; additional

**mentor** /ˈmentɔː/ (n) = an expert who gives young people useful advice

**nationally** /ˈnæʃənəli/ (adv) = in the whole country

**point out** /ˌpɔɪnt ˈaʊt/ (phr v) = to make sb notice sth

**promote** /prəˈməʊt/ (v) = to encourage people to pursue or achieve sth

**reach (an age)** /riːtʃ/ (v) = to become a certain age

**run (a programme)** /rʌn/ (v) = to organise and manage a programme

## Values C: Compassion

**a shoulder to cry on** (phr) = a person who listens with sympathy to sb's troubles

**appropriate** /ə'prəupriət/ (adj) = acceptable; suitable

**be all ears** (phr) = to show great interest in what sb is going to say

**comforting** /'kʌmfətɪŋ/ (adj) = making you less worried, anxious or unhappy

**compassion** /kəm'pæʃən/ (n) = a feeling of pity, sympathy and understanding for sb who is suffering and wanting help

**deserve** /dɪ'zɜːv/ (v) = to earn the right to sth, or to be given sth, thanks to your actions or behaviour

**emotionally** /ɪ'məʊʃənəli/ (adv) = in a way that affects sb's feelings

**encourage** /ɪn'kʌrɪdʒ/ (v) = to give sb the confidence and support to do sth

**gesture** /'dʒestʃə/ (n) = a movement of your hands to express how you feel about sb

**hug** /hʌg/ (n) = putting your arms around sb; an embrace

**mindset** /'maɪndset/ (n) = the way sb thinks; mental attitude

**physical contact** /,fɪzɪkəl 'kɒntækt/ (n) = the act of touching sb else

**physically** /'fɪzɪkli/ (adv) = relating to your body

**positive thinking** /,pɒzətɪv 'θɪŋkɪŋ/ (n) = an optimistic attitude

**respectful** /rɪ'spektfəl/ (adj) = showing consideration for sb

**supportive** /sə'pɔːtɪv/ (adj) = encouraging; helpful

**take the next step** (phr) = to move on to the next stage of a situation

## Public Speaking Skills C

**achievement** /ə'tʃiːvmənt/ (n) = the act of succeeding in doing sth difficult; an accomplishment

**attitude** /'ætɪtjuːd/ (n) = the way you feel or think which people can see in your behaviour

**highlight** /'haɪlaɪt/ (n) = the most interesting, enjoyable or important part of an event

**honour** /'ɒnə/ (n) = a privilege

**honour** /'ɒnə/ (v) = to celebrate and show respect for sb publicly

**host** /həʊst/ (v) = to be the presenter of an event

**incredible** /ɪn'kredəbəl/ (adj) = amazing

**limited** /'lɪmɪtɪd/ (adj) = not in large amounts or quantities; restricted

**present** /prɪ'zent/ (v) = to give sth to sb at a ceremony, such as an award, etc

**without further ado** (phr) = not delaying sth; not wasting any more time

## Unit 10 – Green minds

### 10a

**acid rain** /,æsɪd 'reɪn/ (n) = rain that contains harmful chemicals from pollution

**air pollution** /'eə pə,luːʃən/ (n) = harmful waste/ chemicals in the air

**alone** /ə'ləʊn/ (adv) = being the only thing that can make sth happen

**bacteria** /bæk'tɪəriə/ (pl n) = types of very small organisms that can cause illness

**break down** /,breɪk 'daʊn/ (phr v) = to reduce sth; to break sth into smaller parts

**clean** /kliːn/ (adj) = not polluted; fresh

**clear** /klɪə/ (adj) = that can be seen through easily; transparent

**climate change** /'klaɪmət ,tʃeɪndʒ/ (n) = differences over time in the weather conditions and temperature on the Earth, usually as a result of human activity

**dead** /ded/ (adj) = not alive

**deadly** /'dedli/ (adj) = very harmful

**endangered species** /ɪn,deɪndʒəd 'spiːʃiːz/ (n) = an animal that is at risk of going extinct

**global warming** /,gləʊbəl 'wɔːmɪŋ/ (n) = the increase in the planet's temperature caused either naturally or as the result of human activity

**head for** /'hed fə/ (phr v) = to move or travel towards a place or a situation

**head off** /,hed 'ɒf/ (phr v) = 1) to stop sb/sth and make them change direction; 2) to prevent sth bad from happening; 3) to leave and go somewhere else

**head out** /,hed 'aʊt/ (phr v) = to go out

**head up** /,hed 'ʌp/ (phr v) = to be in charge of sth

**hyena** /haɪ'iːnə/ (n) = a wild animal from Africa that looks like a dog and has a distinctive call that sounds like a human laugh

**infection** /ɪn'fekʃən/ (n) = the condition of having a disease or illness

**jackal** /'dʒækɔːl/ (n) = a wild animal from Africa that looks like a dog and searches for food

**light pollution** /'laɪt pə,luːʃən/ (n) = brightening of the evening sky due to artificial light sources

**lonely** /'ləʊnli/ (adj) = being unhappy due to being by yourself

**mess** /mes/ (n) = sth that is in a state of being dirty and untidy

**noise pollution** /'nɔɪz pə,luːʃən/ (n) = noise that is harmful to nature or irritating for people

**plain** /pleɪn/ (n) = an area of flat land

**population growth** /,pɒpjə'leɪʃən grəʊθ/ (n) = the increase in the number of people living in a country, area or globally

**purifying** /'pjʊərɪfaɪɪŋ/ (adj) = cleansing

**push** /pʊʃ/ (n) = an attempt to achieve sth

**rotting** /'rɒtɪŋ/ (adj) = decaying

**scavenger** /'skævɪndʒə/ (n) = an animal that eats the flesh of dead creatures that it did not kill

**sea cucumber** /'siː ,kjuːkʌmbə/ (n) = a sea creature with a long thick body that looks like a fat worm

**sign** /saɪn/ (n) = an indication of sth

**signal** /'sɪgnəl/ (n) = a sound or action that gives a warning

**stomach acid** /'stʌmək ,æsɪd/ (n) = acid inside the body that helps the digestive process

**suck up** /,sʌk 'ʌp/ (phr v) = to pull sth into the mouth with a lot of force

# Word List

**turkey vulture** /tɜːki ˌvʌltʃə/ (n) = a bird that looks like a small vulture

**under threat** (phr) = in a position where sth/sb is in danger

**vulture** /ˈvʌltʃə/ (n) = a large bird with a bald head and neck which eats dead animals

**wander** /ˈwɒndə/ (v) = to walk around a place without any specific destination

**waste production** /weɪst prəˈdʌkʃən/ (n) = the collection of rubbish or waste materials as the result of an activity

**water pollution** /ˈwɔːtə pəˌluːʃən/ (n) = harmful waste/chemicals in the sea, rivers, etc

## 10b

**admit** /ədˈmɪt/ (v) = to own up to sth, especially when you don't want to

**bare** /beə/ (adj ) = uncovered; without wearing protective clothing

**bird sanctuary** /bɜːd ˌsæŋktʃuəri/ (n) = a place where birds are kept and treated

**boast** /bəʊst/ (v) = to brag about sth

**construction** /kənˈstrʌkʃən/ (n) = the process of building homes and other structures

**growth** /grəʊθ/ (n) = the development of plants, animals or people

**guidelines** /ˈgaɪdlaɪnz/ (pl n) = information that tells people how to do sth

**organic food shop** /ɔːˈgænɪk ˈfuːd ʃɒp/ (n) = a shop that sells fruit, vegetables and other food grown without chemical fertilisers

**radical** /ˈrædɪkəl/ (adj) = extreme

**remind** /rɪˈmaɪnd/ (v) = to tell sb again about sth that they might have forgotten

**target** /ˈtɑːgɪt/ (n) = a goal

**warn** /wɔːn/ (v) = to make sb aware of a problem or threat

## 10c

**carpool** /ˈkɑːpuːl/ (v) = to share your car when travelling somewhere

**cleaning supplies** /ˈkliːnɪŋ səˌplaɪz/ (pl n) = chemicals and products used to clean

**compost** /ˈkɒmpɒst/ (n) = rotting plants that are used in gardening to help other plants grow

**detergent** /dɪˈtɜːdʒənt/ (n) = a chemical used to wash clothes

**digitally** /ˈdɪdʒɪtəli/ (adv) = in a way that uses computers, especially opposed to paper

**drastic** /ˈdræstɪk/ (adj) = very sudden or severe

**economy class** /ɪˈkɒnəmi ˌklɑːs/ (adv) = booking one of the most inexpensive seats available on a plane

**energy consumption** /ˈenədʒi kənˌsʌmpʃən/ (n) = the amount of power used by sth/sb

**energy-efficient** /ˈenədʒi ɪˌfɪʃənt/ (adj) = using little power/fuel to operate

**food waste** /ˈfuːd weɪst/ (n) = unwanted, leftover food

**generation** /ˌdʒenəˈreɪʃən/ (n) = all of the people of roughly the same age in a society

**homeless shelter** /ˈhəʊmləs ˈʃeltə/ (n) = a place for people to stay who live on the streets

**in a good condition** (phr) = in a decent state

**LED light bulb** /ˌled ˈlaɪt bʌlb/ (n) = an energy-efficient bulb that uses light-emitting diodes as a source of light

**locally-sourced** /ˌləʊkəli ˈsɔːst/ (adj) = coming from a nearby area

**management** /ˈmænɪdʒmənt/ (n) = the people in charge of a company or business

**motivate** /ˈməʊtɪveɪt/ (v) = to encourage

**organic food** /ɔːˈgænɪk ˈfuːd/ (n) = fruit, vegetables and other food grown without chemical fertilisers

**paperless** /ˈpeɪpələs/ (adj) = not using any printed material; electronic

**pick (sth) up** /ˌpɪk ˈʌp/ (phr v) = to take sth off the floor, table or surface

**propose** /prəˈpəʊz/ (v) = to suggest sth

**rely on (sb/sth)** /rɪˈlaɪ ɒn/ (phr v) = to be able to expect sb to do sth for you; to be able to trust sb to do sth

**reusable** /riːˈjuːzəbəl/ (adj) = able to be used more than once

**straightaway** /ˈstreɪtəweɪ/ (adv) = right now

**toxic** /ˈtɒksɪk/ (adj) = harmful; poisonous

## Culture 10

**annually** /ˈænjuəli/ (adv) = every year

**driftwood** /ˈdrɪftwʊd/ (n) = wood that washes up on beaches or floats in water

**face** /feɪs/ (v) = to encounter a problem and have to deal with it

**participant** /pɑːˈtɪsɪpənt/ (n) = sb who is involved in sth

**promote** /prəˈməʊt/ (v) = to inform a lot of people about sth and ask for their support

**raise awareness** (phr) = to draw sth to people's attention

**run** /rʌn/ (v) = to organise and manage sth

**sign up** /ˌsaɪn ˈʌp/ (phr v) = to put your name down for an activity

**supervision** /ˌsuːpəˈvɪʒən/ (n) = the act of overseeing sth/sb

**update** /ˈʌpdeɪt/ (n) = the latest information about sth

**wonder** /ˈwʌndə/ (n) = an object that amazes and inspires sb

## Unit 11 – Buying, buying, bought!

### 11a

**advertising slogan** (phr) = a short phrase that is easy to remember and that is used to promote products; a catchy phrase

**advertising spot** (phr) = a short period of time on TV or radio that is used to promote products to consumers

**annoying** /əˈnɔɪɪŋ/ (adj) = irritating

**aware (of)** /əˈweə/ (adj) = informed about sth

**call after** /ˈkɔːl ɑːftə/ (phr v) = to name sb/sth after sb/sth else

**call back** /ˌkɔːl ˈbæk/ (phr v) = to return a phone call

**call for** /ˈkɔːl fə/ (phr v) = 1) to demand sth; 2) to pick up sb

**call in** /ˌkɔːl ˈɪn/ (phr v) = to make a short visit

**call off** /ˌkɔːl ˈɒf/ (phr v) = to cancel sth

**client** /ˈklaɪənt/ (n) = a person that pays a professional or organisation for a service

**create** /kriˈeɪt/ (v) = to make sth; to produce sth

**customer** /ˈkʌstəmə/ (n) = a person who buys sth from a shop; a consumer

**decision** /dɪˈsɪʒən/ (n) = a choice

**deeply** /ˈdiːpli/ (adv) = seriously

**digital marketing** /ˌdɪdʒɪtəl ˈmɑːkɪtɪŋ/ (n) = the use of the Internet, social media, etc to reach customers

**effective** /ɪˈfektɪv/ (adj) = successful

**encourage** /ɪnˈkʌrɪdʒ/ (v) = to persuade sb to do sth

**example** /ɪgˈzɑːmpəl/ (n) = a representative person, object, etc that is used to show what is typical of a larger group

**experience** /ɪkˈspɪəriəns/ (v) = to be exposed to sth

**grab sb's attention** (phr) = to make sb notice you

**jingle** /ˈdʒɪŋgəl/ (n) = a short simple piece of music used to advertise sth

**limit** /ˈlɪmɪt/ (n) = a restriction

**market research** /ˌmɑːkɪt rɪˈsɜːtʃ/ (n) = the collection and study of information relating to what consumers like to buy

**positive** /ˈpɒzətɪv/ (adj) = making you feel happy

**prime time** /praɪm ˌtaɪm/ (n) = the hours when most people watch TV

**produce** /ˈprɒdjuːs/ (n) = fruit, vegetables, etc for sale that are grown on a farm in large quantities

**product** /ˈprɒdʌkt/ (n) = a manufactured thing

**receipt** /rɪˈsiːt/ (n) = a piece of paper that you get when you buy sth showing its value, the money that you paid and any change that you received

**recipe** /ˈresɪpi/ (n) = the ingredients and instructions for cooking a specific type of food

**retail** /ˈriːteɪl/ (n) = the activity of selling products directly to the public (in shops, etc)

**roadside hoarding** /ˌrəʊdsaɪd ˈhɔːdɪŋ/ (n) = a very large board placed on the side of roads, etc where an advertisement is placed

**rush** /rʌʃ/ (v) = to hurry

**sample** /ˈsɑːmpəl/ (n) = a small quantity of sth that you try in order to see what the whole product is like

**scarce** /skeəs/ (adj) = insufficient; available only in small numbers or quantities

**sneaky** /ˈsniːki/ (adj) = cunning; sly

**spend** /spend/ (v) = to pay money in order to buy sth

**spot** /spɒt/ (v) = to identify sb/sth

**support** /səˈpɔːt/ (v) = to help sb/sth because you approve of them

**target audience** /ˈtɑːgɪt ˌɔːdiəns/ (n) = the group of viewers, listeners, etc that companies aim at for advertising purposes

**TV commercial** /ˌtiː viː kəˈmɜːʃəl/ (n) = an advertisement shown on TV

**window display** /ˈwɪndəʊ dɪˌspleɪ/ (n) = the products presented in the front window of a shop and their arrangement that attracts customers inside

**worry** /ˈwʌri/ (n) = anxiety; concern

## 11b

**assistance** /əˈsɪstəns/ (n) = help

**bargain** /ˈbɑːgɪn/ (n) = sth that you buy at a lower price than its usual price; a special offer or discount running at a certain time

**deal** /diːl/ (n) = the best price that you can pay to buy sth

**outfit** /ˈaʊtfɪt/ (n) = a set of matching clothes worn together, such as a suit, etc

**pot** /pɒt/ (n) = a container used to make and serve tea or coffee; a small round container for foods such as yogurt, jam, cream, etc

**rely on** /rɪˈlaɪ ɒn/ (phr v) = to depend on

**retailer** /ˈriːteɪlə/ (n) = a person or business that sells products to consumers in a shop

**sales** /seɪlz/ (pl n) = the period of time when shops, etc sell their products or services at lower prices than usual

**try on** /ˌtraɪ ˈɒn/ (phr v) = to wear clothes to see if they fit or suit you before you buy them

**tube** /tjuːb/ (n) = a long thin container where toothpaste, sun cream, etc is kept

**voucher** /ˈvaʊtʃə/ (n) = a document which represents a sum of money that can be used to buy sth

## 11c

**assure** /əˈʃʊə/ (v) = to inform sb that sth is certainly true, so they do not worry

**broken** /ˈbrəʊkən/ (adj) = wrecked; damaged and separated into pieces

**cracked** /krækt/ (adj) = (of glass, etc) having one or more lines on its surface but not totally broken

**damaged** /ˈdæmɪdʒd/ (adj) = broken; ruined

**dead** /ded/ (adj) = (of equipment/batteries) not working because there is no power

**exchange (sth for sth else)** /ɪksˈtʃeɪndʒ/ (v) = to replace sth with sth else

**in advance** (phr) = beforehand

**missing** /ˈmɪsɪŋ/ (adj) = lost and not in its usual place

**refund** /ˈriːfʌnd/ (n) = the money that you get back when you return a purchase to a shop

**scratched** /skrætʃt/ (adj) = having a small cut or a long thin mark made with a sharp object

**spare** /speə/ (adj) = extra and not needed at present

**stick** /stɪk/ (v) = to remain in the same place

**torn** /tɔːn/ (adj) = (of paper, cloth, etc) ripped

**weak** /wiːk/ (adj) = not strong

**wireless** /ˈwaɪələs/ (adj) = operating with radio signals rather than with the use of connected cables

## Culture 11

**accounts** /əˈkaʊnts/ (pl n) = the documents that show a company's financial situation

**bankrupt** /ˈbæŋkrʌpt/ (adj) = not having enough money to pay your debts

# Word List

**bargain** /ˈbɑːɡɪn/ (n) = sth that you buy at a lower price than its usual price; a special offer or discount running at a certain time

**crash** /kræʃ/ (n) = the fact that a stock market fails

**Cyber Monday** /ˈsaɪbə ˌmʌndeɪ/ (n) = the Monday after the Thanksgiving holiday in the USA when shops encourage consumers to shop online by offering low prices for their products

**estimated** /ˈestɪmeɪtɪd/ (adj) = calculated; guessed at

**financial crisis** /faɪˌnænʃəl ˈkraɪsɪs/ (n) = the period when a country's economy is in serious trouble or danger

**include** /ɪnˈkluːd/ (v) = to incorporate sth; to make sth part of another thing

**investor** /ɪnˈvestə/ (n) = sb who puts money in a company, business, etc in order to make money

**originate (from sth)** /əˈrɪdʒəneɪt/ (v) = to come from sth

**profit** /ˈprɒfɪt/ (n) = the money that you make when you sell sth for more money than you paid to buy it

**record** /rɪˈkɔːd/ (v) = to document sth; to register sth

**retailer** /ˈriːteɪlə/ (n) = a person or business that sells products to consumers in a shop

**shoplifting** /ˈʃɒpˌlɪftɪŋ/ (n) = the act of stealing items from a shop

**spread** /spred/ (v) = to cover a larger area or affect more people; to expand

**stock** /stɒk/ (n) = a part of the ownership of a company that can be sold to the public; a share

**traffic jam** /ˈtræfɪk ˌdʒæm/ (n) = a long line of vehicles that are moving slowly, or not at all

**worldwide** /ˌwɜːldˈwaɪd/ (adv) = in all parts of the world; globally

## Unit 12 – Health is wealth

### 12a

**absorb** /əbˈsɔːb/ (v) = to take a substance into your body

**affect** /əˈfekt/ (v) = to influence sb/sth

**affordable** /əˈfɔːdəbəl/ (adj) = not expensive; having a reasonable price

**audience** /ˈɔːdiəns/ (n) = the people watching an event or show

**breakthrough** /ˈbreɪkθruː/ (n) = an important discovery

**carbohydrate** /ˌkɑːbəʊˈhaɪdreɪt/ (n) = a substance, such as sugar or starch, that gives energy; the food that contains it, such as bread or pasta

**choice** /tʃɔɪs/ (n) = the act of making a selection

**coconut** /ˈkəʊkənʌt/ (n) = a large hard fruit with a brown shell and clear liquid inside

**concerned (about sth)** /kənˈsɜːnd/ (adj) = worried about sth; mindful of sth

**creature** /ˈkriːtʃə/ (n) = an animal; a living thing

**culture** /ˈkʌltʃə/ (n) = a preparation of cells artificially developed in a laboratory

**cut down (on sth)** /ˌkʌt ˈdaʊn/ (phr v) = to eat, drink or use less of sth

**cut in** /ˌkʌt ˈɪn/ (phr v) = to interrupt (sb/sth)

**cut off** /ˌkʌt ˈɒf/ (phr v) = 1) to isolate (sb/sth); 2) to stop providing sth; 3) to disconnect sb (while on the phone)

**(be) cut out (for sth)** /ˌkʌt ˈaʊt/ (phr v) = to have the qualities to do sth

**dairy product** /ˈdeəri ˌprɒdʌkt/ (n) = a food product from animals, such as milk and cheese

**develop** /dɪˈveləp/ (v) = to cause sth to change or become bigger

**digestive system** /daɪˌdʒestɪv ˈsɪstəm/ (n) = the organs that deal with absorbing nutrients from food and breaking them down

**effect** /ɪˈfekt/ (n) = the result of sth

**fat** /fæt/ (n) = a substance found in the body of people and animals that stores energy

**fertiliser** /ˈfɜːtəlaɪzə/ (n) = a substance put on soil to help plants grow

**fibre** /ˈfaɪbə/ (n) = a substance found in fruit, vegetables and brown bread that helps the digestive system

**lean meat** /ˌliːn ˈmiːt/ (n) = meat that does not contain much fat

**lentil** /ˈlentɪl/ (n) = a small dried bean that is cooked to be eaten

**moral** /ˈmɒrəl/ (adj) = relating to what is accepted as good behaviour

**muscle tissue** /ˈmʌsəl ˌtɪʃuː/ (n) = the cells that make up the muscles in the body which enable movement

**mushy** /ˈmʌʃi/ (adj) = (of food) very soft

**nut** /nʌt/ (n) = a dry fruit usually inside a shell

**oily fish** /ˌɔɪli ˈfɪʃ/ (n) = a type of fish that contains a lot of oil in its body, such as mackerel or sardines

**option** /ˈɒpʃən/ (n) = a possibility from a group of things

**organ** /ˈɔːɡən/ (n) = a part of the body that performs a specific function, such as the lungs or heart

**pea** /piː/ (n) = a round green seed

**pesticide** /ˈpestɪsaɪd/ (n) = a chemical used to kill insects and pests

**point** /pɔɪnt/ (n) = a purpose

**poultry** /ˈpəʊltri/ (n) = birds that are bred for food, such as chicken and turkey

**produce** /prəˈdjuːs/ (v) = to make or grow sth

**protein** /ˈprəʊtiːn/ (n) = a substance found in meat, milk, cheese and eggs that helps the body grow and stay strong

**raise** /reɪz/ (v) = to make sth increase in value or amount

**rise** /raɪz/ (v) = to move higher; to stand up

**seafood** /ˈsiːfuːd/ (n) = animals from the sea that can be eaten, such as fish, crab and octopus

**seed** /siːd/ (n) = a small round object found in plants that makes new plants grow

**set up** /ˌset ˈʌp/ (phr v) = to start a new company, organisation, etc

**soy product** /ˌsɔɪ ˈprɒdʌkt/ (n) = a type of food made from small beans from Asia

**vegan** /ˈviːɡən/ (n) = sb who doesn't eat any animal products

**vitamin** /ˈvɪtəmɪn/ (n) = a natural substance found in food that helps the growth of the body

**wholegrain** /ˈhəʊlgreɪn/ (adj) = containing seeds in their natural form

## 12b

**ankle** /ˈæŋkəl/ (n) = the part of your body that connects your leg to your foot

**blood test** /ˈblʌd test/ (n) = a medical examination of a small amount of your blood to see if you have a health problem

**consumer** /kənˈsjuːmə/ (n) = a person who buys things; a shopper

**flu** /fluː/ (n) = an illness similar to a cold but more serious

**intake** /ˈɪnteɪk/ (n) = the amount of food, drink, etc that you take into your body

**mood** /muːd/ (n) = the way you feel at a specific time

**nutrients** /ˈnjuːtriənts/ (pl n) = the substances found in food that help you grow and stay healthy

**nutritious** /njuˈtrɪʃəs/ (adj) = containing substances that are good for your health; nourishing

**portion** /ˈpɔːʃən/ (n) = the amount of food you are given at a meal; a helping

**pregnant** /ˈpregnənt/ (adj) = (of a woman) carrying an unborn baby inside the body

**qualified** /ˈkwɒlɪfaɪd/ (adj) = having the qualifications (e.g. a degree, a certificate, etc) to do a job

**serving** /ˈsɜːvɪŋ/ (n) = the amount of food you are given at a meal

**shift** /ʃɪft/ (n) = the period of time that a group of people work before being replaced by another group

**upset stomach** /ˌʌpset ˈstʌmək/ (n) = a stomach ache

## 12c

**apply** /əˈplaɪ/ (v) = to cover the surface of the body (with sun lotion in order to protect it)

**backpacking** /ˈbækpækɪŋ/ (n) = the activity of travelling and carrying all your belongings in a backpack

**balanced diet** /ˌbælənst ˈdaɪət/ (n) = the combination of the right amounts of various foods in order to keep your body healthy

**bump into (sth)** /ˈbʌmp ɪntə/ (phr v) = to hit or knock against sth by accident

**consume** /kənˈsjuːm/ (v) = to eat or drink sth

**disease** /dɪˈziːz/ (n) = an illness

**eliminate** /ɪˈlɪmɪneɪt/ (v) = to remove sth from sth; to get rid of sth

**emergency** /ɪˈmɜːdʒənsi/ (n) = a crisis; an unexpected, dangerous and urgent situation

**exercise** /ˈeksəsaɪz/ (v) = to do a sport or other physical activity in order to keep your body in shape; to work out

**fair skin** (phr) = a light skin tone

**fire extinguisher** /ˈfaɪər ɪkˌstɪŋgwɪʃə/ (n) = a piece of equipment in the shape of a cylinder which is filled with a chemical used to put out small fires

**fizzy drink** /ˌfɪzi ˈdrɪŋk/ (n) = a drink that contains bubbles of carbon dioxide

**floss** /flɒs/ (v) = to clean the spaces between your teeth and gums using a special thread

**germ** /dʒɜːm/ (n) = a very small organism that causes a disease

**health expenses** /helθ ɪkˌspensɪz/ (pl n) = the money you spend on medical treatment

**limit** /ˈlɪmɪt/ (v) = to restrict sth below a certain number or amount

**maintain** /meɪnˈteɪn/ (v) = to keep sth at a certain level

**mental health** /ˌmentəl ˈhelθ/ (n) = the general wellness of a person's mind

**minor burn** (phr) = an injury caused by fire, sth hot, etc that is not very serious

**pot handle** /ˈpɒt ˌhændəl/ (n) = the part of a round, deep, cooking container that you use to hold or pick up

**remove (yourself from sth)** /rɪˈmuːv/ (v) = to get away from sth in order to avoid a difficult situation

**sunscreen** /ˈsʌnskriːn/ (n) = a cream that you use on your body to protect it from getting burnt by the sun

**take out (sth)** /ˌteɪk ˈaʊt/ (phr v) = to arrange to get sth, such as a loan, insurance, etc, officially from a bank, insurance company, etc

**travel insurance** /ˈtrævəl ɪnˌʃʊərəns/ (n) = the money that travellers pay to a company to protect themselves against injuries, health problems, loss of belongings, etc

**vaccine** /ˈvæksiːn/ (n) = an injection given to people to protect them against specific diseases

## Culture 12

**budget** /ˈbʌdʒɪt/ (n) = the amount of money that is available to a person, organisation, government, etc

**healthcare** /ˈhelθkeə/ (n) = the activity of looking after people's health and well-being

**in vitro fertilisation (IVF)** (phr) = the scientific technique that helps a woman become pregnant

**launch** /lɔːntʃ/ (v) = to start a business, organisation, etc

**life expectancy** /ˈlaɪf ɪkˌspektənsi/ (n) = how long a person, animal or plant is likely to live

**limited** /ˈlɪmɪtɪd/ (adj) = not in large numbers or quantities; restricted

**mention** /ˈmenʃən/ (v) = to discuss sth; to cover sth

**National Insurance contributions** (phr) = a routine payment made by workers to their employers or the government for their pension and medical expenses

**peace of mind** (phr) = the feeling of being calm, happy and not worried about anything

**quality** /ˈkwɒləti/ (adj) = of an excellent standard

**resident** /ˈrezɪdənt/ (n) = a person who lives in a city or town legally

**set up** /ˌset ˈʌp/ (phr v) = to start a new company, organisation, etc

**structure** /ˈstrʌktʃə/ (n) = the way sth is organised

**unique** /juˈniːk/ (adj) = very special

**vision** /ˈvɪʒən/ (n) = an idea, a dream or plan of what you would like sb/sth to be

# Word List

**wipe out** /ˌwaɪp 'aʊt/ (phr v) = to cause sth to stop existing; to eliminate

## Values D: Commitment

**abandon** /əˈbændən/ (v) = to give up sth

**client** /ˈklaɪənt/ (n) = a person that pays a professional or organisation for a service

**commitment** /kəˈmɪtmənt/ (n) = dedication

**committed (to sth/sb)** /kəˈmɪtɪd/ (adj) = dedicated to sth/sb

**dread** /dred/ (v) = to feel anxious before doing sth

**habit** /ˈhæbɪt/ (n) = sth that you do on a regular basis

**intensive** /ɪnˈtensɪv/ (adj) = demanding; requiring a lot of effort

**journal** /ˈdʒɜːnəl/ (n) = a diary

**keep on track** (phr) = to continue doing sth as planned

**motivated** /ˈməʊtɪveɪtɪd/ (adj) = feeling inspired

**progress** /ˈprəʊgres/ (n) = development; improvement

**realistic** /ˌrɪəˈlɪstɪk/ (adj) = practical; sensible

**stick to** /ˈstɪk tə/ (phr v) = to continue doing sth; to not give up

**turn (sth) around** /tɜːn əˈraʊnd/ (phr v) = to change sth that has become unsuccessful into sth successful again

**uncomplicated** /ʌnˈkɒmplɪkeɪtɪd/ (adj) = simple

## Public Speaking Skills D

**average** /ˈævərɪdʒ/ (n) = a typical number or amount of sth

**blood pressure** /ˈblʌd preʃə/ (n) = the force with which blood flows in your body

**consequence** /ˈkɒnsɪkwəns/ (n) = sth that happens as a result or effect of a specific action

**dehydration** /ˌdiːhaɪˈdreɪʃən/ (n) = the condition In which your body has lost too much water making you feel weak or sick

**immune system** /ɪˈmjuːn ˌsɪstəm/ (n) = the structure in your body consisting of various organs and mechanisms that protect you against diseases

**lack (of sth)** /læk/ (n) = the fact that there is not enough of sth; a shortage

**memory loss** /ˈmeməri lɒs/ (n) = the state of not being able to remember

**nutrition** /njuːˈtrɪʃən/ (n) = the process of eating the right food in order to keep your body healthy

**squat** /skwɒt/ (n) = a type of exercise in which you lower your body and bend your knees, then stand up

**strength training** /ˈstreŋθ ˌtreɪnɪŋ/ (n) = a type of exercise in which you lift weights or use your body weight to make your body stronger

**weaken** /ˈwiːkən/ (v) = to become less strong

**weight gain** /ˈweɪt geɪn/ (n) = the situation in which your body becomes heavier

## CLIL A
### PSHE

**account for** /əˈkaʊnt fə/ (phr v) = to be part of a total number, percentage, etc of sth

**approved** /əˈpruːvd/ (adj) = having the accepted standards or level that are decided by a government, committee, etc

**brake** /breɪk/ (v) = to stop or reduce the speed of a vehicle by using a device designed to slow a vehicle's movement

**campaign** /kæmˈpeɪn/ (n) = a course of actions to inform the public about a specific matter

**distract** /dɪˈstrækt/ (v) = to cause sb to lose their concentration

**fatality** /fəˈtæləti/ (n) = a death caused by an accident, attack, etc

**handheld** /ˈhændheld/ (adj) = (of a device) able to be operated using one hand

**illuminated clothing** (phr) = special clothes worn by cyclists, bikers, etc to make them visible to other drivers or people at night

**junction** /ˈdʒʌŋkʃən/ (n) = the place where a road meets another road but doesn't cross it

**motorway** /ˈməʊtəweɪ/ (n) = a road with many lanes for vehicles travelling over long distances; a highway

**pavement** /ˈpeɪvmənt/ (n) = a path at the side of a road for people to walk on

**pedestrian** /pəˈdestriən/ (n) = a person who is on foot and not using a vehicle

**require** /rɪˈkwaɪə/ (v) = to think that sth is necessary

**rural** /ˈrʊərəl/ (adj) = of the countryside

**speed limit** /ˈspiːd ˌlɪmɪt/ (n) = the maximum speed at which a vehicle is allowed to move

**term** /tɜːm/ (n) = the word or phrase for sth

**zebra crossing** /ˌzebrə ˈkrɒsɪŋ/ (n) = a place on a road marked with black and white lines for people to walk across

## CLIL B
### Biology

**communication tool** /kəˌmjuːnɪˈkeɪʃən ˌtuːl/ (n) = the way we use to exchange information, ideas, feelings, etc with other people

**diaphragm** /ˈdaɪəfræm/ (n) = the muscle separating your lungs and stomach

**larynx** /ˈlærɪŋks/ (n) = the organ in the upper part of the throat where the vocal chords are

**lung** /lʌŋ/ (n) = each of the pair of organs in your body that you use to breathe

**nasal cavity** /ˌneɪzəl ˈkævəti/ (n) = the space inside your nose

**oral cavity** /ˌɔːrəl ˈkævəti/ (n) = the mouth and the area inside your mouth

**pitch** /pɪtʃ/ (n) = the tone; how high or low sb's voice is

**power source** /ˈpaʊə sɔːs/ (n) = what you can get energy from, such as electricity, etc

**powerful** /ˈpaʊəfəl/ (adj) = very loud or strong

**release** /rɪˈliːs/ (v) = to let sth come out

**resonance tract** /ˈrezənəns ˌtrækt/ (n) = the system of organs and tubes in your body that help you speak

**resonator** /ˈrezəneɪtə/ (n) = a device the makes sounds vibrate

**rush** /rʌʃ/ (v) = to move quickly

**sinuses** /ˈsaɪnəsɪz/ (pl n) = the spaces in the bones of your head that are connected with your nose

**situated** /ˈsɪtʃueɪtɪd/ (adj) = being in a particular place

**stream** /striːm/ (n) = a flow of air, water, etc

**swallow** /ˈswɒləʊ/ (v) = to cause food, drink, etc to go from your mouth down to your stomach

**tension** /ˈtenʃən/ (n) = pressure

**throat** /θrəʊt/ (n) = the inside part of your neck

**trachea** /trəˈkiːə/ (n) = the tube in your body that takes the air you breathe in to your lungs; the windpipe

**transformed** /trænsˈfɔːmd/ (pp) = changed from one thing to another

**vibrate** /vaɪˈbreɪt/ (v) = to shake in a quick continuous motion; to pulse

**vibration** /vaɪˈbreɪʃən/ (n) = a continuous, gentle, shaking movement causing sth to go to and fro

## CLIL C
### History

**academic qualifications** /ˌækədemɪk ˌkwɒlɪfɪˈkeɪʃənz/ (pl n) = the certificates, diplomas, degrees, etc you acquire after studying at a university, college, etc

**agricultural** /ˌægrɪˈkʌltʃərəl/ (adj) = rural

**compulsory** /kəmˈpʌlsəri/ (adj) = obligatory

**establish** /ɪˈstæblɪʃ/ (v) = to start an organisation, company, etc

**governess** /ˈgʌvənəs/ (n) = (in the past) a female teacher that lived with a rich family and taught their children

**grant** /grɑːnt/ (n) = a sum of money given by the government, etc for educational or other purposes

**logic** /ˈlɒdʒɪk/ (n) = the science of analysing arguments and reaching conclusions

**luxury** /ˈlʌkʃəri/ (n) = sth expensive that you enjoy but is not essential

**manufacturing** /ˌmænjuˈfæktʃərɪŋ/ (n) = the production of goods in a factory

**medieval times** (phr) = the Middle Ages (between AD 500 and AD 1500)

**mining** /ˈmaɪnɪŋ/ (n) = the work done to get metals and other substances out of the ground

**rhetoric** /ˈretərɪk/ (n) = the study of the techniques for using spoken or written language in a convincing way

**sewing lesson** (phr) = a class that teaches how to make or repair clothes, etc using a needle and thread

**support** /səˈpɔːt/ (v) = to look after sb, such as children, etc, by giving them money or things they need in order for them to live

**time off** /ˌtaɪm ˈɒf/ (n) = the period you are officially allowed not to work or study

**tutor** /ˈtjuːtə/ (n) = a teacher who gives private lessons

## CLIL D
### Environmental Studies

**bottle bank** /ˈbɒtl bæŋk/ (n) = a place where used glass bottles are put for recycling

**chase** /tʃeɪs/ (v) = to follow sth

**citizen** /ˈsɪtɪzən/ (n) = sb who lives in a town or city as a legal resident

**compost heap** /ˈkɒmpɒst hiːp/ (n) = a pile of rotten plants, vegetables, leaves, etc used on soil to help plants grow

**council** /ˈkaʊnsəl/ (n) = the organisation that governs a local area

**fertiliser** /ˈfɜːtəlaɪzə/ (n) = a chemical or natural substance that you put on soil to help plants grow

**manage** /ˈmænɪdʒ/ (v) = to deal with sth

**remind (sb to do sth)** /rɪˈmaɪnd/ (v) = to help sb to remember to do sth

**scrunch** /skrʌntʃ/ (v) = to turn sth into a small ball by twisting and crushing it

**seedling** /ˈsiːdlɪŋ/ (n) = a young plant or tree that is grown from a seed

**steel** /stiːl/ (n) = a very strong metal made from a mixture of iron and carbon

**tin foil** /ˈtɪn fɔɪl/ (n) = thin flexible sheets of metal used for wrapping food, etc

**wrapper** /ˈræpə/ (n) = the piece of paper or plastic that covers an item before it is sold

# Pronunciation

## Vowels

| | | |
|---|---|---|
| a | /eə/ | care, rare, scare, dare, fare, share |
| | /eɪ/ | name, face, table, lake, take, day, age, ache, late, snake, make |
| | /æ/ | apple, bag, hat, man, flat, lamp, fat, hand, black, cap, fan, cat, actor, factor, manner |
| | /ɔː/ | ball, wall, call, tall, small, hall, warn, walk, also, chalk |
| | /ɒ/ | want, wash, watch, what, wasp |
| | /ə/ | alarm, away, America |
| | /ɑː/ | arms, dark, bar, star, car, ask, last, fast, glass, far, mask |
| e | /e/ | egg, end, hen, men, ten, bed, leg, tell, penny, pet, bell, pen, tent |
| i | /ɪ/ | in, ill, ink, it, is, hill, city, sixty, fifty, lip, lift, silly, chilly |
| | /ɜː/ | girl, sir, skirt, shirt, bird |
| | /aɪ/ | ice, kite, white, shine, bite, high, kind |
| o | /əʊ/ | home, hope, bone, joke, note, rope, nose, tone, blow, know, no, cold |
| | /ɒ/ | on, ox, hot, top, chop, clock, soft, often, box, sock, wrong, fox |
| | /aʊ/ | owl, town, clown, how, brown, now, cow |
| oo | /ʊ/ | book, look, foot |
| | /uː/ | room, spoon, too, tooth, food, moon, boot |
| | /ʌ/ | blood, flood |
| | /ɔː/ | floor, door |
| u | /ɜː/ | turn, fur, urge, hurl, burn, burst |
| | /ʌ/ | up, uncle, ugly, much, such, run, jump, duck, jungle, hut, mud, luck |
| | /ʊ/ | pull, push, full, cushion |
| | /j/ | unique, union |
| y | /aɪ/ | sky, fly, fry, try, shy, cry, by |

## Consonants

| | | |
|---|---|---|
| b | /b/ | box, butter, baby, bell, bank, black |
| c | /k/ | cat, coal, call, calm, cold |
| | /s/ | cell, city, pencil, circle |
| d | /d/ | down, duck, dim, double, dream, drive, drink |
| f | /f/ | fat, fan, first, food, lift, fifth |
| g | /g/ | grass, goat, go, gold, big, dog, glue, get, give |
| | /dʒ/ | gem, gin, giant |
| h | /h/ | heat, hit, hen, hand, perhaps |
| | | BUT hour, honest, dishonest, heir |
| j | /dʒ/ | jam, just, job, joke, jump |
| k | /k/ | keep, king, kick |
| l | /l/ | lift, let, look, lid, clever, please, plot, black, blue, slim, silly |
| m | /m/ | map, man, meat, move, mouse, market, some, small, smell, smile |
| n | /n/ | next, not, tenth, month, kind, snake, snip, noon, run |
| p | /p/ | pay, pea, pen, poor, pink, pencil, plane, please |
| q | /kw/ | quack, quarter, queen, question, quiet |
| r | /r/ | rat, rich, roof, road, ready, cry, grass, bring, fry, carry, red, read |
| s | /s/ | sit, set, seat, soup, snow, smell, glass, dress, goose |
| | /z/ | houses, cousin, husband |
| t | /t/ | two, ten, tooth, team, turn, tent, tool, trip, train, tree |
| v | /v/ | veal, vet, vacuum, vote, arrive, live, leave, view |
| w | /w/ | water, war, wish, word, world |
| y | /j/ | youth, young, yes, yacht, year |
| z | /z/ | zoo, zebra, buzz, crazy |

## Diphthongs

| | | |
|---|---|---|
| ea | /eə/ | pear, wear, bear |
| | /ɪə/ | ear, near, fear, hear, clear, year, dear |
| | /iː/ | eat, each, heat, leave, clean, seat, neat, tea |
| | /ɜː/ | earth, pearl, learn, search |
| ee | /iː/ | keep, feed, free, tree, three, bee |
| | /ɪə/ | cheer, deer |
| ei | /eɪ/ | eight, freight, weight, vein |
| | /aɪ/ | height |
| ai | /eɪ/ | pain, sail, tail, main, bait, fail, mail |
| ie | /aɪ/ | die, tie, lie |
| ou | /ʌ/ | tough, touch, enough, couple, cousin, trouble |
| | /aʊ/ | mouse, house, round, trout, shout, doubt |
| oi | /ɔɪ/ | oil, boil, toil, soil, coin, choice, voice, join |
| oy | /ɔɪ/ | boy, joy, toy, annoy, employ |
| ou | /ɔː/ | court, bought, brought |
| au | /ɔː/ | naughty, caught, taught |

## Double letters

| | | |
|---|---|---|
| sh | /ʃ/ | shell, ship, shark, sheep, shrimp, shower |
| ch | /tʃ/ | cheese, chicken, cherry, chips, chocolate |
| ph | /f/ | photo, dolphin, phone, elephant |
| th | /θ/ | thief, throne, three, bath, cloth, earth, tooth |
| | /ð/ | the, this, father, mother, brother, feather |
| ng | /ŋ/ | thing, king, song, sing |
| nk | /ŋk/ | think, tank, bank |

# Rules of punctuation

## Capital letters

A capital letter is used:

- to begin a sentence. *It is cold today.*
- for days of the week, months and public holidays.
  *Sunday, August, May Day Bank Holiday*
- for names of people and places.
  *This is Paul and he's from New York.*
- for people's titles.
  *Mr and Mrs Jones, Dr Miller, Prince William, etc.*
- for nationalities and languages.
  *She is Mexican.*
  *Can you speak Spanish?*
  **Note:** The personal pronoun *I* is always a capital letter.
  *Jenny and I are friends.*

## Full stop (.)

A full stop is used to end a sentence that is not a question or an exclamation.

*Sue is away on holiday. She's in Brazil.*

## Comma (,)

A comma is used:

- to separate words in a list.
  *There's lettuce, tomatoes, cucumber and olives in the salad.*
- to separate a non-essential relative clause (i.e. a clause giving extra information which is not essential to the meaning of the main clause) from the main clause.
  *Mary, who has moved here, is a teacher.*
- after certain joining words/transitional phrases (e.g. **in addition to this**, **moreover**, **for example**, **however**, **in conclusion**, etc).
  *For example, I like playing tennis and swimming.*
- when a complex sentence begins with an **if-clause** or other dependent clauses.
  *If Bob isn't there, ask for Ann.*
  **Note:** No comma is used, however, when they follow the main clause.
- to separate questions tags from the rest of the sentence.
  *It's hot, isn't it?*
- before the words **asked**, **said**, etc when followed by direct speech.
  *Max said, "It was late to call them."*

## Question mark (?)

A question mark is used to end a direct question.

*What time does Sheila arrive?*

## Exclamation mark (!)

An exclamation mark is used to end an exclamatory sentence (i.e. a sentence showing admiration, surprise, joy, anger, etc).

*He's so tall!*

*What a nice dress!*

## Quotation marks (" ", ' ')

- Double quotes are often used in direct speech to report the exact words someone said.
  *"Nora called for you," Mark said to me.*
- Single quotes are used when you are quoting someone in direct speech (nested quotes).
  *"She got up, shouted 'I'm late' and ran out of the room," Bob said.*

## Colon (:)

A colon is used to introduce a list.

*To make an omelette we need the following: eggs, milk, butter, cheese, salt and pepper.*

## Semicolon (;)

A semicolon is used to join two independent clauses without using a conjunction.

*We can go to the aquarium; Tuesdays are quiet there.*

## Brackets ( )

Brackets are used to separate extra information from the rest of the sentence.

*The Taj Mahal (built between 1622 and 1653) is in India.*

## Apostrophe (')

An apostrophe is used:

- in short forms to show that one or more letters or numbers have been left out.
  *She's* (= she is) *sleeping now.*
  *This restaurant opened in '99.* (= 1999)
- before or after the possessive **-s** to show ownership or the relationship between people.
  *Charlee's dog, my dad's sister* (singular noun + **'s**)
  *the twins' sister* (plural noun + **'** )
  *the children's balls* (irregular plural + **'s**)

157

# American English – British English Guide

| American English | British English | American English | British English |
|---|---|---|---|
| **A** | | **P** | |
| account | bill/account | pants/trousers | trousers |
| airplane | aeroplane | pantyhose/nylons | tights |
| anyplace/anywhere | anywhere | parking lot | car park |
| apartment | flat | pavement | road surface |
| **B** | | pedestrian crossing | zebra crossing |
| bathrobe | dressing gown | (potato) chips | crisps |
| bathtub | bath | public school | state school |
| bill | banknote | purse | handbag |
| billion=thousand million | billion=million million | **R** | |
| busy (phone) | engaged (phone) | railroad | railway |
| **C** | | rest room | toilet/cloakroom |
| cab | taxi | **S** | |
| call/phone | ring up/phone | sales clerk/sales girl | shop assistant |
| can | tin | schedule | timetable |
| candy | sweets | shorts (underwear) | pants |
| check | bill (restaurant) | sidewalk | pavement |
| closet | wardrobe | stand in line | queue |
| connect (telephone) | put through | store, shop | shop |
| cookie | biscuit | subway | underground |
| corn | sweetcorn, maize | **T** | |
| crazy | mad | truck | lorry, van |
| **D** | | two weeks | fortnight/two weeks |
| desk clerk | receptionist | **V** | |
| dessert | pudding/dessert/sweet | vacation | holiday(s) |
| downtown | (city) centre | vacuum (v.) | hoover |
| drapes | curtains | vacuum cleaner | hoover |
| drugstore/pharmacy | chemist's (shop) | vest | waistcoat |
| duplex | semi-detached | **W** | |
| **E** | | with or without (milk/cream in coffee) | black or white |
| eggplant | aubergine | **Y** | |
| elevator | lift | yard | garden |
| **F** | | **Z** | |
| fall | autumn | (pronounced, "zee") | (pronounced, "zed") |
| faucet | tap | zero | nought |
| first floor, second floor, etc | ground floor, first floor, etc | zip code | postcode |
| flashlight | torch | | |
| French fries | chips | | |
| front desk (hotel) | reception | | |

## Grammar

| American English | British English |
|---|---|
| He just went out./ He has just gone out. | He has just gone out. |
| Hello, is this Steve? | Hello, is that Steve? |
| Do you have a car?/ Have you got a car? | Have you got a car? |

| American English | British English |
|---|---|
| **G** | |
| garbage/trash | rubbish |
| garbage can | dustbin/bin |
| gas | petrol |
| gas station | petrol station/garage |
| grade | class/year |
| **I** | |
| intermission | interval |
| intersection | crossroads |
| **J** | |
| janitor | caretaker/porter |
| **K** | |
| kerosene | paraffin |
| **L** | |
| lawyer/attorney | solicitor |
| line | queue |
| lost and found | lost property |
| **M** | |
| mail | post |
| make a reservation | book |
| motorcycle | motorbike/motorcycle |
| movie | film |
| movie house/theater | cinema |
| **N** | |
| news-stand | newsagent |
| **O** | |
| office (doctor's/dentist's) | surgery |
| one-way (ticket) | single (ticket) |
| overalls | dungarees |

## Spelling

| American English | British English |
|---|---|
| aluminum | aluminium |
| analyze | analyse |
| center | centre |
| check | cheque |
| color | colour |
| honor | honour |
| jewelry | jewellery |
| practice(n,v) | practice(n) practise(v) |
| program | programme |
| realize | realise |
| tire | tyre |
| trave(l)ler | traveller |

## Expressions with prepositions and particles

| American English | British English |
|---|---|
| different from/than | different from/to |
| live on X street | live in X street |
| on a team | in a team |
| on the weekend | at the weekend |
| Monday through Friday | Monday to Friday |

# Irregular Verbs

| Infinitive | Past | Past Participle | Infinitive | Past | Past Participle |
|---|---|---|---|---|---|
| be /biː/ | was /wɒz/ | been /biːn/ | learn /lɜːn/ | learnt (learned) /lɜːnt (lɜːnd)/ | learnt (learned) /lɜːnt (lɜːnd)/ |
| bear /beə/ | bore /bɔː/ | born(e) /bɔːn/ | leave /liːv/ | left /left/ | left /left/ |
| beat /biːt/ | beat /biːt/ | beaten /ˈbiːtən/ | lend /lend/ | lent /lent/ | lent /lent/ |
| become /brˈkʌm/ | became /brˈkeɪm/ | become /brˈkʌm/ | let /let/ | let /let/ | let /let/ |
| begin /brˈgɪn/ | began /brˈgæn/ | begun /brˈgʌn/ | lie /laɪ/ | lay /leɪ/ | lain /leɪn/ |
| bite /baɪt/ | bit /bɪt/ | bitten /ˈbɪtən/ | light /laɪt/ | lit /lɪt/ | lit /lɪt/ |
| blow /bləʊ/ | blew /bluː/ | blown /bləʊn/ | lose /luːz/ | lost /lɒst/ | lost /lɒst/ |
| break /breɪk/ | broke /brəʊk/ | broken /ˈbrəʊkən/ | | | |
| bring /brɪŋ/ | brought /brɔːt/ | brought /brɔːt/ | make /meɪk/ | made /meɪd/ | made /meɪd/ |
| build /bɪld/ | built /bɪlt/ | built /bɪlt/ | mean /miːn/ | meant /ment/ | meant /ment/ |
| burn /bɜːn/ | burnt (burned) /bɜːnt (bɜːnd)/ | burnt (burned) /bɜːnt (bɜːnd)/ | meet /miːt/ | met /met/ | met /met/ |
| burst /bɜːst/ | burst /bɜːst/ | burst /bɜːst/ | pay /peɪ/ | paid /peɪd/ | paid /peɪd/ |
| buy /baɪ/ | bought /bɔːt/ | bought /bɔːt/ | put /pʊt/ | put /pʊt/ | put /pʊt/ |
| can /kæn/ | could /kʊd/ | (been able to /bɪn ˈeɪbəl tə/) | read /riːd/ | read /red/ | read /red/ |
| | | | ride /raɪd/ | rode /rəʊd/ | ridden /ˈrɪdən/ |
| catch /kætʃ/ | caught /kɔːt/ | caught /kɔːt/ | ring /rɪŋ/ | rang /ræŋ/ | rung /rʌŋ/ |
| choose /tʃuːz/ | chose /tʃəʊz/ | chosen /ˈtʃəʊzən/ | rise /raɪz/ | rose /rəʊz/ | risen /ˈrɪzən/ |
| come /kʌm/ | came /keɪm/ | come /kʌm/ | run /rʌn/ | ran /ræn/ | run /rʌn/ |
| cost /kɒst/ | cost /kɒst/ | cost /kɒst/ | say /seɪ/ | said /sed/ | said /sed/ |
| cut /kʌt/ | cut /kʌt/ | cut /kʌt/ | see /siː/ | saw /sɔː/ | seen /siːn/ |
| deal /diːl/ | dealt /delt/ | dealt /delt/ | sell /sel/ | sold /səʊld/ | sold /səʊld/ |
| dig /dɪg/ | dug /dʌg/ | dug /dʌg/ | send /send/ | sent /sent/ | sent /sent/ |
| do /duː/ | did /dɪd/ | done /dʌn/ | set /set/ | set /set/ | set /set/ |
| draw /drɔː/ | drew /druː/ | drawn /drɔːn/ | sew /səʊ/ | sewed /səʊd/ | sewn /səʊn/ |
| dream /driːm/ | dreamt (dreamed) /dremt (driːmd)/ | dreamt (dreamed) /dremt (driːmd)/ | shake /ʃeɪk/ | shook /ʃʊk/ | shaken /ˈʃeɪkən/ |
| | | | shine /ʃaɪn/ | shone /ʃɒn/ | shone /ʃɒn/ |
| drink /drɪŋk/ | drank /dræŋk/ | drunk /drʌŋk/ | shoot /ʃuːt/ | shot /ʃɒt/ | shot /ʃɒt/ |
| drive /draɪv/ | drove /drəʊv/ | driven /ˈdrɪvən/ | show /ʃəʊ/ | showed /ʃəʊd/ | shown /ʃəʊn/ |
| eat /iːt/ | ate /eɪt/ | eaten /ˈiːtən/ | shut /ʃʌt/ | shut /ʃʌt/ | shut /ʃʌt/ |
| | | | sing /sɪŋ/ | sang /sæŋ/ | sung /sʌŋ/ |
| fall /fɔːl/ | fell /fel/ | fallen /ˈfɔːlən/ | sit /sɪt/ | sat /sæt/ | sat /sæt/ |
| feed /fiːd/ | fed /fed/ | fed /fed/ | sleep /sliːp/ | slept /slept/ | slept /slept/ |
| feel /fiːl/ | felt /felt/ | felt /felt/ | smell /smel/ | smelt (smelled) /smelt (smeld)/ | smelt (smelled) /smelt (smeld)/ |
| fight /faɪt/ | fought /fɔːt/ | fought /fɔːt/ | | | |
| find /faɪnd/ | found /faʊnd/ | found /faʊnd/ | speak /spiːk/ | spoke /spəʊk/ | spoken /ˈspəʊkən/ |
| fly /flaɪ/ | flew /fluː/ | flown /fləʊn/ | spell /spel/ | spelt (spelled) /spelt (speld)/ | spelt (spelled) /spelt (speld)/ |
| forbid /fəˈbɪd/ | forbade /fəˈbeɪd/ | forbidden /fəˈbɪdən/ | | | |
| forget /fəˈget/ | forgot /fəˈgɒt/ | forgotten /fəˈgɒtən/ | spend /spend/ | spent /spent/ | spent /spent/ |
| forgive /fəˈgɪv/ | forgave /fəˈgeɪv/ | forgiven /fəˈgɪvən/ | stand /stænd/ | stood /stʊd/ | stood /stʊd/ |
| freeze /friːz/ | froze /frəʊz/ | frozen /ˈfrəʊzən/ | steal /stiːl/ | stole /stəʊl/ | stolen /ˈstəʊlən/ |
| | | | stick /stɪk/ | stuck /stʌk/ | stuck /stʌk/ |
| get /get/ | got /gɒt/ | got /gɒt/ | sting /stɪŋ/ | stung /stʌŋ/ | stung /stʌŋ/ |
| give /gɪv/ | gave /geɪv/ | given /ˈgɪvən/ | swear /sweə/ | swore /swɔː/ | sworn /swɔːn/ |
| go /gəʊ/ | went /went/ | gone /gɒn/ | sweep /swiːp/ | swept /swept/ | swept /swept/ |
| grow /grəʊ/ | grew /gruː/ | grown /grəʊn/ | swim /swɪm/ | swam /swæm/ | swum /swʌm/ |
| hang /hæŋ/ | hung (hanged) /hʌŋ (hæŋd)/ | hung (hanged) /hʌŋ (hæŋd)/ | take /teɪk/ | took /tʊk/ | taken /ˈteɪkən/ |
| | | | teach /tiːtʃ/ | taught /tɔːt/ | taught /tɔːt/ |
| have /hæv/ | had /hæd/ | had /hæd/ | tear /teə/ | tore /tɔː/ | torn /tɔːn/ |
| hear /hɪə/ | heard /hɜːd/ | heard /hɜːd/ | tell /tel/ | told /təʊld/ | told /təʊld/ |
| hide /haɪd/ | hid /hɪd/ | hidden /ˈhɪdən/ | think /θɪŋk/ | thought /θɔːt/ | thought /θɔːt/ |
| hit /hɪt/ | hit /hɪt/ | hit /hɪt/ | throw /θrəʊ/ | threw /θruː/ | thrown /θrəʊn/ |
| hold /həʊld/ | held /held/ | held /held/ | understand /ˌʌndəˈstænd/ | understood /ˌʌndəˈstʊd/ | understood /ˌʌndəˈstʊd/ |
| hurt /hɜːt/ | hurt /hɜːt/ | hurt /hɜːt/ | | | |
| keep /kiːp/ | kept /kept/ | kept /kept/ | wake /weɪk/ | woke /wəʊk/ | woken /ˈwəʊkən/ |
| know /nəʊ/ | knew /njuː/ | known /nəʊn/ | wear /weə/ | wore /wɔː/ | worn /wɔːn/ |
| | | | win /wɪn/ | won /wʌn/ | won /wʌn/ |
| lay /leɪ/ | laid /leɪd/ | laid /leɪd/ | write /raɪt/ | wrote /rəʊt/ | written /ˈrɪtən/ |
| lead /liːd/ | led /led/ | led /led/ | | | |